CLAIM YOUR BIRTHRIGHT

PRESENTED TO: _____
ON: _____
MESSAGE: _____
_____
_____
_____
_____
_____
_____
_____
_____
_____
_____
_____
_____

PRESENTED BY: _____

"Claim Your Birthright is a thorough and comprehensive study of the true Israel, which will challenge both the student and the scholar."
—Carl Nine,
Pastor and Greek scholar

"What I like most about this book is McKeever's head-on, no-nonsense tackling of a tough and controversial biblical teaching. He presents not simply his conclusions, but he unfolds for everyone's examination, the detailed logic used to reach them."
—Ed Gruman,
World Vision management

"I think that this book is one of the most challenging that I have ever read because of what he goes into and what his conclusions are. As a Zionist, I was somewhat circumspect in reading it. I think every Christian owes it to himself to read this book."
—Roger Minor,
Attorney

"This book has really been needed for a long time. We talk of our inheritance, but we can never know our inheritance without knowing our birthright. This is a vital message for a vital time."
—Jim Spillman,
Evangelist and Greek scholar

CLAIM YOUR BIRTH-RIGHT

Dr. James McKeever

Unless otherwise indicated, all Scripture quotations are taken from the *New American Standard Bible (NAS)*, Copyright © The Lockman Foundation 1960, 1962, 1963, 1968, 1971, 1973, 1975, 1977. Used by permission.

Scripture quotations identified **KJV** are from the *King James Version* of the Bible. Those identified **NKJV** are from the *New King James Version*, Copyright © Thomas Nelson, Inc. 1979, 1980, 1982. Any identified **RSV** are from the *Revised Standard Version*, Copyright © Division of Christian Education of the National Council of the Churches of Christ 1952 (O.T.), 1946, 1971 (N.T.). Those identified **NIV** are from the *New International Version*, Copyright © International Bible Society 1973, 1978. Those identified **Amplified** are taken from *The Amplified Bible*, Copyright © Zondervan Publishing House 1965, 1979. Used by permission.

CLAIM YOUR BIRTHRIGHT

Copyright © 1989 by James M. McKeever

All rights reserved. No part of this book may be reproduced or transmitted in any form or by any means, electronic or mechanical, including photocopying, recording, or by any information storage retrieval system, without permission from the Publisher.

Printed in the United States of America
First printing June, 1989

Omega Publications
P. O. Box 4130
Medford, Oregon 97501 (U.S.A.)

ISBN #0-86694-112-6 (Softback)

TABLE OF CONTENTS

1. Give Away Your Birthright? 21
2. The Two Covenants 29
3. Others Included in Israel 55
4. Hebrews Excluded From Israel 71
5. Who Is Israel Today? 81
6. Unfulfilled Promises and Prophecies 107
7. Ezekiel 36-37—The Gathering of Israel 119
8. Ezekiel 38-39—Gog-Magog Battle 133
9. Jerusalem Made Desolate 145
10. The Ten Lost Tribes 155
11. The One "Found Tribe" 167
12. What About the State of Israel? 183
13. Will All of Israel be Saved? 219
14. Claim Your Birthright 235

Appendices

A. How to Become a Christian 247
B. The Star of David and the Menorah 253
C. Modern Judaism is Very Different from Biblical Judaism 265
D. Meet the Author 281

"This brand-new book is obviously going to win another Angel Award for you. All saints should thank God for your God-given gift to express the word of God in readable terms."
—Jack Hoskins,
Attorney

"This book set the joy bells ringing, to realize that my full inheritance in Christ is based upon the gifts and calling of God, which are irrevocable."
—Carlton Booth,
Retired Fuller Seminary professor

"This book really helped me to understand prophecy and just pulled the different issues in biblical prophecy together for me. I think that is what was most important about it to me. It is the most meaningful work I have ever seen in making that understanding of those issues accessible."
—Dan Biskind,
Executive and entrepreneur

"Anyone with deep Dispensational roots will cringe, but the contents of this book need to be communicated—especially to the average Christian. James has done his homework and communicated well!"
—Gary Matsdorf,
Pastor and Greek scholar

INTRODUCTION

Dear Reader,

We're going to have an exciting journey together, as we look afresh at Jesus Christ and the fabulous inheritance we have with Him. We Christians have an inheritance as part of Israel and in the fact that we are joint heirs with Jesus Christ.

You may have raised your eyebrows when I said that Christians are part of Israel, but I believe that before you complete this book there will be agreement both in your mind and in your spirit that this is the case.

Christians have many behavioral patterns and even beliefs that they cling to, as a frightened child clings to his mother. But if you ask many Christians why they are clinging to a particular belief and where in the Scriptures they found the basis for it, oftentimes they would be hard-pressed to give you an answer.

It reminds me of a short story in the book, *The Almost Forgotten Day*, by Mark A. Finley. He relates this story:

> *One day during the time of Imperial Russia, the czar was walking through one of the beautiful parks connected with his palace. He came upon a sentry standing guard near a patch of shrubs. Surprised to find a guard in that place, he inquired, "What are you doing?" "I don't know," answered the sentry, "I am following the captain's orders." The czar asked the captain,*

"Why do you have a sentry standing guard over a patch of shrubs?" "Regulations have always been that way," the captain responded, "but I don't know the reason for it." After a thorough investigation, the czar discovered that nobody in his court could remember a time when it had not been that way. So the czar turned to the archives containing the ancient records and, to his surprise, this is what he discovered. One hundred years before, Catherine the Great ordered a rose bush to be planted and had stationed a sentry nearby so that no one would trample on the young plant. The plant had long since died. Now a guard stood watching. But he didn't know what he was guarding.

"How incredible!", you might exclaim. But that, my friend, is what scores of people in Christian churches are doing—guarding, believing and defending a doctrine that has slipped into the church through tradition—a doctrine that is a myth and not a commandment of God.

In this chapter [Editor: this book] we'll discover exactly how tradition has been exalted above God's word. . . .

Jesus Himself condemned the Pharisees for holding to the tradition of the elders rather than listening to the word of God. If you take the time to examine them, there are many beliefs held firmly by Christians today that are not biblically based—in fact they are contrary to the Scriptures—and people do not know how the belief got started or why, yet they hold to it with great tenacity.

For example, some teachers have stated that "the fig tree is Israel." I have looked up every verse in the Bible that contains "fig" or "fig tree," and there is not a single verse wherein Israel is depicted as a fig tree. You can check that out for yourself. Yet there are many Christians who would almost fight and die to defend this belief, which is obviously not scriptural. (We will deal with the fig tree in a chapter of this book.)

Speaking of the subject of Israel, almost everyone would agree that the group of people who wandered in the wilderness and who occupied Palestine during the time of Christ would be considered "Israel." However, there is much confusion and diverse opinion on who Israel was during New Testament times and even today. There are three major views on the subject of who Israel is today:

1. The Jews are Israel. This view is held primarily by teachers of the dispensational theory of biblical interpretation. They would tend to include, in their definition of "Israel," Jews living in any nation, and especially those living in the State of Israel.

2. There is a physical Israel and a spiritual Israel. Those who hold this view would think that the Jews are physical Israel and that the church—made up of every true believer in Jesus Christ—is spiritual Israel. They would quote a large number of Scriptures, most of which we will examine in this book, that point out that the church is Israel, and yet they would continue to classify the Jew as part of Israel, but only physical Israel.

3. Only the born-again believers in Jesus Christ are Israel. This is a position that is growing rapidly in popularity. This is the view that Israel is only a spiritual entity, and that the requirements to become a part of Israel—in both the Old Testament and the New Testament—are spiritual requirements and not physical requirements. Unfortunately, some of the believers in this position have been classified as "anti-Semitic," but it is my observation that they are not. These people tend to be very pro-Jewish, except when it comes to classifying them as the Israel of God.

I thought it might be of help in understanding this book, and the varying facets concerning Israel, to define a few terms for you:

HEBREW: Since Abraham was a Hebrew, all of his descendants technically would also be Hebrew. This would include the descendants of Ishmael and Esau. However, it was from these two gentlemen that the Arab nations sprang. So even though they are technically Hebrew, we will not use the term in that way. We will restrict the use of the term "Hebrew" to those who descended through Abraham, Isaac and Jacob.

STATE OF ISRAEL: This is the nation that was created in 1948 by declaration of Ben Gurion, and which is composed of a diverse mixture. There are Jews of various races, Hebrews (some of which are followers of the religion of Judaism and others of which are atheists and agnostics), some Palestinians, including both Arab Muslims and Arab Christians. In addition, there are a few immigrants of other nationalities and religions.

ISRAELI: An Israeli is a citizen of the State of Israel.

ISRAELITE: An Israelite is one who is a member of the spiritual group of people which I would call the true Israel of God.

JEW: This term is used in many ways today. It could denote someone who was raised in a "Jewish" culture and home, even if he were an agnostic or atheist. However, we will not normally be using the term "Jew" in that way in this book. We will usually look at a Jew as someone who embraces Judaism as his religion. There are Jews from many races, such as Chinese Jews and Egyptian Jews.

Based on this set of terms, it is interesting that there can be no such thing as a Christian Jew. A

Christian is one who follows the Christian religion and a Jew is one who follows the religion of Judaism, and these religions are mutually exclusive. You can be one or the other, but not both. A Jew is one trying to get to God through the Law, and a Christian is one trying to get to God through Jesus Christ, the only begotten Son of God.

You could have a Christian Hebrew, for we look at "Hebrew" as a biological or racial term, whereas "Jew" and "Christian" are spiritual terms, denoting adherence to a given religion.

VARIETY WITHIN UNITY

Among the readers of this book will be people of various Protestant denominations, Catholics, Jews and perhaps those of other beliefs or of no belief at all. Thus, we each come to the subject of *Israel* and the inheritance and the birthright of Israelites from totally different perspectives and backgrounds.

However, the exciting thing is that we do have one major thing in common. We are all seekers of the truth, and most likely seekers of God and His will. We all need to have a love and respect for each other.

For those who know Jesus Christ as Lord and Savior, we have something additionally in common—we know and love Jesus Christ, the only begotten Son of God. It is in Him that we have our fellowship and unity. We may differ in our beliefs regarding the proper form of baptism or eternal security. We may differ in our beliefs about the timing of the rapture. We may differ in our beliefs regarding who Israel is. Those things are not important. The important thing is lifting up Jesus Christ, and He will draw all men unto Himself.

Many years ago, I was president of a Christian businessmen's group in Dallas, Texas (which is my home town). I usually invited in a guest speaker, not wanting to put myself forward. However, there began to be some bickering between the Baptists and men of other denominations about the form of baptism. There was some stress and strong words concerning the baptism of the Holy Spirit arising between the Full Gospel Assembly of God men and others. With all this conflict going on, I felt that I should address the group. The Lord led me to speak out of Philippians, and I read these verses:

> **15** Some, to be sure, are preaching Christ even from envy and strife, but some also from good will;
> **16** the latter do it out of love, knowing that I am appointed for the defense of the gospel;
> **17** the former proclaim Christ out of selfish ambition, rather than from pure motives, thinking to cause me distress in my imprisonment.
> **18** What then? Only that in every way, whether in pretense or in truth, Christ is proclaimed; and in this I rejoice, yes, and I will rejoice.
> —Philippians 1

I pointed out that, while Paul was in jail there in Rome, there were people out preaching Christ with a wide variety of motives. Some preached Christ trying to create strife. Some did it because they were envious of Paul. Still others did it out of love and good will. So some had pure motives and others preached Christ out of selfish ambition. Paul certainly did not agree with those who were preaching out of selfish ambition, envy and strife. But verse 18 is so beautiful—Paul rejoiced that Christ was being preached, whether it was in pretense or in truth. And he said that because Christ was being proclaimed, he would rejoice, and would continue to rejoice.

I shared with these good brothers that even if we differed in our views of the proper form of baptism, the baptism of the Holy Spirit, predestination versus free will, and other theological subjects, as long as a brother was preaching Jesus Christ as the only Son of God, and the only way to heaven, I would rejoice in the fact that he was proclaiming Christ.

Some years earlier I had learned a significant lesson from the Lord. I was living in Los Angeles at the time and, as I walked across the square in the center of town, there was a man standing on a soapbox whose clothes were ten sizes too large. He had a large Bible and was screaming for people to repent and to turn to Christ. I walked by on the other side of the wide sidewalk, wishing that he would be quiet, because he was being so offensive. About thirty minutes later I came by again, and this same man was still screaming out the truth about Christ. The Lord really convicted me, reminding me that this man would be able to reach people that I would never be able to reach, and that regardless of his form and style, so different from my own, Christ was being proclaimed and I should rejoice in that. I walked the rest of the way back to the office with tears in my eyes, asking the Lord to forgive me.

You might find something in this book with which you disagree, and that is fine. But our fellowship is still about the precious person of Jesus Christ, isn't it? And we can still love each other and rejoice in each other.

I AM AN ISRAELITE

I am an Israelite, and I am very happy to be one. In the Old Testament, God gave the Israelites a beautiful lampstand for the tabernacle:

> **31 "Then you shall make a lampstand of pure gold. The lampstand and its base and its shaft are to be made of hammered work; its cups, its bulbs and its flowers shall be of one piece with it.**
> **32 "And six branches shall go out from its sides; three branches of the lampstand from its one side, and three branches of the lampstand from its other side...."**
>
> —Exodus 25

Today, we call this seven-candle lampstand the "menorah." All through the Old Testament, the menorah was the symbol of the Israel of God.

It is interesting to note that the six-pointed star, which is erroneously called the Star of David, has been introduced within the last two hundred years as a symbol of the State of Israel. As far as we can find in history, David neither saw nor used that star. It was evidently first used by King Solomon, primarily when he was worshiping the gods of his foreign wives, especially the goddess Astarte.

But let's return to the point that the menorah was the symbol of Israel throughout the Old Testament. Since I am an Israelite, my wife and I joyfully display our menorah in a prominent place in our home. We want the world to know that we are Israelites and a part of the Israel of God.

Since there is no record that God ever wanted the six-pointed star or suggested that it be used, we would rather remain solidly in God's camp and, if we are going to utilize a symbol at all, I would like to use the one that God designed—the menorah, with the three candlesticks on either side of the central one.

The menorah reminds me of the crucifixion of our Lord and Savior, Jesus Christ. If you look at His upraised hands and the upraised hands of the thieves on either side of Him, there are three upraised hands on each side of the Light of the world, Jesus Christ.

I trust that this book will be a blessing to you, and that it will help you understand what your birthright is and help you to claim it. This could be one of the most important books you will ever read, because it affects your inheritance and your birthright.

If there is anything in this book that is not the truth of God, I pray that the Holy Spirit will eradicate it from your mind. The things that are God's truth, I pray that the Holy Spirit will burn into your heart. I pray that this book may be used to lift a veil from your eyes and to help you to lay aside preconceived ideas about Israel, your place in it, and about your birthright. May it help you see exactly how you fit into Israel, and what it means and implies for you, both now and in eternity.

God bless you as you read,

DR. JAMES McKEEVER

This book is dedicated first and foremost
to the glory of God
and His only begotten Son,
Jesus Christ,
with special thanks to the Holy Spirit
for His teaching, guidance and insights.

A special dedication is made
to the Omega Family, Omega Team and Omega staff,
without whose prayers and support
this book could never have been written.

In addition, this book is dedicated
to all of my brothers in Christ
who have a dispensational leaning and to the Jews.
I want you to know that I love you in Christ
and I trust that you, like me, are seekers
of God's pure and perfect truth,
even if it means a change in our present theology.

I am also excited to dedicate this book
to those Christians who, after reading this work,
will stop giving away their birthright
and take their rightful place as part of Israel.

ACKNOWLEDGEMENTS

Once someone asked me when I was going to write my next book. I replied that it might be tomorrow, a year from now, five years from now or maybe never. I shared with that individual that I could not simply sit down and write a book anytime I wanted to. I could only write a book when God told me to and told me what to write.

Unfortunately, I think that many Christian books today are written because the author decided that he would sit down and write a book, rather than doing so under the compulsion of the Holy Spirit.

Therefore, the first and foremost acknowledgement must be to God the Father, Jesus Christ and the Holy Spirit, who led me to write this book. Actually, they did more than that—they forced me to write this book. I did not want to write it, because I knew that there would be some Christians who would be offended by it. I have already had enough opposition for my views on the rapture, the Gog-Magog war and so forth. I really don't need any more opposition or rotten tomatoes thrown at me because of my beliefs concerning Israel.

On the human level, the major person I would applaud and thank for bringing this book into being is my precious wife, Jeani. She edited the book and actually wrote a portion of it. In addition, she was my loving, supporting, encouraging wife. What a wonderful partner to have by my side, laboring for the Lord together with me.

As a close second would be my good brother, Jim Andrews, who oversaw the typesetting and proofreading. He is also a valuable colaborer in the ministry, in the economic activities and here on the Living Waters Ranch.

I also appreciate the ladies who faithfully typed the book, Jackie Cunningham and Judy McClure. I am also indebted to Ellen Thorsen, who helped with the proofreading.

There were a number of men of God to whom I submitted copies of the manuscript for their comments prior to submitting the book for publication. I incorporated most of their comments and suggestions into the book. However, I will absolve them by stating that probably not one of them agrees with every single statement in this book. I need men of God like them to whom I can submit my work, so that I do not go off on a tangent or drift into error. These men are:

> Jim Andrews, executive
> Dan Biskind, executive and entrepreneur
> Carlton Booth, retired Fuller Seminary professor
> Jamie Buckingham, pastor and author
> Giff Claiborne, advertising executive and pastor
> Ed Gruman, World Vision management
> Jack Hoskins, attorney
> Gary Matsdorf, pastor and Greek scholar
> Roger Minor, attorney
> Carl Nine, pastor and Greek scholar
> Jim Spillman, evangelist and Greek scholar
> Harry Stiritz, CPA and ordained minister

My heartfelt thanks goes out to these brothers who did a labor of love in reading the rough manuscript and giving their godly suggestions and input.

I am also indebted to the Omega staff, the Omega Family and the Omega Team, who prayed for me faithfully during the writing of this book, and who

ACKNOWLEDGEMENTS

undergirded me and lifted me up during the spiritual warfare that inevitably occurs when I write a book.

In addition, I am indebted to you, the reader, for without you there would be no need to write a book. My earnest prayer and expectation is that this book will indeed help you. I pray that it will lift up Jesus Christ, and that it also might help any unbeliever who may be reading it to find the peace and joy that comes from having Jesus Christ as your very own personal Savior.

Many thanks to you all and God bless you.

James McKeever

Dr. James McKeever

But the goal of our instruction is love from a pure heart and a good conscience and a sincere faith.

—James McKeever
(Also found in 1 Timothy 1:5)

"The understanding of the scriptures that the Lord is bringing forth in these latter days is sweeping away some age old 'traditions of the elders' and 'manmade doctrines.'

"Manmade doctrines are always fragmentary, fleshy, forced, and with no pleasing continuity. They conflict with spiritual harmony and leave one with an uneasiness about all the unanswered questions.

"If we are to have absolute truths regarding our salvation, remission of our sins and eternal life, no one can accept such *flimsy, fleshy* evidence.

"It is time that *all* scripture is thoroughly examined again, 'to see that it is so,' with a pure heart and a clear *spiritual* eye."

—Bill Owens, Pastor
Christian Service Centers, International
from his book, *No Jew No Gentile*, pp. 1-2

1

GIVE AWAY YOUR BIRTHRIGHT?

When one becomes a born-again Christian, by receiving Jesus Christ as his Savior and his Master, he acquires a birthright, in addition to his salvation. This birthright is fabulous, beyond comprehension.

Sadly, many Christians are giving away their birthright with the words of their mouths, just as Esau gave away his birthright with the words of his mouth. This book will help you see what your fantastic birthright is and how to claim it.

God made certain promises to Abraham which were to pass on to his seed. God promised some land, and he also promised to bless those who blessed him (Abraham) and his seed (offspring) and many other promises. Do you know who the seed or offspring of Abraham are today? The Bible plainly tells us:

> 29 And if you belong to Christ then you are Abraham's offspring, heirs according to promise.
> —Galatians 3, NAS

> 29 And if ye be Christ's, then are ye Abraham's seed, and heirs according to the promise.
> —Galatians 3, KJV

Isn't that exciting? This tells us that if anyone belongs to Jesus Christ personally—is a born again believer in Jesus Christ—then he is an heir to all the promises made to Abraham! This is a rich inheritance, and yet most Christians are giving it away.

Incidentally, if you are not absolutely sure that you know Jesus Christ personally as your Savior and Master, I would encourage you to pause and read Appendix A at the back of this book. This shares how you can know for sure that you have a relationship with Jesus Christ. Consequently, you can know that you have both salvation and an incredible birthright.

Being the seed or offspring of Abraham (according to Galatians 3:29), Christians are thus part of Israel. In this book, I hope to show you solidly through the Scriptures that every true believer in Jesus Christ is a bona fide, no reservations, part of Israel. Jesus loves you and wants you to have your full birthright.

WHO OR WHAT IS ISRAEL?

This vital subject of "Israel" is extremely important, especially for every Christian, yet so many Christians and Jews alike are totally confused about it. You cannot properly understand prophecy without a clear understanding of who the true Israel of God is. Without understanding this, you cannot understand the proper place of both Christians and Jews in the endtimes of this age, and you will not know what your true birthright really is.

Let me say at this point that there is not an anti-Semitic cell in my body. In our trips to the Mideast, the Lord has given me an appreciation and a real love for the Hebrews and Jews in the "State of Israel." They are a tough, resilient people whom I admire a great deal. I think that, as a nation, we should help them more than we are. They are our only ally in the Mideast. I say this so that you will clearly understand my feelings toward them, because some of the things that I will share might, on the surface, be interpreted as negative toward them, but they definitely are not

GIVE AWAY YOUR BIRTHRIGHT? 23

intended to be. I will have more to say about the incredible State of Israel in a later chapter.

One of the reasons that the subject of "Israel" is so confusing is that there are at least seven different entities in the Bible called Israel. They are as follows:

1. A man formerly called Jacob
2. A piece of real estate in the Mideast
3. The ten northern tribes
4. The entire twelve tribes
5. The Jews who lived in Judea
6. The seed of Abraham
7. Old Testament saints combined with New Testament believers

To complicate things further, some teachers try to divide Israel into two parts, a physical Israel and a spiritual Israel. As we will see later, I do not believe the Bible will allow us to do that. I believe we will find from the Scriptures that the true Israel, the Israel of God, is a single group of people that cannot be divided.

True Israel is the group of people who are the inheritors of the promises made originally to Abraham. *If* Christians are in some way the inheritors or joint inheritors of those promises, then to give away our inheritance would be as foolish as doing what Esau did when he gave away his birthright.

ESAU ACTED FOOLISHLY

To realize afresh how foolish it is to give away your birthright, let us review the story of how Esau came back hungry from hunting and traded his birthright for some stew. Let's reread it from the Scriptures, so it will be alive in our minds:

29 And when Jacob had cooked stew, Esau came in from the field and he was famished;

30 and Esau said to Jacob, "Please let me have a swallow of that red stuff there, for I am famished." Therefore his name was called Edom.
31 But Jacob said, "First sell me your birthright."
32 And Esau said, "Behold, I am about to die; so of what use then is the birthright to me?"
33 And Jacob said, "First swear to me"; so he swore to him, and sold his birthright to Jacob.
34 Then Jacob gave Esau bread and lentil stew; and he ate and drank, rose and went on his way. Thus Esau despised his birthright.

—Genesis 25

Esau was willing to give up his inheritance, his birthright, for a trivial amount of food. Most people would look at that act as a very foolish one and would almost pity Esau. He gave away his inheritance by the words of his mouth.

We see later that Esau came to his aged father who wanted to bless him before he died and give him his inheritance:

1 Now it came about, when Isaac was old, and his eyes were too dim to see, that he called his older son Esau and said to him, "My son." And he said to him, "Here I am."
2 And Isaac said, "Behold now, I am old and I do not know the day of my death.
3 "Now then, please take your gear, your quiver and your bow, and go out to the field and hunt game for me;
4 and prepare a savory dish for me such as I love, and bring it to me that I may eat, so that my soul may bless you before I die."

—Genesis 27

You may remember that verses 5 through 25 describe how Rebekah told her son Jacob to go kill two choice kids and to bring them to her to prepare a

GIVE AWAY YOUR BIRTHRIGHT?

savory stew. She further instructed him to put the skins on his hands and arms, so that he would appear to be his brother Esau. So Jacob took the stew into his father Isaac, who then pronounced a beautiful blessing upon him:

> 26 Then his father Isaac said to him, "Please come close and kiss me, my son."
> 27 So he came close and kissed him; and when he smelled the smell of his garments, he blessed him and said,
>> "See, the smell of my son
>> Is like the smell of a field which the Lord
>>   has blessed;
> 28 Now may God give you of the dew of heaven,
>> And of the fatness of the earth,
>> And an abundance of grain and new wine;
> 29 May peoples serve you,
>> And nations bow down to you;
>> Be master of your brothers,
>> And may your mother's sons bow down to you.
>> Cursed be those who curse you,
>> And blessed be those who bless you."
> 30 Now it came about, as soon as Isaac had finished blessing Jacob, and Jacob had hardly gone out from the presence of Isaac his father, that Esau his brother came in from his hunting.
> 31 Then he also made savory food, and brought it to his father; and he said to his father, "Let my father arise, and eat of his son's game, that you may bless me."
> 32 And Isaac his father said to him, "Who are you?" And he said, "I am your son, your first-born, Esau."
> 33 Then Isaac trembled violently, and said, "Who was he then that hunted game and brought it to me, so that I ate of all of it before you came, and blessed him? Yes, and he shall be blessed."

34 When Esau heard the words of his father, he cried out with an exceedingly great and bitter cry, and said to his father, "Bless me, even me also, O my father!"

35 And he said, "Your brother came deceitfully, and has taken away your blessing."

36 Then he said, "Is he not rightly named Jacob, for he has supplanted me these two times? He took away my birthright, and behold, now he has taken away my blessing." And he said, "Have you not reserved a blessing for me?"

37 But Isaac answered and said to Esau, "Behold, I have made him your master, and all his relatives I have given to him as servants; and with grain and new wine I have sustained him. Now, as for you then, what can I do, my son?"

—Genesis 27

So we see that, not only did Esau give away his birthright by his foolish behavior and lust over some lentil stew, but here Jacob also became the inheritor of what should have been Esau's blessing as the elder son. Like they say in the old country, Esau was "dumber than dirt." He gave away his entire, glorious inheritance for a little bit of food. He took himself and his descendants out of the line to inherit the promises God made to Abraham, and he did so with the words of his mouth.

CHRISTIANS TODAY ARE JUST LIKE ESAU

Many of the seed or offspring of Abraham—those who know Jesus Christ as their Savior and Master—are doing the same foolish thing that Esau did. They are giving away their birthright by the words of their mouths (we are talking about inheritance, not salvation). They do this by stating that some other group of people are the seed of Abraham and the inheritor of God's promises. They do this when they say that some other

GIVE AWAY YOUR BIRTHRIGHT? 27

group of people are the Israel of God, which means that other group is the inheritor of the promises made to Abraham. When they do that with their mouths, they are giving away their birthright to someone else.

I think that our denial of our birthright is as foolish as what Esau did, if not more so, because at least he got a bowl of stew for his birthright! Christians today are giving away their birthright and getting absolutely nothing in return.

This may be a new way of looking at this entire subject for you, and we need to give it time to sink in. We also need to examine numerous passages to see if this is consistent with what the Bible teaches.

The first thing to look at is the old covenant and the new covenant, and the relation between the two. We need to consider how all of those who became part of Israel through the old covenant relate to those who become part of Israel through the new covenant, through the precious blood of Jesus, who loved us and shed His blood so that followers of Christ could be part of the chosen family of God.

In order to help you to understand how Christians are part of Israel, we need to look back at who was part of Israel in the Old Testament. The answer may be surprising to you, because much of Israel was not physically or biologically descended from Abraham.

Don't let that statement shock you. Simply read on, and find out from the Bible itself who the true Israel of God really is, your part in it and the birthright you have because of being part of it. This book, *Claim Your Birthright*, can be one of the most exciting, enlightening and rewarding books that you have ever read.

2

THE TWO COVENANTS

We are all familiar with the "Old Testament" and the "New Testament." Actually those terms are synonymous with the "old covenant" and the "new covenant." In our modern terminology, we would think of these as:

1. The old contract
2. The new contract

A very important question which arises is this: did the old covenant (contract) end and the new covenant (contract) take its place *or* did the old covenant continue and the new covenant simply take a place in parallel with it? To put it in other words, is there only one way to God the Father or are there two ways? You can view these two possible relationships between the old contract and the new contract this way:

A. Parallel

old covenant   old covenant

                      new covenant

OR

B. Successive

old covenant   new covenant

CHAPTER 2

THE OLD COVENANT VERSUS THE NEW COVENANT

Much of people's thinking concerning who Israel is depends on their view of the old covenant and the new covenant. If one believes that the old covenant still continues and the new covenant simply took a place parallel to it two thousand years ago, and that both are still valid, one would come out with one view of Israel. On the other hand, if one believes that the old covenant ended (was fulfilled) and the new covenant replaced it, then one would arrive at a different conclusion about Israel. I believe that the Scriptures support the second view (successive) as the valid one.

Christ said that He came to fulfill the Law (Matthew 5:17). He fulfilled all of the requirements of the old contract, thus completing and terminating it as a means of coming into a right relationship with God. This means that the old contract is no longer valid as a means of justification, and that the only way to God is through the new contract (new covenant). Christ is the only means of salvation today.

This is not to say that the Old Testament is not still of value; it certainly is. Romans 3:19-24 lets us know that through the Law comes the knowledge of sin and our accountability to God. Yet the same passage reemphasizes the new covenant fact that redemption is in Jesus Christ alone:

> 20 ... by the works of the Law no flesh will be justified in His sight; for through the Law comes the knowledge of sin. . . .
>
> 23 for all have sinned and fall short of the glory of God,
> 24 being justified as a gift by His grace through the redemption which is in Christ Jesus; . . .
> —Romans 3

We all know that Christ declared all foods clean (Mark 7:18, 19) and, thus, negated the ceremonial part of the old covenant. But what about the ten commandments? Another passage in Romans tells us this:

> **14 For sin shall not be master over you, for you are not under law, but under grace.**
> —Romans 6

Here we see that we are no longer under the Law (of the Old Testament), but we are under grace instead. What does it mean by "the Law"? Is this just the ceremonial law? A verse in Romans 7 clears this up:

> **7 What shall we say then? Is the Law sin? May it never be! On the contrary, I would not have come to know sin except through the Law; for I would not have known about coveting if the Law had not said, "YOU SHALL NOT COVET."**
> —Romans 7

Here we see one of the ten commandments quoted as being part of "the Law." This means that Christians are no longer even under the ten commandments. (If they were, they should worship on Saturday rather than on Sunday.) So the entire old contract has been fulfilled in Jesus Christ and no longer applies to anyone, whether he be Hebrew or Christian. (Let me hasten to restate that there are very valid reasons for studying the Old Testament and for singing songs from the Old Testament. We can still learn many things about our God from the Law, even though we are not under it.)

We have seen briefly that the old covenant consists of the Old Testament ceremonial and behavioral laws, and the ten commandments. It also obviously comprises the promises (covenants) that God made to the patriarchs. We have also seen that we are no longer under "the Law," which is the old covenant.

CHAPTER 2

The book of Hebrews goes into this even more explicitly. There, we read these words:

> 6 But now He has obtained a more excellent ministry, by as much as He is also the mediator of a better covenant, which has been enacted on better promises.
> 7 For if that first covenant had been faultless, there would have been no occasion sought for a second.
> 8 For finding fault with them, He says,
> "BEHOLD, DAYS ARE COMING, SAYS THE LORD,
> WHEN I WILL EFFECT A NEW COVENANT WITH THE HOUSE OF ISRAEL AND WITH THE HOUSE OF JUDAH;
> 9 NOT LIKE THE COVENANT WHICH I MADE WITH THEIR FATHERS
> ON THE DAY WHEN I TOOK THEM BY THE HAND
> TO LEAD THEM OUT OF THE LAND OF EGYPT;
> FOR THEY DID NOT CONTINUE IN MY COVENANT,
> AND I DID NOT CARE FOR THEM, SAYS THE LORD.
> 10 "FOR THIS IS THE COVENANT THAT I WILL MAKE WITH THE HOUSE OF ISRAEL
> AFTER THOSE DAYS, SAYS THE LORD:
> I WILL PUT MY LAWS INTO THEIR MINDS,
> AND I WILL WRITE THEM UPON THEIR HEARTS.
> AND I WILL BE THEIR GOD,
> AND THEY SHALL BE MY PEOPLE.
> 11 "AND THEY SHALL NOT TEACH EVERYONE HIS FELLOW CITIZEN,
> AND EVERYONE HIS BROTHER, SAYING, 'KNOW THE LORD,'

> FOR ALL SHALL KNOW ME,
> FROM THE LEAST TO THE GREATEST OF THEM.
> 12 "FOR I WILL BE MERCIFUL TO THEIR INIQUITIES,
> AND I WILL REMEMBER THEIR SINS NO MORE."
> 13 When He said, "A new covenant," He has made the first obsolete. But whatever is becoming obsolete and growing old is ready to disappear.
>
> —Hebrews 8

We see clearly from this passage in Hebrews that the first covenant (the old covenant) is obsolete and was ready to disappear in the first century. Thus, I would have to conclude that the old covenant has been fulfilled and terminated, and the new covenant has replaced it.

Because of this, I cannot get excited about the present day Jews worshiping on the Sabbath (Saturday). They are simply trying to reach the God of Abraham through an invalid means—through a cancelled contract. In that respect, they are no better off than the Arabs, who try to reach the God of Abraham through the Muslim religion. They, too, are trying to reach Him through an invalid means.

This is heavy, but we need to let it sink in. Later in this chapter, we will examine the fact that Jesus Himself said that He was the only way to God. That was either the truth or it was a lie. I believe it was truth, and that Jesus Christ is the only way to God. God cannot be reached through any other means, and that would include the old covenant.

I would like to share one additional thought about the old covenant before we move on. Many have taught that the old covenant was "unconditional." As we will see later in this chapter, that certainly was not true. There were three conditions that God laid down for the old covenant. However, God also said that this covenant was going to be everlasting, and this certainly is true.

All of the promises that God made to Abraham, which passed on to Israel, will be kept. God will indeed keep His side of the bargain. What God did was to change our side of the covenant. He changed what we have to do in order to inherit those promises and blessings. That is what the new covenant is all about. God's side has not changed, but He changed the rules as to how a man comes into a right relationship with Himself. It is no longer through the laws of the old covenant—now it is only by believing in His only begotten Son.

When we say that we are no longer under the Old Testament Law, that includes the ten commandments, as we said. (This does not mean that the Law does not still have a valid function in our lives to reveal the character and desires of our heavenly Father. The Old Testament still has a great deal of value to us, as we get to know God better.) Lest you misunderstand and think that not being under the law gives us a license to sin, I would hasten to remind you that in the New Testament we are called to an even higher and purer way to live. An illustration may help you to understand what I mean by this.

Let us say that someone was driving down a highway that had a speed limit of 50 miles per hour posted all along it. Now if someone were to absolutely guarantee that individual that there was not a policeman within 200 miles, how fast would he drive? My guess is that he would tend to drive 60 or maybe 70 miles per hour.

On the other hand, let's say that all of the 55 miles-per-hour speed limit signs were taken down and a policeman was riding in the front seat with the driver. If he told the driver to drive 55, how fast would that individual drive? Probably 53 miles per hour. (If the policeman told that individual to drive 30 miles per hour or, in some rare circumstances, even 70 miles per hour, the driver would obey precisely what the policeman said, regardless of the signs along the highway.)

So it is with God in His relationship with man. In the Old Testament, we had the written Law (the signs along the highway). In the New Testament, we have the Holy Spirit living inside us (sitting in the front seat with us). If we are really following God, we are thereby called to live in a higher and purer way.

In the Old Testament, one was not to commit adultery, but under the guidance of the Holy Spirit we are not even to lust (Matthew 5:27,28). Under the old covenant, one was not to commit murder, but under the new covenant, with the Holy Spirit in our hearts, we are not even to remain angry with a brother (Matthew 5:21, 22). So we are called to an even higher, purer and more righteous way of life than that which was required under the old covenant.

Paul sums this up well in Romans. He points out that we are not under the Law (the old covenant), but we are under grace. The question might then arise as to whether we should not sin more so that God's grace would be even more abundant. This is Paul's answer:

> 1 What shall we say then? Are we to continue in sin that grace might increase?
> 2 May it never be! How shall we who died to sin still live in it?
> —Romans 6

As we have seen, we are no longer under the old covenant, which has been completed, finished, and made obsolete. We are now under the new covenant, but it requires a higher and purer way to live. It is not a license to sin.

Thank you, Jesus, that you lived a perfect life, died and rose again to fulfill the old covenant and establish the new covenant! That's good news!

Even though the Law still has a function in our lives (to show us our sin and to reveal the character and desires of our heavenly Father) the old covenant, as a contract, is no longer viable. The only way to God is through Jesus Christ—for everyone, including the Hebrews.

THE OLD COVENANT HAS ENDED

Now let's look at some other places in the book of Hebrews that show that the old covenant ended and the new covenant replaced it:

> 8 After saying above, "SACRIFICES AND OFFERINGS AND WHOLE BURNT OFFERINGS AND sacrifices FOR SIN THOU HAST NOT DESIRED, NOR HAS THOU TAKEN PLEASURE in them" (which are offered according to the Law),
> 9 then He said, "BEHOLD, I HAVE COME TO DO THY WILL." He takes away the first in order to establish the second.
> —Hebrews 10

Here we see that God Himself is going to "take away" the first (covenant) so that He can establish a second covenant.

> 10 We have an altar, from which those who serve the tabernacle have no right to eat.
> —Hebrews 13

In this last verse, we see that those who serve under the tabernacle (the old covenant) have no right to partake of the altar from which we eat the bread of life.

I would like now to share with you a fairly long passage from Hebrews 7, drawing your attention to a few points of specific interest and relevance to our subject, as we read through it.

> 11 Now if perfection was through the Levitical priesthood (for on the basis of it the people received the Law), what further need was there for another priest to arise according to the order of Melchizedek, and not be designated according to the order of Aaron?
> 12 For when the priesthood is changed, of necessity there takes place a change of law also.
> —Hebrews 7

In the two preceding verses, we see that the Bible says that the priesthood was changed from the Levitical priesthood to the priesthood of Jesus (Melchizedek). It clearly states that when the priesthood was changed, the Law (covenant) as to how one rightly relates to God, also had to change. The author of Hebrews then goes on to show that the priesthood was taken away from the tribe of Levi and was given to the Lion of the tribe of Judah—to Jesus Christ:

> 13 For the one concerning whom these things are spoken belongs to another tribe, from which no one has officiated at the altar.
> 14 For it is evident that our Lord was descended from Judah, a tribe with reference to which Moses spoke nothing concerning priests.
> 15 And this is clearer still, if another priest arises according to the likeness of Melchizedek,
> 16 who has become such not on the basis of a law of physical requirement, but according to the power of an indestructible life.
> 17 For it is witnessed of Him,
> "THOU ART A PRIEST FOREVER
> ACCORDING TO THE ORDER OF
> MELCHIZEDEK."
> —Hebrews 7

The author of Hebrews proceeds to tell us that the former commandment (covenant) was set aside and that Jesus Himself has become a guarantee of a better covenant, one that replaced the old covenant:

> **18** For, on the one hand, there is a setting aside of a former commandment because of its weakness and uselessness
> **19** (for the Law made nothing perfect), and on the other hand there is a bringing in of a better hope, through which we draw near to God.
> **20** And inasmuch as it was not without an oath
> **21** (for they indeed became priests without an oath, but He with an oath through the One who said to Him,
> "THE LORD HAS SWORN
> AND WILL NOT CHANGE HIS MIND,
> 'THOU ART A PRIEST FOREVER'");
> **22** so much the more also Jesus has become the guarantee of a better covenant.
> **23** And the former priests, on the one hand, existed in greater numbers, because they were prevented by death from continuing,
> **24** but He, on the other hand, because He abides forever, holds His priesthood permanently.
> **25** Hence, also, He is able to save forever those who draw near to God through Him, since He always lives to make intercession for them.
> —Hebrews 7

In the verse 25, we see that our wonderful high priest, Jesus, holds that status permanently and is able to save anyone who draws near to God *through Him*. Remember, there is no other way to God except through our glorious Savior, Jesus Christ, who loves us so very much.

> **26** For it was fitting that we should have such a high priest, holy, innocent, undefiled, separated from sinners and exalted above the heavens;
> **27** who does not need daily, like those high priests, to offer up sacrifices, first for His own sins, and then

for the sins of the people, because this He did once for all when He offered up Himself.

28 For the Law appoints men as high priests who are weak, but the word of the oath, which came after the Law, appoints a Son, made perfect forever.
—Hebrews 7

Verse 28 shows that the old Law appointed men as priests, but the new word of the oath *"which came after the Law"* appointed Jesus. Obviously, the Law had to end if Christ's way to God, the new covenant, came "after the Law."

OTHER PASSAGES WHICH SHOW THAT THE NEW COVENANT REPLACED THE OLD COVENANT

There are numerous verses in both the Old Testament and the New Testaments which clearly show that the old covenant was replaced by the new covenant. In fact, back in the days of Jeremiah, the Lord told the people that He was going to do away with the old covenant and make a new covenant:

31 "Behold, days are coming," declares the LORD, "when I will make a new covenant with the house of Israel and with the house of Judah,

32 not like the covenant which I made with their fathers in the day I took them by the hand to bring them out of the land of Egypt, My covenant which they broke, although I was a husband to them," declares the LORD.

33 "But this is the covenant which I will make with the house of Israel after those days," declares the LORD, "I will put My law within them, and on their heart I will write it; and I will be their God, and they shall be My people.

34 "And they shall not teach again, each man his neighbor and each man his brother, saying, 'Know the

Lord,' for they shall all know Me, from the least of them to the greatest of them," declares the LORD, "for I will forgive their iniquity, and their sin I will remember no more."

—Jeremiah 31

Paul puts it very beautifully when he says that all the people who were under the old covenant were blind—they could not see spiritually; but when they received Jesus Christ as their Savior, then the blindness was removed:

> 14 But their minds were hardened; for until this very day at the reading of the old covenant the same veil remains unlifted, because it is removed in Christ.
> 15 But to this day whenever Moses is read, a veil lies over their heart;
> 16 but whenever a man turns to the Lord, the veil is taken away.
>
> —2 Corinthians 3

What this says is that anyone under the old covenant is blind spiritually, and the only way to have that blindness removed is to receive Jesus Christ as one's personal Savior. It is sad that the Jewish rabbis and the Jews attending their synagogues are going through some motions, but their hearts are hardened and their eyes are blind, according to this passage of Scripture.

Paul's message to the Gentile Christians in Galatia makes it even clearer:

> 21 Tell me, you who want to be under law, do you not listen to the law?
> 22 For it is written that Abraham had two sons, one by the bondwoman and one by the free woman.
> 23 But the son by the bondwoman was born according to the flesh, and the son by the free woman through the promise.

24 This is allegorically speaking: for these women are two covenants, one proceeding from Mount Sinai bearing children who are to be slaves; she is Hagar.

25 Now this Hagar is Mount Sinai in Arabia, and corresponds to the present Jerusalem, for she is in slavery with her children.

26 But the Jerusalem above is free; she is our mother.

27 For it is written,
> "REJOICE, BARREN WOMAN WHO DOES NOT BEAR;
> BREAK FORTH AND SHOUT, YOU WHO ARE NOT IN LABOR;
> FOR MORE ARE THE CHILDREN OF THE DESOLATE THAN
> OF THE ONE WHO HAS A HUSBAND."

28 And you brethren, like Isaac, are children of promise.

29 But as at that time he who was born according to the flesh persecuted him who was born according to the Spirit, so it is now also.

30 But what does the Scripture say?
> "CAST OUT THE BONDWOMAN AND HER SON,
> FOR THE SON OF THE BONDWOMAN SHALL NOT BE AN HEIR WITH THE SON OF THE FREE WOMAN."

31 So then, brethren, we are not children of a bondwoman, but of the free woman.

—Galatians 4

Before we analyze this passage, I would like to repeat verse 28, which is so important:

> 28 And you brethren, like Isaac, are children of promise.
>
> —Galatians 4

Paul was putting these Gentile Christians on an equivalent basis with Isaac as the children of promise. He states this very explicitly, leaving no doubt whatsoever. These Gentile believers in Jesus Christ were children of promise just as much as Isaac, father of Jacob (Israel). Let that sink in.

Looking at the broader teaching of the passage, it talks about the two sons of Abraham, but it equates Hagar to Mount Sinai—all those who are under the old covenant. Paul says that people who follow that old covenant are in slavery. He also equates Hagar, the mother of slavery, to the present city of Jerusalem.

Then Paul switches to talk about the new Jerusalem (the one from above) as a mother of believers in Jesus Christ. They are children of the free woman, whereas all of the people who were under the old covenant were children of the bondwoman. Here once again, he declares the superiority of the new covenant over the old covenant, and includes all non-Hebrew (as well as Hebrew) believers in Jesus Christ as the chosen people of God—as children of promise.

When these writers say "old covenant," I believe they are including all of the covenants in the Old Testament. There was a major covenant made with Abraham as well as a covenant that God made with Israel during the time of Moses, and one with David. There are teachers who would attempt to break up this "old covenant," claiming that the covenant of Moses has been invalidated, but not the covenant of Abraham. I see absolutely no biblical justification for this. In fact, God never made a covenant with Moses; He made a covenant with Israel, using Moses as a scribe. Of course, Moses was included in Israel:

> 1 These are the words of the covenant which the LORD commanded Moses to make with the sons of Israel in the land of Moab, besides the covenant which He had made with them at Horeb.
> —Deuteronomy 29

8 So Moses took the blood and sprinkled it on the people, and said, "Behold the blood of the covenant, which the LORD has made with you in accordance with all these words."

—Exodus 24

16 And the LORD said to Moses, "Behold, you are about to lie down with your fathers; and this people will arise and play the harlot with the strange gods of the land, into the midst of which they are going, and will forsake Me and break My covenant which I have made with them. . . ."

—Deuteronomy 31

10 There was nothing in the ark except the two tablets which Moses put there at Horeb, where the LORD made a covenant with the sons of Israel, when they came out of Egypt.

—2 Chronicles 5

When the Bible says that the old covenant has disappeared, that is *all* of the old covenants found in the Old Testament, including the one with Abraham and the one with Israel during the time of Moses.

CIRCUMCISION IS A KEY

It is interesting that the covenant that God made with Abraham was conditional, contrary to popular teaching. Abraham was to "walk before God and be blameless" as his part of the covenant. Some people teach that this covenant was unconditional, as we mentioned earlier. That simply is not correct, according to Scripture.

1 Now when Abram was ninety-nine years old, the LORD appeared to Abram and said to him,
"I am God Almighty;
Walk before Me, and be blameless.

44 CHAPTER 2

> 2 "And I will establish My covenant between Me and you,
> And I will multiply you exceedingly."
> 3 And Abram fell on his face, and God talked with him, saying,
> 4 "As for Me, behold, My covenant is with you,
> And you shall be the father of a multitude of nations.
> 5 "No longer shall your name be called Abram,
> But your name shall be Abraham;
> For I will make you the father of a multitude of nations.
> 6 "And I will make you exceedingly fruitful, and I will make nations of you, and kings shall come forth from you.
> 7 "And I will establish My covenant between Me and you and your descendants after you throughout their generations for an everlasting covenant, to be God to you and to your descendants after you.
> 8 "And I will give to you and to your descendants after you, the land of your sojournings, all the land of Canaan, for an everlasting possession; and I will be their God."
>
> —Genesis 17

There was another condition to the old covenant, and that was circumcision. The passage continues with God telling Abraham about that:

> 9 God said further to Abraham, "Now as for you, you shall keep My covenant, you and your descendants after you throughout their generations.
> 10 "This is My covenant, which you shall keep, between Me and you and your descendants after you: every male among you shall be circumcised.
> 11 "And you shall be circumcised in the flesh of your foreskin; and it shall be the sign of the covenant between Me and you.

12 "And every male among you who is eight days old shall be circumcised throughout your generations, a servant who is born in the house or who is bought with money from any foreigner, who is not of your descendants.

13 "A servant who is born in your house or who is bought with your money shall surely be circumcised; thus shall My covenant be in your flesh for an everlasting covenant.

14 "But an uncircumcised male who is not circumcised in the flesh of his foreskin, that person shall be cut off from his people; he has broken My covenant."
—Genesis 17

In this passage, we hear clearly from God's own mouth that circumcision was a requirement of the old covenant and that any male who was not circumcised was cut off from Israel because he had broken God's covenant.

Abraham followed this very religiously:

4 Then Abraham circumcised his son Isaac when he was eight days old, as God had commanded him.
—Genesis 21

During the time of Moses, at the very first Passover, circumcision was reemphasized by God as a requirement to be part of the old covenant:

43 And the LORD said to Moses and Aaron, "This is the ordinance of the Passover: no foreigner is to eat of it;

44 but every man's slave purchased with money, after you have circumcised him, then he may eat of it.

45 "A sojourner or a hired servant shall not eat of it.

> 46 "It is to be eaten in a single house; you are not to bring forth any of the flesh outside of the house, nor are you to break any bone of it.
> 47 "All the congregation of Israel are to celebrate this.
> 48 "But if a stranger sojourns with you, and celebrates the Passover to the LORD, let all his males be circumcised, and then let him come near to celebrate it; and he shall be like a native of the land. But no uncircumcised person may eat of it. . . ."
> —Exodus 12

This was later incorporated into the Law which God gave to Moses:

> 1 Then the LORD spoke to Moses, saying,
> 2 "Speak to the sons of Israel, saying, 'When a woman gives birth and bears a male child, then she shall be unclean for seven days, as in the days of her menstruation she shall be unclean.
> 3 'And on the eighth day the flesh of his foreskin shall be circumcised. . . .'"
> —Leviticus 12

Before God would let the children of Israel conquer the promised land, they had to be sure all the males were circumcised, in order to be partakers of the old covenant:

> 2 At that time the LORD said to Joshua, "Make for yourself flint knives and circumcise again the sons of Israel the second time."
> 3 So Joshua made himself flint knives and circumcised the sons of Israel at Gibeath-haaraloth.
> 4 And this is the reason why Joshua circumcised them: all the people who came out of Egypt who were males, all the men of war, died in the wilderness along the way, after they came out of Egypt.

THE TWO COVENANTS 47

> 5 For all the people who came out were circumcised, but all the people who were born in the wilderness along the way as they came out of Egypt had not been circumcised.
>
> —Joshua 5

It was plain that one had to be circumcised under the old covenant in order to be part of Israel.

The three conditions of the covenant with Abraham were:

1. To walk before God
2. To be blameless
3. To have all males circumcised

In the time of Peter, Paul and the early disciples, a rousing argument came up as to whether the Gentile believers needed to be circumcised in order to become part of Israel. In actuality, this was an argument as to whether or not they were under the old covenant. In fact, the old covenant was called "the covenant of circumcision":

> 8 "And He gave him the covenant of circumcision; and so Abraham became the father of Isaac, and circumcised him on the eighth day; and Isaac became the father of Jacob, and Jacob of the twelve patriarchs...."
>
> —Acts 7

There were some who claimed that the old covenant still existed and the new covenant simply took its place beside it. Therefore, they tried to get all of the Gentile Christians to be circumcised. The entire chapter of Acts 15 deals with this. We will look at a portion of it:

> 1 And some men came down from Judea and began teaching the brethren, "Unless you are circum-

cised according to the custom of Moses, you cannot be saved."

2 And when Paul and Barnabas had great dissension and debate with them, the brethren determined that Paul and Barnabas and certain others of them should go up to Jerusalem to the apostles and elders concerning this issue.

—Acts 15

Reading on, we find out what happened when they arrived in Jerusalem:

4 And when they arrived at Jerusalem, they were received by the church and the apostles and the elders, and they reported all that God had done with them.

5 But certain ones of the sect of the Pharisees who had believed, stood up, saying, "It is necessary to circumcise them, and to direct them to observe the Law of Moses."

6 And the apostles and the elders came together to look into this matter.

7 And after there had been much debate, Peter stood up and said to them, "Brethren, you know that in the early days God made a choice among you, that by my mouth the Gentiles should hear the word of the gospel and believe.

8 "And God, who knows the heart, bore witness to them, giving them the Holy Spirit, just as He also did to us;

9 and He made no distinction between us and them, cleansing their hearts by faith.

10 "Now therefore why do you put God to the test by placing upon the neck of the disciples a yoke which neither our fathers nor we have been able to bear?

11 "But we believe that we are saved through the grace of the Lord Jesus, in the same way as they also are."

—Acts 15

In these verses, we see that good old Peter states that there is *no distinction* between Jewish believers and Gentile believers—they are all saved through the grace of the Lord Jesus and they all have their hearts cleansed by faith. But let us go on to see what happened. If the apostles and elders concluded that they were still under the old covenant, they would require these Gentile believers to be circumcised. If, on the other hand, they felt that the old covenant was dead and the new covenant had replaced it, then they would not place the burden of circumcision upon these Gentile believers. Here is what happened next:

12 And all the multitude kept silent, and they were listening to Barnabas and Paul as they were relating what signs and wonders God had done through them among the Gentiles.
13 And after they had stopped speaking, James answered, saying, "Brethren, listen to me.
14 "Simeon has related how God first concerned Himself about taking from among the Gentiles a people for His name.
15 "And with this the words of the Prophets agree, just as it is witten,
16   'AFTER THESE THINGS I will return,
      AND I WILL REBUILD THE TABERNACLE OF DAVID WHICH HAS FALLEN,
      AND I WILL REBUILD ITS RUINS,
      AND I WILL RESTORE IT,
17   IN ORDER THAT THE REST OF MANKIND MAY SEEK THE LORD,
      AND ALL THE GENTILES WHO ARE CALLED BY MY NAME,'
18   SAYS THE LORD, WHO MAKES THESE THINGS KNOWN FROM OF OLD.
19 "Therefore it is my judgment that we do not trouble those who are turning to God from among the Gentiles,

> **20** but that we write to them that they abstain from things contaminated by idols and from fornication and from what is strangled and from blood.
> **21** "For Moses from ancient generations has in every city those who preach him, since he is read in the synagogues every Sabbath."
>
> —Acts 15

Here we see that the decision was made that the Gentile Christians did not have to be circumcised (and, by implication, any new-born Jewish Christians did not have to be circumcised). The old covenant had been fulfilled, completed and had ended through Jesus Christ and His life, His precious blood and His powerful resurrection.

It is wonderful when a group of believers have one mind. Here all the apostles and prophets came to one mind on the subject that circumcision was not required. They wrote a letter to that effect:

> **22** Then it seemed good to the apostles and the elders, with the whole church, to choose men from among them to send to Antioch with Paul and Barnabas—Judas called Barsabbas, and Silas, leading men among the brethren,
> **23** and they sent this letter by them,
>> "The apostles and the brethren who are elders, to the brethren in Antioch and Syria and Cilicia who are from the Gentiles, greetings.
>> **24** "Since we have heard that some of our number to whom we gave no instruction have disturbed you with their words, unsettling your souls,
>> **25** it seemed good to us, having become of one mind, to select men to send to you with our beloved Barnabas and Paul,
>> **26** men who have risked their lives for the name of our Lord Jesus Christ.

27 "Therefore we have sent Judas and Silas, who themselves will also report the same things by word of mouth.

28 "For it seemed good to the Holy Spirit and to us to lay upon you no greater burden than these essentials:

29 that you abstain from things sacrificed to idols and from blood and from things strangled and from fornication; if you keep yourselves free from such things, you will do well. Farewell."

30 So, when they were sent away, they went down to Antioch; and having gathered the congregation together, they delivered the letter.

31 And when they had read it, they rejoiced because of its encouragement.

—Acts 15

They clearly understood that, by not requiring believers in Jesus Christ to be circumcised, they were pronouncing the "covenant of circumcision" as completed, over, finished. Later, when Paul came back to Jerusalem, all the Jews there—both believers in Jesus Christ and non-believers—knew what Paul was teaching:

21 and they have been told about you, that you are teaching all the Jews who are among the Gentiles to forsake Moses, telling them not to circumcise their children nor to walk according to the customs.

—Acts 21

In teaching the Jews as well as the Gentiles not to circumcise their children, Paul was telling them that the old covenant (of circumcision) was over and no longer valid and the new covenant had replaced it.

In fact, Paul went even further by calling the circumcision of the old covenant a *false* circumcision. He pointed out that there is only one valid circumcision now:

> 2 Beware of the dogs, beware of the evil workers, beware of the false circumcision;
> 3 for we are the true circumcision, who worship in the Spirit of God and glory in Christ Jesus and put no confidence in the flesh.
> —Philippians 3

The only people who are truly circumcised are those who glory in Christ Jesus. Do you glory in Christ? If you do, you are of the true circumcision. If someone has been circumcised in the flesh and does not glory in our precious Savior, his circumcision is false, invalid.

As we pointed out earlier, Paul also expressed this thought in writing to the believers in Rome, who were a combination of Hebrews and non-Hebrews:

> 28 For he is not a Jew who is one outwardly; neither is circumcision that which is outward in the flesh.
> 29 But he is a Jew who is one inwardly; and circumcision is that which is of the heart, by the Spirit, not by the letter; and his praise is not from men, but from God.
> —Romans 2

To net it down, the old covenant was conditional and required circumcision to make it valid to an individual. In the New Testament, when it was decided not to require believers to be circumcised, the leaders were saying that the old covenant was dead and that the new covenant of Jesus Christ replaced it. And today, the only valid way to God is through Jesus Christ. We are no longer under the old covenant, and we are no longer under the Law. We are under the Spirit which is a higher requirement of holiness. We yearn to be like our Savior and Example, Jesus Christ.

THE TWO COVENANTS 53

JESUS AND THE NEW COVENANT

When Jesus makes absolute statements, there are no exceptions. For example, in John 3:16, when He said "Whosoever," there are no exceptions. When He told Nicodemus that "no one" can even see the kingdom of God unless he is born again, there are not any exceptions (John 3:1-15). Even a Jewish leader, who kept the Old Testament laws like Nicodemus did, could no longer get into the kingdom of heaven by the old covenant—he had to be born again. The same was true for any other Hebrew or Jew of that day.

Jesus stated this even more clearly:

> 6 Jesus said to him, "I am the way, and the truth, and the life; no one comes to the Father, but through Me. . . ."
>
> —John 14

When Jesus said that "no one" comes to the Father but through Himself, He invalidated all other possible roads of access to God the Father. This would include attempting to come to God through the old covenant.

Jesus also tells us that if we deny Him before men, He will deny us in eternity:

> 8 "And I say to you, everyone who confesses Me before men, the Son of Man shall confess him also before the angels of God;
> 9 but he who denies Me before men shall be denied before the angels of God. . . ."
>
> —Luke 12

This concept—that the only way to God is through Jesus Christ—is found throughout the New Testament:

> 23 Whoever denies the Son does not have the Father; the one who confesses the Son has the Father also.
>
> —1 John 2

This passage states clearly that whoever denies Jesus Christ, as the Son of God, does *not* have the Father. In this quote, "whoever" is all-inclusive and there are no exceptions. Even if a person is attempting to follow the old covenant perfectly, but he denies Jesus Christ, there is absolutely no way that he can have the Father.

To believe that there is another way to the Father, other than through Jesus Christ, contradicts our Savior Himself. The price of the new covenant was high. Jesus poured out His own precious blood in order to pay for the new covenant:

> 20 And in the same way He took the cup after they had eaten, saying, "This cup which is poured out for you is the new covenant in my blood. . . ."
>
> —Luke 22

With the shedding of His blood and the establishing of the new covenant, Jesus Christ eliminated any other means of access to God the Father, because He says He is the "only" way. In effect, He declared that the old covenant had ended and that His precious blood had established the new covenant.

Now that we have seen the proper relationship between the two covenants, let us move on to examine who was included in Israel, beginning in the time when the old covenant was still valid.

3

OTHERS INCLUDED IN ISRAEL

There are some Christian teachers today who say that the Hebrews and Jews living on the shores of Palestine are "physical Israel" and the Christians are "spiritual Israel." (We will see why they make this comment on "spiritual Israel" in a later chapter.) I would like to humbly suggest that Israel has always been and always will be a group of people based on spiritual criteria; it was never anything but that.

PROMISES MADE TO ABRAHAM AND HIS OFFSPRING

God made certain promises to Abraham that He said would pass on to his seed or offspring. However, apparently this did not apply to all of his biological offspring, since Ishmael (from whom come the Arabs) was not an inheritor of the divine promises made to Abraham.

If we go the next step to Abraham's son Isaac, whose sons were Jacob and Esau, we likewise find that Esau was not an inheritor of the promises (from him come the Edomites.) The promises only went down to Jacob, whose name was subsequently changed to "Israel."

In addition to the well-known sons of these men, there were many other sons as well. For example,

Abraham took another wife after Sarah, and she bore him six sons:

> 1 Now Abraham took another wife, whose name was Keturah.
> 2 And she bore to him Zimran and Jokshan and Medan and Midian and Ishbak and Shuah.
> 3 And Jokshan became the father of Sheba and Dedan. And the sons of Dedan were Asshurim and Letushim and Leummim.
> 4 And the sons of Midian were Ephah and Epher and Hanoch and Abida and Eldaah. All these were the sons of Keturah.
> 5 Now Abraham gave all that he had to Isaac;
> 6 but to the sons of his concubines, Abraham gave gifts while he was still living, and sent them away from his son Isaac eastward, to the land of the east.
> —Genesis 25

Thus, the blessings of God were not to these biological children of Abraham but only to his spiritual seed. If we were to regard the promises made to Abraham as purely biological, of necessity we would need to include all these people who were biologically from Abraham. Should they not also receive all of the promises?

Why then should only Isaac, of all Abraham's sons, and only Jacob, of Isaac's two sons, receive the promise? What was the basis? The basis was certainly not biological, or else all of them would have been included. The basis must have been spiritual.

RUTH, RAHAB AND OTHERS

There are only four women mentioned in the genealogy of Christ. Two of these are Ruth and Rahab, and neither of them was biologically from Abraham. In fact, if you want to trace the genealogy of these two women, Ruth was a Moabite woman, and

OTHERS INCLUDED IN ISRAEL

yet was the great grandmother of David, and Rahab was a harlot in Jericho, who was taken as a wife by a Hebrew named Salmon. She was the great, great grandmother of David.

> 5 and to Salmon was born Boaz by Rahab; and to Boaz was born Obed by Ruth; and to Obed, Jesse; 6 and to Jesse was born David the king.
> —Matthew 1

So, if we want to think of it this way, Boaz—son of Rahab—was only 50 percent from Abraham biologically. Then Boaz married Ruth, who was not biologically from Abraham, so their offspring, Obed (David's grandfather), was only 25 percent from Abraham biologically. If we carry that down through the time of Christ, since Christ came from the line of David biologically, it is very possible that Jesus might have been a very small percentage biologically from Abraham, particularly with the infusion of foreign blood brought in from wives taken in Egypt, in wars and in the Babylonian captivity. We know that, at most, Jesus was only 25 percent genealogically from Abraham.

Ruth and Rahab are but two specific examples of people being assimilated into Israel. The Old Testament is absolutely loaded with other people who became a part of Israel, who were not genealogically from Abraham. Before we look at some of them, I would like to define my use of a couple of words.

We know from the Scriptures that Abraham is called a Hebrew:

> 13 Then a fugitive came and told Abram the Hebrew. Now he was living by the oaks of Mamre the Amorite, brother of Eschcol and brother of Aner, and these were allies with Abram.
> —Genesis 14

Since the term "Hebrew" referred to his biological heritage, in this book we will use the word "Hebrews" in referring to those who are biologically from Abraham through Isaac and Jacob. On the other hand, we will use "Israel" and "Israelite" to refer to the spiritual group of people that God chose. As we will see, not all of these (as with Ruth and Rahab) were biologically from Abraham.

I would like to suggest that trying to look at this whole subject of Israel biologically will tie you in knots. It has to be looked at spiritually. When Ruth and Rahab were assimilated into Israel, they became 100 percent Israelites, and Jesus Christ was spiritually 100 percent from Abraham and David. The confusion arises because most people have not yet understood that Israel is a spiritual entity and not a physical entity. If you try to approach all of this on a biological basis, Ruth and Rahab were not biologically from Abraham, and we do not know how many of the other men in the genealogy of Christ had wives who were not of Abrahamic descent. I think Christians should stop playing biological roulette and let Ruth and Rahab be completely a part of Israel. When you do that, you have just agreed that Israel is a spiritual entity.

Others are included in "Israel" as well. All through the Old Testament, foreigners, strangers and aliens were assimilated into Israel, and God looked at them as part of the congregation of Israel. For example:

> 43 And the Lord said to Moses and Aaron, "This is the ordinance of the Passover: no foreigner is to eat of it;
> 44 But every man's slave purchased with money, after you have circumcised him, then he may eat of it.
> 45 "A sojourner or a hired servant shall not eat of it.

OTHERS INCLUDED IN ISRAEL

> 46 "It is to be eaten in a single house; you are not to bring forth any of the flesh outside of the house, nor are you to break any bone of it.
> 47 "All the congregation of Israel are to celebrate this.
> 48 "But if a stranger sojourns with you, and celebrates the Passover to the Lord, let all his males be circumcised, and then let him come near to celebrate it; and he shall be like a native of the land. But no uncircumcised person may eat of it. . . ."
> —Exodus 12

Here we see that, after being circumcised, every slave purchased by a Hebrew could eat of the Passover. Any stranger who lived among them or who visited a Hebrew, and who had all his males circumcised, could also come and eat of the Passover, and be assimilated into the congregation of Israel. However, during the days of the Passover, there was to be no leaven found in their houses. This is what would happen if there was:

> 19 'Seven days there shall be no leaven found in your houses; for whoever eats what is leavened, that person shall be cut off from the congregation of Israel, whether he is an alien or a native of the land. . . .'
> —Exodus 12

Here we see that anyone who had leaven in his house during that time would be cut off from the congregation of Israel, whether it was an alien or a native Hebrew. Thus, we see that assimilated aliens were considered by God to be a part of Israel, at least from the first Passover forward. To try to differentiate between biological decendants of Abraham, who are part of the congregation of Israel, and those who are not biologically decended from Abraham, but who are also a part of the congregation of Israel, would be splitting hairs, if not impossible. This is not the way God looked at it. I always want to try to have God's perspective on things, as much as is possible. We too should look at all these people (including Ruth and Rahab) as 100 percent part of Israel, because Israel is a spiritual entity and not a physical entity. It was spiritual, not physical, even in the times of the Old Testament.

FOREIGN WIVES ASSIMILATED INTO ISRAEL

Ruth and Rahab were not exceptions. Under the Old Testament Law, the Israelite men had permission from God to take wives from among their enemies. Ultimately, such wives and the offspring of their marriages would be part of Israel. One place we read about this is in Deuteronomy:

> 10 "When you go out to battle against your enemies, and the LORD your God delivers them into your hands, and you take them away captive,
> 11 and see among the captives a beautiful woman, and have a desire for her and would take her as a wife for yourself,
> 12 then you shall bring her home to your house, and she shall shave her head and trim her nails.
> 13 She shall also remove the clothes of her captivity and shall remain in your house, and mourn her father and mother a full month; and after that you may go in to her and be her husband and she shall be your wife...."
>
> —Deuteronomy 21

From this passage, we can see that Ruth and Rahab were not the only foreign wives incorporated into Israel. A whole host of foreign woman were taken as wives by the Israelite men, and they became part of Israel in the Old Testament. These women were not genealogically descended from Abraham, yet they became part of Israel.

MANY BECAME JEWS

The events described in the book of Esther took place at Susa, the Persian capital during the reign of Ahasuerus, which was 486-465 B.C. I am sure that you are familiar with the story of Esther, wherein the old queen fell out of favor with the king and was deposed. The king then searched for a new queen and chose Esther.

Esther was a cousin of Mordecai. They had been carried away by Nebuchadnezzar, with the other captives, from Jerusalem into Babylon. Esther was the daughter of Mordecai's uncle. She had neither father nor mother, so Mordecai raised her. Mordecai uncovered a plot to kill the king and revealed this, so that the king was saved.

The king's second in command, Haman, hated the Jews who lived there in Persia and wanted to destroy them. He got a decree passed to execute the Jews. After fasting for three days, along with all the other Jews in that area, Esther risked her life to intercede with the king on behalf of the Jews.

King Ahasuerus could not rescind the previous edict issued in his name and sealed with his signet ring, but He gave a new order that the Jews could defend themselves:

> 9 So the king's scribes were called at that time in the third month (that is, the month Sivan), on the twenty-third day; and it was written according to all that Mordecai commanded to the Jews, the satraps, the governors, and the princes of the provinces which extended from India to Ethiopia, 127 provinces, to every province according to its script, and to every people according to their language, as well as to the Jews according to their script and their language.
>
> 10 And he wrote in the name of King Ahasuerus, and sealed it with the king's signet ring, and sent

letters by couriers on horses, riding on steeds sired by the royal stud.

11 In them the king granted the Jews who were in each and every city the right to assemble and to defend their lives, to destroy, to kill, and to annihilate the entire army of any people or province which might attack them, including children and women, and to plunder their spoil,

12 on one day in all the provinces of King Ahasuerus, the thirteenth day of the twelfth month (that is, the month Adar).

13 A copy of the edict to be issued as law in each and every province, was published to all the peoples, so that the Jews should be ready for this day to avenge themselves on their enemies.

14 The couriers, hastened and impelled by the king's command, went out, riding on the royal steeds; and the decree was given out in Susa the capital.

—Esther 8

The king rewarded Mordecai, and the Jews celebrated an incredible victory that day:

15 Then Mordecai went out from the presence of the king in royal robes of blue and white, and a large crown of gold and a garment of fine linen and purple; and the city of Susa shouted and rejoiced.

16 For the Jews there was light and gladness and joy and honor.

17 And in each and every province, and in each and every city, wherever the king's commandment and his decree arrived, there was gladness and joy for the Jews, a feast and a holiday. And many among the peoples of the land became Jews, for the dread of the Jews had fallen on them.

—Esther 8

Did you get the last part of verse 17? Many of the people of the land (the Persians) *became Jews*—they became part of Israel. So we see that in the Old Testament, being a Jew was a spiritual matter, not a matter of biology. Being a Jew meant to follow the religion of Judaism, and "a Jew" could be someone of any race or nation.

Now let's see what happened upon the return of the Jews from the Babylonian captivity.

RETURN FROM THE BABYLONIAN CAPTIVITY

We read in the books of Ezra and Nehemiah that many of those who came up from Tel-melah and some other places could not trace their ancestry back to their fathers' households and many others had married foreign wives:

> 59 Now these are those who came up from Tel-melah, Tel-harsha, Cherub, Addan, and Immer, but they were not able to give evidence of their fathers' households, and their descendants, whether they were of Israel: . . .
> —Ezra 2

> 44 All these had married foreign wives, and some of them had wives by whom they had children.
> —Ezra 10

Of those who came up out of Babylon, only those who were priests put aside their foreign wives. Still, all of the people—including the foreign wives—who came up from the Babylonian captivity were ultimately considered "Israel," whether or not they were biologically from Abraham. (Most of the Jews remained in Babylon.)

Thus, we see one more building block to attest to the fact that God has regarded Israel a spiritual entity, and never a physical one. It is His family and He can allow anyone into it that He wants. Who are we to sit as judge and say, "Ruth and Rahab cannot become part of Israel"? If God wants them in, and evidently He did, let's treat them as 100 percent Israel, and let's put aside this biological nonsense.

ASSIMILATING PROSELYTES

God knew that foreigners would be assimilated into Israel. In fact, in the Old Testament times there were clearly-outlined procedures for assimilating proselytes (those not physically descended from Abraham) who wanted to become part of Israel. Hebrews who did not follow God were removed from Israel.

One of the passages of Scripture that deals with assimilating those who were not born physically to Abraham's offspring, into Old Testament Israel, is found in Isaiah:

> 3 Let not the foreigner who has joined himself to the LORD say,
> "The LORD will surely separate me from His people."
> Neither let the eunuch say, "Behold, I am a dry tree."
> 4 For thus says the LORD,
> "To the eunuchs who keep My sabbaths
> And choose what pleases Me,
> And hold fast My covenant,
> 5 To them I will give in My house and within My walls a memorial,
> And a name better than that of sons and daughters;
> I will give them an everlasting name which will not be cut off.
> 6 "Also the foreigners who join themselves to the LORD,
> To minister to Him, and to love the name of the LORD,
> To be His servants, every one who keeps from profaning the sabbath,

And holds fast My covenant;
7 Even those I will bring to My holy mountain,
And make them joyful in My house of prayer.
Their burnt offerings and their sacrifices will be acceptable on My altar;
For my house will be called a house of prayer for all the peoples."
8 The Lord God, who gathers the dispersed of Israel, declares,
"Yet others I will gather to them, to those already gathered."
—Isaiah 56

Another passage of Scripture that deals with this subject is the following:

21 "So you shall divide this land among yourselves according to the tribes of Israel.
22 "And it will come about that you shall divide it by lot for an inheritance among yourselves and among the aliens who stay in your midst, who bring forth sons in your midst. And they shall be to you as the native-born among the sons of Israel; they shall be allotted an inheritance with you among the tribes of Israel.
23 "And it will come about that in the tribe with which the alien stays, there you shall give him his inheritance," declares the Lord God.
—Ezekiel 47

Earlier in this chapter we quoted some verses that also apply here:

43 And the LORD said to Moses and Aaron, "This is the ordinance of the Passover: no foreigner is to eat of it;
44 but every man's slave purchased with money, after you have circumcised him, then he may eat of it.
45 "A sojourner or a hired servant shall not eat of it. . . .

> 47 "All the congregation of Israel are to celebrate this.
>
> 48 "But if a stranger sojourns with you, and celebrates the Passover to the LORD, let all his males be circumcised, and then let him come near to celebrate it; and he shall be like a native of the land. But no uncircumcised person may eat of it.
>
> 49 "The same law shall apply to the native as to the stranger who sojourns among you."
>
> —Exodus 12

As you can see from the preceding passages, if a stranger or an alien wanted to eat the Passover, to be circumcised, and to follow God, then he was no longer considered to be an alien, but rather part of the congregation of Israel.

JEWS FROM EVERY NATION

We have seen that there were many who were not biologically from Abraham who were part of the congregation of Israel. There was a process to assimilate the proselytes. In fact, the non-Hebrew followers of Jehovah God, who had been circumcised, were called proselytes. There was a large number of them in Jerusalem on the day of Pentecost, when the disciples who were gathered together were all filled with the Holy Spirit and began to speak with other tongues:

> 5 Now there were Jews living in Jerusalem, devout men, from every nation under heaven.
>
> 6 And when this sound occurred, the multitude came together, and were bewildered, because they were each one hearing them speak in his own language.
>
> 7 And they were amazed and marveled, saying, "Why, are not all these who are speaking Galileans?
>
> 8 "And how is it that we each hear them in our own language to which we were born?

> 9 "Parthians and Medes and Elamites, and residents of Mesopotamia, Judea and Cappadocia, Pontus and Asia,
> 10 Phrygia and Pamphylia, Egypt and the districts of Libya around Cyrene, and visitors from Rome, both Jews and proselytes,
> 11 Cretans and Arabs—we hear them in our own tongues speaking of the mighty deeds of God."
> —Acts 2, NAS

> 10 Phrygia and Pamphylia, Egypt and the parts of Libya near Cyrene; visitors from Rome
> 11 (both Jews and converts to Judaism); Cretans and Arabs—we hear them declaring the wonders of God in our own tongues!"
> —Acts 2, NIV

People from every single nation who were there heard native tongues being spoken. If they were from Egypt, they heard apostles speaking in Egyptian. If they were native born in Cyrene, they heard the apostles speaking in the Cyrenian language, and so forth. These obviously were not Hebrews returning from various countries where they resided or these other languages would not have been their native tongues. These Jews (proselytes according to verse 10) had moved to Jerusalem and were now living there. Of course, there could have been some Hebrews mixed in with the proselytes. Thus, we see that even in the time of Jesus, many of the "Jews" were not Hebrews. They were, in fact, from every race and "every nation under the sun."

Jesus Himself acknowledged that proselytes, gentiles converted to Judaism, were being made and they became Jews:

> 15 "Woe to you, scribes and Pharisees, hypocrites, because you travel about on sea and land to make one

> proselyte; and when he becomes one, you make him twice as much a son of hell as yourselves...."
>
> —Matthew 23

A proselyte from Antioch was one of the first deacons:

> 5 And the statement found approval with the whole congregation; and they chose Stephen, a man full of faith and of the Holy Spirit, and Philip, Prochorus, Nicanor, Timon, Parmenas and Nicolas, a proselyte from Antioch.
>
> —Acts 6

All through history, there were those not genealogically descended from Abraham who were being converted to Judaism, and thus became Jews.

If someone today makes a statement such as "God loves the Jews" or "the Jews are God's chosen people," what are they really saying? Based on the definitions of the Jews themselves, they are saying that God's chosen people are the Japanese and other Oriental Jews, Black Jews, Indian Jews and Caucasian Jews. This is not a definition that I invented. Just go to the Great Synagogue in Jerusalem and ask to see a Japanese rabbi, and you will meet one. Being a Jew is spiritual, not physical.

Christians today really are confused when they talk about the Jews or the State of Israel being God's chosen people. Are they saying that all Hebrews, even those who hate and reject God, are God's chosen people, *or* are they saying that all people, regardless of race, who embrace Judaism are God's chosen people, but not the atheistic Hebrew? As we will see before this book is over, neither one of these definitions will hold water when held up to the light of Scripture. The Israel of God is something totally different.

Since God is a spirit, the key identity of God's chosen people would not be of the flesh; it would be of the spirit.

ALIENS BEING MERGED INTO "JEWS" TODAY

Today, there are Jews from almost every race and nation in the world. Just as in the Old Testament, being a Jew today means embracing Judaism as your religion. In the Great Synagogue in Jerusalem, there is an entire wing for the Japanese Jews, for example.

There is the story that Abe Goldstein went to Tokyo and went to the synagogue on Saturday. Of course, the rabbi and all the Jews there were Japanese. When Abe Goldstein met the rabbi at the back door of the synagogue after the meeting, the rabbi said, "Funny, you don't look Jewish."

There was a situation where a group of black Jews in Africa had been airlifted into the State of Israel from Ethiopia. The Ethiopian Jews were airlifted by the Israeli government by the thousands on January 4th, 1985, in an operation code-named "Operation Moses."

Ethiopian Jews have been generally known as "Falashas" which means "stranger" or "exile" in Ge'ez (ancient Ethiopic). In general, the Ethiopian Jews consider this term as a derogatory one, and they refer to themselves as "Beta Israel" (House of Israel) or, in more simple terms, "Ethiopian Jews."

"Operation Moses" is only one of many rescue operations that have taken place with many immigrants migrating to Palestine, as the State of Israel has provided a haven for oppressed Jews from all over the globe. This migration has been referred to as "the ingathering of the exiles."

Jewish immigrants have been arriving from some 80 countries—Russia, the United States, South Africa, Canada, Argentina, Australia, Iraq, Turkey, Iran, Tunisia, India, China, as well as from the Atlas Mountains in Morocco. They come from Western cultures, Eastern cultures and from tribal cultures as primitive as those of the Stone Age. Some were hunters with blowpipes, clubs, bows and arrows and some were doctors and lawyers, but all of them are Jews.

People of various races and nations are considered "Jews" today—that is, they are following the Judaic religion. This shows very dramatically that we are dealing with spiritual entities and not physical entities.

4

HEBREWS EXCLUDED FROM ISRAEL

Biologically, a person can never change the race of his birth. If you were born Caucasian, you will always be Caucasian. You can change religions, dye your hair, change your name, but you are still Caucasian. There is nothing that anyone can do to remove himself from the Caucasian race or any other race.

In a similar way, if a person is born a Hebrew—a biological descendant of Abraham—he will always be a Hebrew. Biologically, he cannot change that. However, it is different if we are talking about a group of people of a certain religion. There are numerous people who started life out as Catholics, and switched to a Protestant church, for example. There are those who once were Buddhists, but who switched to Shintoism. There are some who once were atheists, who are now Christians.

In many cases, the individual himself made the decision to change religions and, in some cases, the religious leaders decided to excommunicate him or expel him from the religious order.

HEBREWS EXPELLED FROM ISRAEL

As we have just discussed, there is no way that you could ever expel a Hebrew from being a Hebrew, but if Israel is a spiritual entity, then you could expel

Hebrews from Israel. If God did this, or commanded someone to be cut off from the congregation of Israel, it would solidly prove that Israel is a spiritual entity and not a biological one.

We need to turn our attention to the fact that God did exclude many from Israel who were native-born Hebrews. He excluded those descended from Ishmael, and the other six sons of Abraham; He excluded Esau and his descendants, and so forth. These were people who were descendants of Abraham. We have already looked at one of these situations, when the Passover dinner was given to Moses by God:

> 18 'In the first month, in the fourteenth day of the month at evening, you shall eat unleavened bread, until the twenty-first day of the month at evening.
> 19 'Seven days there shall be no leaven found in your houses; for whoever eats what is leavened, that person shall be cut off from the congregation of Israel, whether he is an alien or a native of the land.
> 20 'You shall not eat anything leavened; in all your dwellings you shall eat unleavened bread.'"
> —Exodus 12

Here we see that there were aliens who were part of Israel. But, in verse 19, we also see that even if a native Hebrew ate leavened bread in his house during the seven days of the Passover, he would be "cut off from the congregation of Israel." In other words, God would kick him out, and he would no longer be part of Israel. He was still a Hebrew; that is physical and cannot change. However, since being part of Israel is spiritual, he could be removed from that spiritual group.

EXCLUSION IN THE BOOK OF LEVITICUS

The book of Leviticus is called the "book of Law." The first chapters give the laws concerning the priests, and the second half of the book gives laws concerning relations of people with each other and with God.

There were things that a man could do that would cause him to be killed or to pay a big penalty, and there were other things that a man could do that would cause him to be cut off from his people, from the congregation of Israel. One of these was as follows:

> 3 "Any man from the house of Israel who slaughters an ox, or a lamb, or a goat in the camp, or who slaughters it outside the camp,
>
> 4 and has not brought it to the doorway of the tent of meeting to present it as an offering to the LORD before the tabernacle of the LORD, bloodguiltiness is to be reckoned to that man. He has shed blood and that man shall be cut off from among his people. . . .
>
> 8 "Then you shall say to them, 'Any man from the house of Israel, or from the aliens who sojourn among them, who offers a burnt offering or sacrifice,
>
> 9 and does not bring it to the doorway of the tent of meeting to offer it to the LORD, that man also shall be cut off from his people. . . .'"
>
> —Leviticus 17

If we read this passage in context, we see that some of the sons of Israel were sacrificing in the open field to goat demons or idols. Therefore, we see that it was commanded that anyone who was going to slaughter a lamb or goat had to first bring it to the doorway of the tabernacle as an offering to the Lord. If he did not do this, he was "cut off from among his people," cut off from among the congregation of Israel. In other words, if he did that, he was no longer a part of Israel. Israel is spiritual.

If a man were to blaspheme God, he was not only cut off spiritually from Israel and was no longer a part of Israel, but he was killed physically:

> 13 Then the LORD spoke to Moses, saying,
> 14 "Bring the one who has cursed outside the camp, and let all who heard him lay their hands on his head; then let all the congregation stone him.
> 15 "And you shall speak to the sons of Israel, saying 'If anyone curses his God, then he shall bear his sin.
> 16 'Moreover, the one who blasphemes the name of the LORD shall surely be put to death; all the congregation shall certainly stone him. The alien as well as the native, when he blasphemes the Name, shall be put to death. . . .'"
>
> —Leviticus 24

It is interesting to note, in verse 16, that this applied to the alien who was a part of Israel, as well as to the native Hebrew who was part of Israel. They were treated exactly the same: they were cut off from physical life and from Israel, if they blasphemed God.

There are other cases that we could examine, wherein God clearly commands the people to cut off a Hebrew from being part of Israel. So we see more evidence that Israel is a spiritual entity and that being a part of it is not something that happens because of genealogy. Israel was never physical, or else these people could not have been "cut off from Israel."

It is impossible to cut off a Japanese person from being Japanese. One born Japanese will always be Japanese, biologically speaking, even if he moves to another country and chooses to change his citizenship. If Israel were the physical descendants of Abraham, none of the Hebrews could be cut off from Israel. But since Israel was always a spiritual group of people, not a biological group of people, one could cut off from Israel those who blasphemed and did other things that displeased God, even Hebrews.

HEBREW PROPHETS CUT OFF FROM ISRAEL

There were some prophets in the Old Testament who were Hebrews, who were claiming to speak for the Lord, but who were not speaking for the Lord at all. We read about them several places in the Bible. For example, we find this in Ezekiel:

> 1 Then the word of the LORD came to me saying,
> 2 "Son of man, prophesy against the prophets of Israel who prophesy, and say to those who prophesy from their own inspiration, 'Listen to the word of the LORD!
> 3 'Thus says the Lord GOD, "Woe to the foolish prophets who are following their own spirit and have seen nothing. . . .
> 6 "They see falsehood and lying divination who are saying, 'The LORD declares,' when the LORD has not sent them; yet they hope for the fulfillment of their word.
> 7 "Did you not see a false vision and speak a lying divination when you said, 'The LORD declares,' but it is not I who have spoken?"'"
> 8 Therefore, thus says the Lord GOD, "Because you have spoken falsehood and seen a lie, therefore behold, I am against you," declares the Lord GOD.
> 9 "So My hand will be against the prophets who see false visions and utter lying divinations. They will have no place in the council of My people, nor will they be written down in the register of the house of Israel, nor will they enter the land of Israel, that you may know that I am the Lord GOD. . . ."
> —Ezekiel 13

Here we see that these prophets were prophesying certain things and "hoping" that they would come to pass. Yet they were doing so in a prophetic manner, declaring that this was what God had said.

God was against this type of false prophesy and, as we see in verse 9, God Himself cut off these people from Israel; He said they would not be written down in the register of the house of Israel. Even though they were Hebrews, they were no longer a part of Israel.

As we said earlier, if being of Israel was a biological, racial thing, then there was no way they could be cut off, because they would always be Hebrews. "Hebrew" is a biological term, whereas "Israel" is a spiritual term. They were cut off from the congregation of Israel, even though they were Hebrews, once more proving that Israel is a spiritual group of people and not a group of people biologically descended from Abraham.

HEBREWS WHO DID NOT LISTEN TO SPIRITUAL LEADERS CUT OFF

The priest in the Old Testament stood as the connecting link between God and man. All of the people of Israel, whether Hebrew or from some other race, were under the priesthood spiritually. Let's look at what happened when they would not listen to their spiritual leaders:

> 12 "And the man who acts presumptuously by not listening to the priest who stands there to serve the LORD your God, nor to the judge, that man shall die; thus you shall purge the evil from Israel.
> 13 "Then all the people will hear and be afraid, and will not act presumptuously again. . . ."
> —Deuteronomy 17

The significant thing here is that God wants evil purged out of His Israel. In the Old Testament, the Israel of that day purged evil out by spiritually cutting off evildoers or by killing them:

HEBREWS EXCLUDED FROM ISRAEL

> 2 "If there is found in your midst, in any of your towns, which the LORD your God is giving you, a man or a woman who does what is evil in the sight of the LORD your God, by transgressing His covenant,
>
> 3 and has gone and served other gods and worshiped them, or the sun or the moon or any of the heavenly host, which I have not commanded,
>
> 4 and if it is told you and you have heard of it, then you shall inquire thoroughly. And behold, if it is true and the thing certain that this detestable thing has been done in Israel,
>
> 5 then you shall bring out that man or that woman who has done this evil deed, to your gates, that is, the man or the woman, and you shall stone them to death. . . ."
>
> —Deuteronomy 17

These verses from Deuteronomy, which is called the "second book of the Law," indicate that God wants to purge evil out of Israel. The same thing is true today—God still wants to purge evil out of Israel.

Concerning the exclusion from Israel of Hebrews who refused to follow God, in the majority of cases, it was God Himself who eliminated them from Israel. For example, consider the following:

> 31 Then Moses returned to the LORD, and said, "Alas, this people has committed a great sin, and they have made a god of gold for themselves.
>
> 32 "But now, if Thou wilt, forgive their sin—and if not, please blot me out from Thy book which Thou has written!"
>
> 33 And the LORD said to Moses, "Whoever has sinned against Me, I will blot him out of My book.
>
> 34 "But go now, lead the people where I told you. Behold, My angel shall go before you; nevertheless in the day when I punish, I will punish them for their sin."

> 35 Then the LORD smote the people, because of what they did with the calf which Aaron had made.
>
> —Exodus 32

> 20 "The LORD shall never be willing to forgive him, but rather the anger of the LORD and His jealousy will burn against that man, and every curse which is written in this book will rest on him, and the LORD will blot out his name from under heaven.
>
> 21 "Then the LORD will single him out for adversity from all the tribes of Israel, according to all the curses of the covenant which are written in this book of the law...."
>
> —Deuteronomy 29

Obviously we could dwell much longer on this subject, but I just wanted to give a little of the Old Testament background to show that the Israel of those days was a congregation based on spiritual criteria, rather than physical criteria.

In the Psalms, there is a beautiful definition of who Israel is: those who are pure in heart, which is a spiritual criterion. The writings of the Hebrews often had a parallel structure; they would say something and then repeat it in other words:

> 1 Surely God is good to Israel,
> To those who are pure in heart!
>
> —Psalms 73

JESUS EXCLUDED SOME HEBREWS FROM ISRAEL

We have been looking at some of the descendants of Abraham, Isaac and Jacob being excluded from Israel in the Old Testament. Now let us turn to what our Lord and Savior had to say. In the time of Jesus Christ, there were some Pharisees (who were Hebrews) who were devoted to the religion of Judaism. They

HEBREWS EXCLUDED FROM ISRAEL

went about trying to convert non-Hebrews to the religion of Judaism. As we discussed in Chapter 3, their converts were called "proselytes." Here is what Jesus had to say about them:

> 15 "Woe to you, scribes and Pharisees, hypocrites, because you travel about on sea and land to make one proselyte; and when he becomes one, you make him twice as much a son of hell as yourselves. . . .
>
> 29 "Woe to you, scribes and Pharisees, hypocrites! For you build the tombs of the prophets and adorn the monuments of the righteous,
> 30 and say, 'If we had been living in the days of our fathers, we would not have been partners with them in shedding the blood of the prophets.'
> 31 "Consequently you bear witness against yourselves, that you are sons of those who murdered the prophets.
> 32 "Fill up then the measure of the guilt of your fathers.
> 33 "You serpents, you brood of vipers, how shall you escape the sentence of hell? . . ."
>
> —Matthew 23

In these verses, we see that Jesus Christ condemns these Hebrews to hell, and certainly no one who is a part of Israel will go to hell. So Jesus Himself excluded some Hebrews from being part of Israel.

SUMMARY AND CONCLUSION

In the previous chapter we saw that there were many who were not genealogically from Abraham, who were assimilated into Israel and became part of Israel. In this chapter, we have observed that there were also many who were descended from Abraham, Isaac and Jacob (Hebrews) who were excluded from Israel. Many times the exclusion was made by God the Father and, in the New Testament, even by Jesus Christ Himself.

This leads us to the tentative conclusion that Israel is not a biological group of people descended from Abraham, but it is a spiritual group of people from various races. If the Israel in the Old Testament was a spiritual group of people, then the question that naturally arises is: "Who is Israel today." And if God does indeed want to purge evil out of Israel today, this question becomes even more pressing. The exciting thing is that the Bible clearly tells us, as we will see in the next chapter.

5

WHO IS ISRAEL TODAY?

The basic problem with Christians today is that they do not know the Scriptures and, if a portion of Scripture is shown to them that contradicts some of their pet doctrines or theories, they will tend to cling to their old beliefs rather than believe the Bible. For example, many Christians do not believe the Bible concerning the "Jews" and Israel. To show you this, let's say that standing before a Christian group were two people: one was a blondheaded young man from Southern California named Johnny Johnson, who knew Christ as his Savior and really loved the Lord; standing beside him was Abe Goldstein, who lived in Jerusalem and did not know Christ. If I asked that Christian group which of the two was a "Jew," most of them would say, "Abe Goldstein from Jerusalem." The reason they would say this is because they really do not believe the Bible, which says this:

> 26 If therefore the uncircumcised man keeps the requirements of the Law, will not his uncircumcision be regarded as circumcision?
> 27 And will not he who is physically uncircumcised, if he keeps the Law, will he not judge you who though having the letter of the Law and circumcision are a trangressor of the Law?
> 28 For he is not a Jew who is one outwardly; neither is circumcision that which is outward in the flesh.

> 29 But he is a Jew who is one inwardly; and circumcision is that which is of the heart, by the Spirit, not by the letter; and his praise is not from men, but from God.
>
> —Romans 2

The only way one can have one's heart circumcised by the Holy Spirit today is by becoming a Christian. The Bible states plainly, in verse 28, that a Jew is not one based on the outward flesh. It tells us that the real Jew is one who has had his heart circumcised by the Holy Spirit. Thus, if you really believe these verses from Romans, in our example, you would say that Johnny Johnson is a Jew and Abe Goldstein is not. Remember, "he is not a Jew who is one outwardly" (verse 28).

You might just pause for a moment and ask yourself which one you really believe is a "Jew." I think you will conclude, as I have, that according to the Bible, anyone who has received Christ as his Savior is a "Jew" and anyone who does not know Christ as his Savior is not a "Jew." This means that all Christians (according to these verses in Romans) are Jews, regardless of racial background, and that even if someone is a Hebrew living in Jerusalem today, if he does not know Christ as his Savior, he is not a "Jew."

This is a very important point. You might just want to pause and pray about this; allow the Holy Spirit to minister to you the significance of what we have just discussed.

However, for the purpose of this book, we will use the term *Jew* as it is popularly used today, meaning a follower of the religion of Judaism.

PROMISES TO ABRAHAM

God made some promises to Abraham, such as this one:

WHO IS ISRAEL TODAY? 83

18 On that day the LORD made a covenant with Abram, saying,
"To your descendants I have given this land, From the river of Egypt as far as the great river, the river Euphrates: . . . "
—Genesis 15

Another promise made to Abraham is also found in Genesis:

3 ". . . And I will bless those who bless you, And the one who curses you I will curse. And in you all the families of the earth shall be blessed."
—Genesis 12

This raises the question of who is heir today of all the promises made to Abraham? This is another way of saying, "Who is Israel?" We get a clear and perfect answer to this in Galatians:

6 Even so Abraham BELIEVED GOD, AND IT WAS RECKONED TO HIM AS RIGHTEOUSNESS.

7 Therefore, be sure that it is those who are of faith who are sons of Abraham. . . .

13 Christ redeemed us from the curse of the Law, having become a curse for us—for it is written, CURSED IS EVERYONE WHO HANGS ON A TREE"—

14 in order that in Christ Jesus the blessing of Abraham might come to the Gentiles, so that we might receive the promise of the Spirit through faith. . . .

28 There is neither Jew nor Greek, there is neither slave nor free man, there is neither male nor female; for you are all one in Christ Jesus.

29 And if you belong to Christ, then you are Abraham's offspring, heirs according to promise.
—Galatians 3, NAS

> **29 And if ye be Christ's, then are ye Abraham's seed, and heirs according to the promise.**
> —Galatians 3, KJV

Verse 7 says that those who have faith are sons of Abraham. The implication there is that those who are not of faith are not sons of Abraham. What faith is that talking about? Verse 14 tells us that it is faith in Jesus Christ. Therefore, verse 7 says that all those who have faith in Jesus Christ are sons of Abraham, and, by implication, all those who do not have faith in Jesus Christ are not sons of Abraham.

Verses 28 and 29 clear this up even more. Here the word of the Lord says that the terms "Jew" and "Greek" do not mean anything any more; if we belong to Christ, then we are Abraham's *seed* or *offspring*. ("Offspring" is a biological term.) All of those who know Jesus Christ are heirs to all of the promises made to Abraham! You and I, as Christians, are heirs to the promises made to Abraham. And those who do not know Jesus Christ (including non-Christian Hebrews living in Jerusalem) are not heirs to the promises made to Abraham.

The sons of Abraham—all of the believers in Jesus Christ—are true Israel. According to these Scriptures, all other people, regardless of their biological origin, are not heirs to the promises made to Abraham. When Christians sing "Awake, O Israel," we are really telling ourselves to wake up to something. When we talk about Israel returning to the promised land, we are really talking about the believers in Christ returning to the promised land, specifically to Mount Zion when Jesus comes back.

To me, this is very exciting! We are God's chosen people. All of the promises made to Abraham, Isaac, Jacob (Israel), Moses and David are ours to inherit! Praise the Lord!

I believe that upon careful examination of the Scriptures (and I hope that you will do this examination for yourself), you will find that Israel always has been and always will be a spiritual entity, and not a physical entity. As I pointed out in Chapter 3, there are only four women mentioned in the genealogy of Christ. Two of these, Ruth and Rahab, were not biologically descended from Abraham, Isaac, and Jacob, and yet they were part of Israel.

Some might say that Christ's lineage came down through the men and not the women. Since Christ did not have any physical father, that argument does not hold up at all. If you say that Ruth and Rahab were not part of Israel, then these two vital links in the chain are broken and this would imply that Christ is not of Israel, which obviously is not true. Therefore, we must conclude that these two women, Ruth and Rahab, are indeed part of Israel.

THE RULES CHANGE

Another example which points out that Israel has always been and is today a spiritual entity, and not a physical entity, is the olive tree described in Romans.

13 But I am speaking to you who are Gentiles. Inasmuch then as I am an apostle of Gentiles, I magnify my ministry,
14 if somehow I might move to jealousy my fellow countrymen and save some of them.
15 For if their rejection be the reconciliation of the world, what will their acceptance be but life from the dead?
16 And if the first piece of dough be holy, the lump is also; and if the root be holy, the branches are too.
17 But if some of the branches were broken off, and you, being a wild olive, were grafted in among them and became partaker with them of the rich root of the olive tree,

> 18 do not be arrogant toward the branches; but if you are arrogant, remember that it is not you who supports the root, but the root supports you.
> 19 You will say then, "Branches were broken off so that I might be grafted in."
> 20 Quite right, they were broken off for their unbelief, but you stand by your faith. Do not be conceited, but fear;
> 21 for if God did not spare the natural branches, neither will He spare you.
> 22 Behold then the kindness and severity of God; to those who fell, severity, but to you, God's kindness, if you continue in His kindness; otherwise you also will be cut off.
> 23 And they also, if they do not continue in their unbelief, will be grafted in; for God is able to graft them in again.
> 24 For if you were cut off from what is by nature a wild olive tree, and were grafted contrary to nature into a cultivated olive tree, how much more shall these who are the natural branches be grafted into their own olive tree?
>
> —Romans 11

The olive tree is Israel. After Christ's sacrificial death, the individual Hebrews who did not believe in Christ were broken off. The Gentiles who believed in Christ were grafted in and, if any of the broken-off branches (the Hebrews) received Christ as their Savior, they were grafted back in. Figure 5.1 shows this graphically.

To repeat, the olive tree is Israel. There is only one olive tree—not two, as some might say. As we mentioned earlier, some would try to claim that there is a physical Israel and a spiritual Israel. I do not find that concept in the Bible. There is only one Israel, as we have seen in previous chapters; it is spiritual and always has been. It is simply that the rules for how one becomes part of Israel changed with Christ. The way

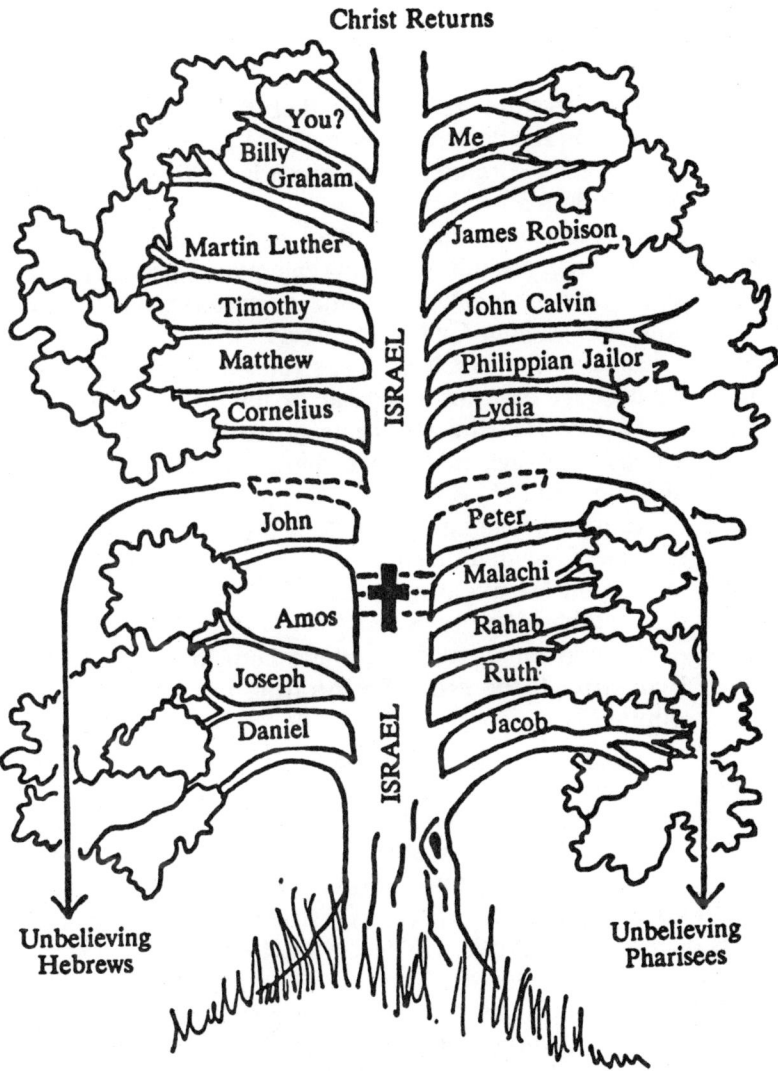

Figure 5.1

one now becomes part of Israel is by believing in Jesus Christ as one's personal Savior. In Old Testament times, one became part of Israel by believing God and obeying Him, looking forward to Christ.

Let's look at another passage which shows that we are dealing with a spiritual entity when we talk about Israel:

> 11 Therefore remember, that formerly you, the Gentiles in the flesh, who are called "Uncircumcision" by the so-called "Circumcision," which is performed in the flesh by human hands—
>
> 12 remember that you were at that time separate from Christ, excluded from the commonwealth of Israel, and strangers to the covenants of promise, having no hope and without God in the world.
>
> 13 But now in Christ Jesus you who formerly were far off have been brought near by the blood of Christ.
>
> 14 For He Himself is our peace, who made both groups into one, and broke down the barrier of the dividing wall,
>
> 15 by abolishing in His flesh the enmity, which is the Law of commandments contained in ordinances, that in Himself He might make the two into one new man, thus establishing peace,
>
> 16 and might reconcile them both in one body to God through the cross, by it having put to death the enmity.
>
> —Ephesians 2

Here the Bible points out that Christ took the Hebrews and the non-Hebrews, who previously were excluded from Israel, and He made them (those out of each group who would receive Christ) into one group by His death on the cross. He made the two into "one new man" (the new, expanded Israel). There are those who would like to pull this one new man apart into "Hebrew Christians" and "non-Hebrew Christians." Again, this is not scriptural, since Christ made the two groups into the new man and that new man is Israel today and consists of all those who believe in Jesus Christ.

Hebrews who do not believe in Jesus Christ are not part of this new man and, thus, are not part of Israel today. (Of course, believers from Old Testament times remain part of Israel.)

Just as an aside, there are those today who think that a "completed Hebrew" (one who has become a Christian) has a superior position spiritually to other Christians. When they say this, they are trying to pull the one new man back into two parts. I am all for reaching the Hebrews for Christ. I am equally for reaching the Chinese, the Irish, and every other nationality for Christ. A Hebrew who has become a Christian is no better or no worse than a Spaniard who becomes a Christian. We are all complete in Christ! Praise the Lord!

This fact, that all those who are physically descended from Jacob (Israel) are not really part of God's Israel (unless they have received Christ as Savior), is clearly stated by Paul in his letter to the Romans:

> 6 But it is not as though the word of God has failed. For they are not all Israel who are descended from Israel;
>
> 7 neither are they all children because they are Abraham's descendants, but: "THROUGH ISAAC YOUR DESCENDANTS WILL BE NAMED."
>
> 8 That is, it is not the children of the flesh who are children of God, but the children of the promise are regarded as descendants.
>
> 9 For this is a word of promise: "AT THIS TIME I WILL COME, AND SARAH SHALL HAVE A SON."
>
> 10 And not only this, but there was Rebekah also, when she had conceived twins by one man, our father Isaac;
>
> 11 for though the twins were not yet born, and had not done anything good or bad, in order that God's

purpose according to His choice might stand, not because of works, but, because of Him who calls,

12 it was said to her, "THE OLDER WILL SERVE THE YOUNGER."

13 Just as it is written, "JACOB I LOVED, BUT ESAU I HATED."

14 What shall we say then? There is no injustice with God, is there? May it never be!

15 For He says to Moses, "I WILL HAVE MERCY ON WHOM I HAVE MERCY, AND I WILL HAVE COMPASSION ON WHOM I HAVE COMPASSION."

16 So then it does not depend on the man who wills or the man who runs, but on God who has mercy.

17 For the Scripture says to Pharaoh, "FOR THIS VERY PURPOSE I RAISED YOU UP, TO DEMONSTRATE MY POWER IN YOU, AND THAT MY NAME MIGHT BE PROCLAIMED THROUGHOUT THE WHOLE EARTH."

18 So then He has mercy on whom He desires, and He hardens whom He desires.

—Romans 9

In verses 6-8 of this passage, we see that biological descendancy from Jacob (Israel) does not make a person part of true Israel. It is only the children of the spiritual promise who are true Israel.

This passage in Romans also brings out the interesting concept that we discussed in Chapter 3: the promises made to Abraham only applied to His spiritual seed, Isaac, and not to his other sons. In addition to Isaac and Ishmael, as we mentioned before, Abraham had six other sons by another wife, as well as sons by concubines:

1 Now Abraham took another wife, whose name was Keturah.

2 And she bore to him Zimran and Jokshan and Medan and Midian and Ishbak and Shuah. . . .

5 Now Abraham gave all that he had to Isaac;

WHO IS ISRAEL TODAY?

> 6 but to the sons of his concubines, Abraham gave gifts while he was still living, and sent them away from his son Isaac eastward, to the land of the east.
> —Genesis 25

Although we know that Abraham had a number of other sons, the promises made to him by God did not pass on to them, nor to Ishmael, but only to Isaac. So again we see that from the very beginning, we were not looking at biological heirs to Abraham's promises, but spiritual heirs. That line of heirship to all of the promises made to Abraham continues today to Abraham's seed. But we have shown that the born-again Christians are today the seed of Abraham.

The fact that God has changed the rules about how an individual becomes part of Israel was made clear by Jesus Christ when He taught about Israel, using the vineyard as an illustration:

> 9 And He began to tell the people this parable: "A man planted a vineyard and rented it out to vine-growers, and went on a journey for a long time.
> 10 "And at the harvest time he sent a slave to the vinegrowers, in order that they might give him some of the produce of the vineyard; but the vine-growers beat him and sent him away empty-handed.
> 11 "And he proceeded to send another slave; and they beat him also and treated him shamefully, and sent him away empty-handed.
> 12 "And he proceeded to send a third; and this one also they wounded and cast out.
> 13 "And the owner of the vineyard said, 'What shall I do? I will send my beloved son; perhaps they will respect him.'
> 14 "But when the vine-growers saw him, they reasoned with one another, saying 'This is the heir; let us kill him that the inheritance may be ours.'

15 "And they threw him out of the vineyard and killed him. What, therefore, will the owner of the vineyard do to them?

16 "He will come and destroy these vine-growers and will give the vineyard to others." And when they heard it, they said, "May it never be!"

17 But He looked at them and said, "What then is this that is written,

> 'THE STONE WHICH THE BUILDERS REJECTED,
> THIS BECAME THE CHIEF CORNER stone'?

18 "Everyone who falls on that stone will be broken to pieces; but on whomever it falls, it will scatter him like dust."

19 And the scribes and the chief priests tried to lay hands on Him that very hour, and they feared the people; for they understood that He spoke this parable against them.

—Luke 20

In this parable, Christ is clearly saying that the Hebrews (vine-growers), who rejected the prophets of God (the slaves) and killed the son (Christ), would eventually have the vineyard (Israel) taken away from them. This "vineyard" will then be given to people who will love and respect the Vineyard Owner (God) and His Son. Thus, the definition of who inherits God's promises definitely changed, as God took away the inheritance from the Hebrews. In verse 19, we see that the scribes and the priests clearly understood what Christ was saying, and they knew that He was speaking this parable against the Jewish leaders and the Jewish system and nation of that day.

We have seen from the Bible that Israel always has been and always will be a spiritual entity. Today, Israel is composed of all those who have received Jesus Christ as their Savior and it excludes anyone, including the Hebrews, who has not received Christ as his Savior.

WHO IS ISRAEL TODAY? 93

The real "Jews" of today are those who have received Christ as their Savior. All of the promises made to Abraham are to be inherited by Israel, by those who have received Christ as their Savior! This includes the promise about the land of Palestine, as we will see later. Another promise to be inherited by Israel (the Christians) is that God will bless those who bless us and curse those who curse us. This is an exciting thing to be remembered during the times of persecution ahead.

THE CHURCH IS ISRAEL IN SONG

Up until now, we have looked at passages in the Bible that clearly show us that the believers in Jesus Christ are Israel. Now we will consider another source which shows that through the centuries people have understood that the church is Israel. We would first like to look at one of the wonderful old hymns that many of us have sung repeatedly that talks about the incredible power in the name of Jesus:

ALL HAIL THE POWER OF JESUS' NAME

1. All hail the power of Jesus' name!
   Let angels prostrate fall;
   Bring forth the royal diadem,
   And crown Him Lord of all;
   Bring forth the royal diadem,
   And crown Him Lord of all!

2. Ye chosen seed of Israel's race,
   Ye ransomed from the fall,
   Hail Him who saves you by His grace,
   And crown Him Lord of all;
   Hail Him who saves you by His grace,
   And crown Him Lord of all!

3. Let every kindred, every tribe,
   On this terrestrial ball,
   To Him all majesty ascribe,

And crown Him Lord of all;
To Him all majesty ascribe,
And crown Him Lord of all!

4. O that with yonder sacred throng
We at His feet may fall!
We'll join the everlasting song,
And crown Him Lord of all;
We'll join the everlasting song,
And crown Him Lord of all!

—Edward Perronet
—John Rippon, alt.

From this precious old hymn, a favorite of many Christians, we can see that those who are ransomed from the fall (Christians) are called the "chosen seed of Israel's race" (second stanza). There was no doubt in the mind of the man who wrote this great hymn that Christians are indeed Israel.

Among the more modern choruses that are popular in charismatic circles, we have ones such as this:

AWAKE, O ISRAEL

1. Awake, O Israel! Put off thy slumber
And the truth shall set you free!
For out of Zion comes thy Deliv'rer,
In the year of Jubilee!

2. For in the furnace of much affliction
I have chosen thee, behold,
And so for iron I'll give thee silver,
And for brass I'll give thee gold.

3. Thou art My chosen, for I have sought thee,
Thou art graven on My hand,
And I will gather all those that gather,
They shall come back to their land.

4. O hallelujah! O hallelujah!
Hallelujah! O, praise the Lord!

> O hallelujah! O hallelujah!
> Hallelujah! Praise the Lord!
>
> —Merla Watson

I do not know what you think about when you sing the words to this song. You are not telling some Hebrews who live in Palestine to get out of bed. It is a song to the church telling us to wake up, reminding us that the truth will set us free. Unfortunately, there is much false teaching being circulated in the body of Christ, but this song says that those who seek and find the truth will be set free! Of course, we know that Christ is the truth. Also, there are evidently some things from which we are going to need to be delivered (verse 1) and our Deliverer is coming again!

The second verse talks about the furnace of affliction that I believe we are going to be going through. God is substituting precious things for base things in our lives through this furnace of affliction.

Then the third verse beautifully points out that Christians today are the chosen people of God. Remember that Christ says, "Ye have not chosen me, but I have chosen you. . . ." (Matthew 15:16, *KJV*). So when you talk about God's chosen people (Israel), that's us! Christians are God's chosen people!

Peter tells us that we are now God's chosen race; even though we once were not a people, He has now made us His people!

> **9** But you are A CHOSEN RACE, A royal PRIESTHOOD, A HOLY NATION, A PEOPLE FOR God's OWN POSSESSION, that you may proclaim the excellencies of Him who has called you out of darkness into His marvelous light;
>
> **10** for you once were NOT A PEOPLE, but now you are THE PEOPLE OF GOD; you had NOT RECEIVED MERCY, but now you have RECEIVED MERCY.
>
> —1 Peter 2

The last half of the third verse of the song, "Awake, O Israel," speaks of something that we will look at in depth a bit later. As is commonly known, the land of Palestine was promised to Abraham (Genesis 15: 18-21). Then in Galatians 3, we found out that all those who believe in Christ are heirs to all of the promises made to Abraham. Then to whom does that land of Palestine belong? I believe we can legitimately conclude that it belongs to Christians. At the end of the tribulation, Christ is going to gather all of the Christians, both the living and the dead, to that land—our land. I believe this is the reason that when Christians visit the land of Israel, they feel like they are "coming home." It is from there that we will rule and reign with Christ for one thousand years. Praise the Lord!

This return of Christians to Zion, which is in our land, is the subject of a beautiful chorus taken from Isaiah 51:11:

THEREFORE THE REDEEMED

Therefore the redeemed of the Lord shall return
And come with singing unto Zion,
And everlasting joy shall be upon their heads.
They shall obtain gladness and joy,
And sorrow and mourning shall flee away.
Therefore the redeemed of the Lord shall return
And come with singing unto Zion,
And everlasting joy shall be upon their heads.

—Ruth Lake

This reminds me of the popular old hymn that says, "We're Marching to Zion." That land and that mountain are our inheritance—that is, the inheritance of "the redeemed," which refers to Christians. I am excited about the day when God will gather us, Israel, to that land. What a time of rejoicing that will be!

There is another exciting prophetic chorus that we sing, taken from Micah 4:2:

WHO IS ISRAEL TODAY?

COME AND LET US GO

Come and let us go unto the mountain of the Lord,
Unto the city of our God.
Come and let us go unto the mountain of the Lord,
Unto the city of our God.
And He will teach us His ways,
And we will walk in His paths,
Come and let us go unto the mountain of the Lord,
Unto the city of our God.

—Unknown

The mountain of the Lord is, of course, Mount Zion and when He gathers us together there, He is going to teach us His ways perfectly and we will walk in His paths. I am excited about going to Zion, the inheritance promised to Abraham, which is the inheritance of Israel (all those who believe in Jesus Christ as Lord and Savior).

I would like to include just one more chorus which states that the Christians are Israel. Many Christians sing this chorus, but, unfortunately, some do not believe the words of it:

THE LION OF THE TRIBE OF JUDAH

He is the Lion of the tribe of Judah, Jesus
Took our chains, broke them and freed us,
Now He is our rock of victory.
He is our strength in the time of weariness,
He is our tower in the time of woe,
O, He is the hope of Israel.

—Unknown

How clearly this chorus expresses our new identity as Israel. Jesus, Lion of Judah, is the victorious King who conquered sin and death, delivering us from the chains of slavery to sin and freeing us to new lives of service and worship to Him. As born-again Christians who submit all to Jesus, the "King of the Jews," we become part of Israel and inheritors of God's promises. Thus, through Jesus—and Him alone—we have hope, not only for salvation from sin, but also for strength and deliverance in times of distress that face us. Jesus is a solid rock in which we may trust completely for victory.

Thank You, Jesus, that You are the liberator, the rock, the strength and the hope of Israel, Your followers.

THE EVIDENCE IS OVERWHELMING

When I began writing this book, I already felt that the Israel of God was composed of the Old Testament saints and the New Testament believers in Jesus Christ, and that the old covenant had ended and the new covenant had replaced it. But the more I began to dig into the subject, the more I began to realize that the evidence from the Scriptures is absolutely overwhelming in support of the fact that today the only living people who are a part of Israel are those who know Jesus Christ as their personal Savior.

There are scores of Scriptures that we could use to attest to this point. I would like just to touch on a few more here. This first one we mentioned in an earlier chapter:

28 And you brethren, like Isaac, are children of promise.
—Galatians 4

This Scripture places the "brethren," who were the writer's fellow Christians, with Isaac as children of promise.

23 Whoever denies the Son does not have the Father; the one who confesses the Son has the Father also.
—1 John 2

WHO IS ISRAEL TODAY? 99

There is no way that anyone can come to the Father except through Jesus Christ. It is about time that Christians strongly proclaim to the Jewish people, whom we love, that their religion of Judaism is a cancelled religion and they cannot come to God that way. As long as we play "buddy-buddy" with them, we are doing them (and Jesus) a great disservice. We should let them know clearly that their religion is dead and that they had better accept their Messiah, Jesus Christ, if they want to have eternal life with God. Otherwise, they are going to hell, just like the Muslim who worships the God of Abraham is going to hell without Jesus Christ. Jesus Himself told the Jewish leaders this, so why should we be afraid?

> 13 "But woe to you, scribes and Pharisees, hypocrites, because you shut off the kingdom of heaven from men; for you do not enter in yourselves, nor do you allow those who are entering to go in.
> 14 "Woe to you, scribes and Pharisees, hypocrites, because you devour widows' houses, even while for a pretense you make long prayers; therefore you shall receive greater condemnation. . . .
> 33 "You serpents, you brood of vipers, how shall you escape the sentence of hell?
> 34 Therefore, behold, I am sending you prophets and wise men and scribes; some of them you will kill and crucify, and some of them you will scourge in your synagogues, and persecute from city to city,
> 35 that upon you may fall the guilt of all the righteous blood shed on earth, from the blood of righteous Abel to the blood of Zechariah, the son of Berechiah, whom you murdered between the temple and the altar. . . ."
> —Matthew 23

As we touched on in Chapter 4, Jesus Himself told the scribes and Pharisees, who were Hebrews biologically and Jews by religion, that they were not going into the kingdom of heaven, but that they were going to receive a greater condemnation—the condemnation of hell. This does not sound like being biologically from Abraham does much good, does it? And these were words out of the mouth of Jesus Christ, God's own Son and our Savior.

It is interesting to note Jesus' manner of addressing those who were self-righteous, such as the scribes and Pharisees. In contrast to His gentleness in dealing with the woman at the well—who already was well aware of the fact that she was a sinner—he came down hard on these men, to jolt them into the realization of their sin and need for salvation. Jesus is our Example, and we can certainly learn much from Him in this regard.

Paul picked up the theme as well:

> **2 Beware of the dogs, beware of the evil workers, beware of the false circumcision;**
>
> **3 for we are the true circumcision, who worship in the Spirit of God and glory in Christ Jesus and put no confidence in the flesh, . . .**
>
> —Philippians 3

Here Paul is warning against those who would want to mutilate the flesh through circumcision and he is telling the non-Hebrew believers in Christ, to whom this letter was addressed, that they are the real circumcision.

> 8 "And to the angel of the church in Smyrna write: The first and the last, who was dead, and has come to life, says this:
>
> 9 'I know your tribulation and your poverty (but you are rich), and the blasphemy by those who say they are Jews and are not, but are a synagogue of Satan. . . .'"
>
> —Revelation 2

In this passage, again Jesus Himself is speaking. If He is speaking of a Jewish synagogue in the first century, He is claiming it is part of Satan's camp and

WHO IS ISRAEL TODAY? 101

no longer part of God's. Christ also validated what Paul said at the end of Romans 2, which we read at the start of this chapter. He said that there are those who claimed to be Jews (evidently because of their physical ancestry) but they really were not "Jews," not part of Israel.

PROOF FROM GALATIANS 6:16

Before we look at Galatians 6:16 specifically, we need to branch off into a little bit of language discussion. Let's say there was a word in English that could have the same effect in a sentence as a comma or it could mean the same as the word "and." For the sake of our discussion, we will use "nad." If we encountered that word, *nad*, in an English sentence, how would we know whether to treat it as a comma or as an "and"? Of course, the only way to know would be from the context.

If there was a paragraph talking about some shepherds and also talking about some Swiss people, and both groups were being discussed in a sentence which read, "the shepherds *nad* the Swiss," we would know that meant "the shepherds and the Swiss."

On the other hand, if there was a paragraph that was only talking about shepherds, and we encountered the phrase right at the end of the paragraph "the shepherds *nad* the Swiss," we would know that this should be translated "the shepherds, the Swiss" which would mean that the shepherds were from Switzerland. This is a common linguistic form that we use often, wherein an individual or group is mentioned and, following that (set off by commas), a synonym is given for that individual or group, or an alternative description of him or them. For example, we might say:

"George Washington, the President, said . . ."
"Pilots, trained aviators, are really . . ."
"The Priests, Levites by birth, daily . . ."

There is a word in Greek that is like the fictional word "nad" that we have been talking about. It can be translated either as a comma or as the word "and." That is the Greek word *kai*. With that background, let us proceed to read this verse from Galatians:

> **16** And those who will walk by this rule, peace and mercy be upon them, and *(kai)* upon the Israel of God.
> —Galatians 6, NAS

Looking at this from a couple of other translations, we have:

> **16** Peace and mercy be upon all who walk by this rule, upon the Israel of God
> —Galatians 6, RSV

> **16** Peace and mercy to all who follow this rule, even to the Israel of God
> —Galatians 6, NIV

> **16** Peace and mercy be upon all who walk by this rule—who discipline themselves and regulate their lives by this principle—even upon the [true] Israel of God!
> —Galatians 6, AMPLIFIED

Just as in our example of the "shepherds and the Swiss," contextually Paul is only talking about one group of people, not two. So, based on context, we have absolutely no choice but to treat *kai* as a comma in this instance. Paul is equating "the Israel of God" to "all who walk by this rule." To see what rule we are discussing, we need to read the preceding verses:

> **13** For those who are circumcised do not even keep the Law themselves, but they desire to have you circumcised, that they may boast in your flesh.
> **14** But may it never be that I should boast, except in the cross of our Lord Jesus Christ, through which the world has been crucified to me, and I to the world.

15 For neither is circumcision anything, nor uncircumcision, but a new creation.
—Galatians 6

Thus, Paul himself is equating Israel to both believing Jews and believing Gentiles, and he is excluding from Israel anyone who does not have Christ as Savior—even the Hebrews, who were biologically descended from Abraham.

Pastor Gary Matsdorf, who taught both Hebrew and Greek for ten years at LIFE Bible College in the Los Angeles area, had this to say about this verse:

1) Translations vary over the use of the *kai*.
2) Grammatically there are two options:
   a) The *kai* is what is known as an epexegetical *kai* in which the last phrase ("the Israel of God") is a renaming of "all who walk" (*RSV*). This would see Paul as addressing only one group and outright calling the Church ("all who walk") the Israel of God. Some scholars are on this side and this view is old, going all the way back to Chrysostom & Martyr.
   b) The *kai* is consecutive, introducing a separate group to whom the blessing is to extend. Scholars in this area take "the Israel of God" to be "the true Israel known to God" (Bruce). Others see "the Israel of God" as Jewish Christians or Jews as a whole.
3) From a purely grammatical point, it could go either way; the majority of English versions go with two groups. The *RSV* boldly differs and says that it is one group; the *NIV* ("even") is fuzzy but sees one group.
4) Contextually, it's hard to see why Paul would throw out a "red herring" and suddenly mention national Israel as a separate group to receive blessing. He's not been dealing with national Israel in the letter. Galatians 6 is no Romans 9-11.

CHAPTER 5

Tyndale Press has a series of commentaries, one book for each book of the New Testament, each written by an expert. This series is called the *Tyndale New Testament Commentaries*. Dr. R. Allan Cole wrote the book on Galatians, and this is what he had to say about this critical verse 16. On pages 183 and 184:

"The second half of verse 16 poses a question of interpretation which hangs on the exact meaning of the introductory *kai*. Does the word mean 'and,' 'in addition to,' or 'even,' 'that is to say'? A strong case can be made for both views. If the word is to be translated 'and,' then Paul's final prayer is directed towards those Gentiles who realize the unimportance of their physical state, and to Jews who likewise realize the unimportance of circumcision. By so doing, they prove themselves to be the true Israel, God's Israel, the 'righteous remnant.' To them circumcision is a matter of the heart, not of the body (Rom. ii. 29). This would link closely with the two groups described in verse 15 as *peritome* and *akrobustia* ('circumcision' and 'uncircumcision'—the latter probably being a Jewish play on words; see Arndt-Gingrich). It would also be a fitting olive-branch stretched out to 'orthodox' Jewish Christianity, lest they should think that they were included in Paul's attacks on the Judaizers (Romans xi probably has the same purpose). It would be a full recognition of the fact that Jew and Gentile alike are fellow-heirs of the grace of life; they have 'communion in the Messiah,' to quote a great Jewish Christian. We may feel that it is an olive-branch on the point of a bayonet; but it is a gesture of peace and reconciliation fitting the closing verses of such an Epistle.

"The other translation is bolder, but Paul is quite capable of it. This is to take *kai* as 'even,' 'that is to say,' 'the equivalent of.' Linguistically, this is quite possible; the question must be solved theologically and exegetically.

"This would identify the new group, the 'third race of men' of whom the Church fathers delighted to talk—neither Jew nor Gentile, but Christian—with God's Israel. This is often put bluntly as 'the Church is the new Israel.' Put thus, we may well want to qualify the statement; but in broad outline, and as stated by Paul, it seems unexceptionable.

"In the first place, if *kai* does not mean 'even,' then Paul is allowing two groups side by side in the kingdom of God; first, those who 'live according to the principle' enunciated in verse 15, and, secondly, God's Israel. But those of Israel who do not have this 'principle' are thereby automatically excluded from the true Israel, God's Israel. This is the inevitable deduction from Paul's reasoning above. In other words, while there is place for the believing Christian Jew in the Kingdom, there is not for the Judaizer. Paul would go further. He would say that the 'believing Jew' belongs to Israel, but that the Judaizer does not. Thus there cannot be two groups; there can only be one. That was the battle Paul was fighting at Antioch, over 'table-fellowship' between Jewish and Gentile Christians.

"Further, in passages like Colossians ii. 2 and (more strongly) Philippians iii. 2, 3, Paul seems to make the identification clear. Admittedly, the second is the famous controversial passage where he has already described the (unbelieving) Jews as 'dogs'—the term used by them to describe Gentiles. He has thus turned the tables. The (unbelieving) Jews are 'Gentile dogs'; they are 'mutilators' (*katatomen*, not *peritomen*); while the Christians are now 'the Jews' (*the peritome*). 'We,' says Paul, 'are the Jews, we who serve God with Spiritual worship, and make our boast of Christ, and do not trust in outward things.' It will be noted that many of the emphases here (*pneumati*, 'Spirit': *kauchomenoi*, 'boasting': *saki*, 'natural condition,' 'outward circumstances') are also those of Galatians. But it is important to remember that, while Paul says that Christians are 'true Jews,' he never says that Gentiles are Jews, nor Jews Gentiles; that is an illegitimate deduction. What he does say is that believing Jew and believing Gentile alike form the 'Israel of God,' the instrument of His purpose. It is interesting to remember in the context of verse 16 that 'Peace upon Israel' is the great Old Testament blessing (Ps. cxxv.5)."

Here you see that both of these scholars, Pastor Gary Matsdorf and Dr. R. Allan Cole, are compelled by the context to translate this key verse equating the "Israel of God" to "all those who walk by this rule," who are the believers in Jesus Christ. You may find this a little technical, but this it is hard, solid Scriptural evidence that Paul considered the Israel of God—the only Israel of God—to be all those who believe in Jesus Christ and walk according to the commandments of Christ.

SUMMARY AND CONCLUSION

We have previously seen that, even in the Old Testament, Israel was a spiritual group of people, not one based on genealogy (those descended from Abraham). It was composed of people from various races and ethnic backgrounds.

With the coming of Christ, the rules changed as to how one becomes part of Israel. Now the *only* way to become part of Israel is to receive Jesus Christ as your personal Savior, for He is the *only* way to God.

The question inevitably arises as to the State of Israel and where it fits in. We will deal with that vital subject later in this book, but first we need to investigate the exciting, unfullfilled promises and prophecies made to Israel, which are our inheritance, our birthright, as a result of our faith in Jesus Christ and our obedience to Him.

6

UNFULFILLED PROMISES AND PROPHECIES

In the Bible, there are unfulfilled promises made to Israel and there are prophecies concerning Israel that have yet to be fulfilled. Hopefully, by now the question of who Israel is, has been settled in your mind, and you know who is the inheritor of those promises made to Abraham. For your quick review, let us reread this verse:

> 29 And if you belong to Christ, then you are Abraham's offspring, heirs according to promise.
> —Galatians 3

Here we see that all of us who know Christ as our personal Savior are Abraham's offspring (seed) and inheritors of the promises made to him.

Remember that true Israel, or the whole house of Israel, is comprised of the Old Testament saints who believed God and all the New Testament saints who have received Jesus Christ as their Savior. In both the Old and New Testaments, a person's status in Israel was determined by his belief and not by his ancestors.

Now let us look at a couple of the promises that God made to Abraham that Israel (the church today) is to inherit:

CHAPTER 6

> 18 On that day the LORD made a covenant with Abram, saying,
> "To your descendants I have given this land,
> From the river of Egypt as far as the great river, the river Euphrates:
> 19 the Kenite and the Kenizzite and the Kadmonite
> 20 and the Hittite and the Perizzite and the Rephaim
> 21 and the Amorite and the Canaanite and the Girgashite and the Jebusite."
> —Genesis 15

Before discussing this fantastic promise made to Abraham which was passed on to Israel, which is ours to inherit, there is something I need to address first, a minor issue that is confusing to some people. God promised some land to Abraham. He promised a smaller amount of land to Moses. We find that all of the land that God promised to Moses was conquered by Joshua and given to the tribes:

> 23 So Joshua took the whole land, according to all that the Lord had spoken to Moses, and Joshua gave it for an inheritance to Israel according to their divisions by their tribes. Thus the land had rest from war.
> —Joshua 11

However, not all of the land that was promised to Abraham, as shown on the following map, has ever been under the control of Israel—neither in Old Testament times nor in New Testament times. Believers in Jesus will some day occupy it, but we will not occupy that land until our King returns.

Let me reiterate—and I certainly hope you do not get weary of my saying this in different ways, but it is so very important to understand—there is only one Israel. In the Old Testament, it was composed of all the saints who believed in God. The rules changed on how one becomes part of Israel with the advent of Jesus Christ.

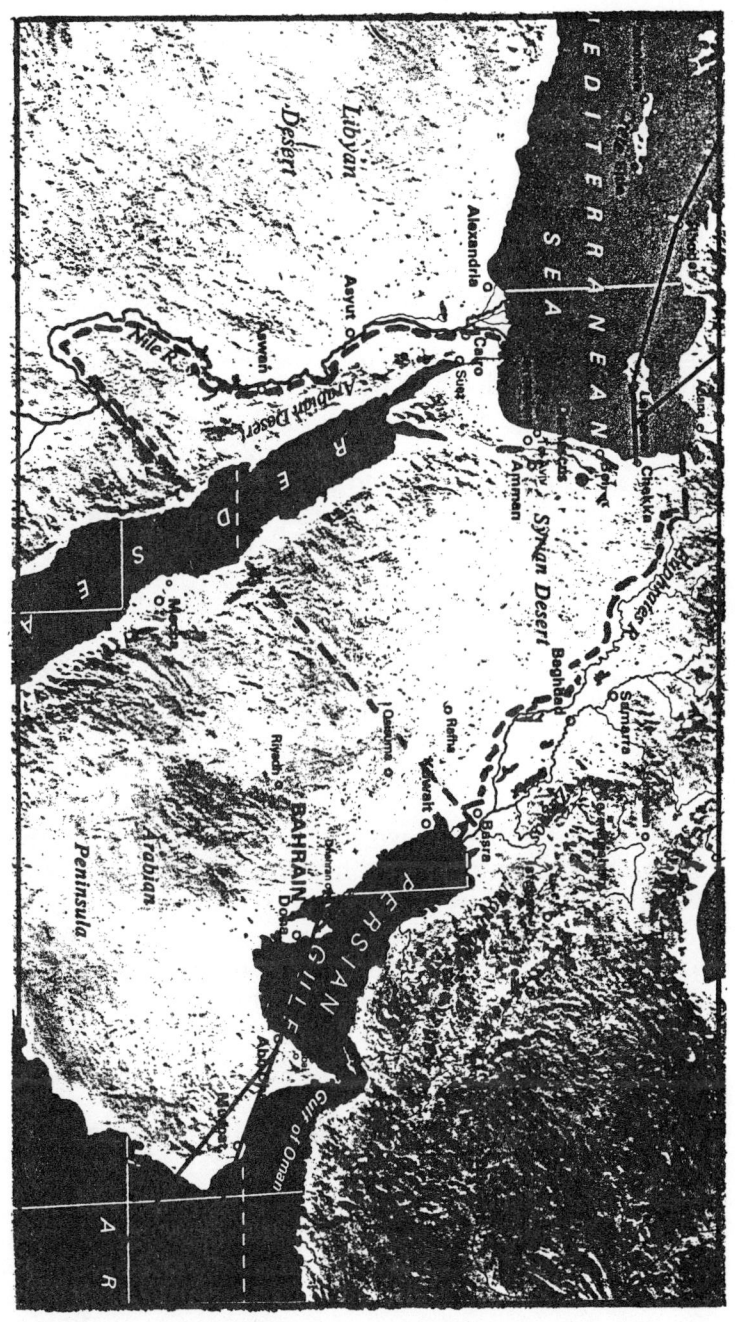

Now Israel is comprised of all those who believe in Jesus Christ, whether they be Hebrews or from some other biological root.

As I mentioned, all of the land that God promised to Abraham has never been under the control of Israel. Figure 6.1 shows a rough map of this area. There are some who would think in terms of the State of Israel possessing all of this land, which contains all or part of Syria, Iraq, Jordan, Egypt, and other countries. Those who suppose that the State of Israel will launch an aggressive war to acquire all of this territory are, I believe, whistling in the dark. There is no way that will occur, nor is it prophesied or intended by God.

However, an exciting thing will occur when all of Israel is raptured and we go to that land with Jesus—then it will all be ours. Incidentally, the Old Testament saints will be raptured along with the believers in Christ. Daniel is told that he will rise again at the end of the age:

> 13 "But as for you, go your way to the end; then you will enter into rest and rise again for your allotted portion at the end of the age."
> —Daniel 12

You can see that we are not talking about the "rapture of the church," as some erroneously would call it. "Israel" is what is going to be raptured and, praise God, Daniel, Abraham, Isaac, Jacob, Moses and all other Old Testament saints will be raptured with us!

When the raptured Israel goes to the Mount of Olives with Jesus Christ, our returning King, and His foot touches down there, the mountain will split apart and, across the Kidron Valley, Mount Zion will be uplifted as chief of the mountains. All the area around Jerusalem will be turned into the "great plain of the earth." Then Israel (and that includes every believer in Jesus Christ) will inherit the land promised to Abraham!

4 And in that day His feet will stand on the Mount of Olives, which is in front of Jerusalem on the east; and the Mount of Olives will be split in its middle from east to west by a very large valley, so that half of the mountain will move toward the north and the other half toward the south. . . .
—Zechariah 14

7 For it will be a unique day which is known to the LORD, neither day nor night, but it will come about that at evening time there will be light.

8 And it will come about in that day that living waters will flow out of Jerusalem, half of them toward the eastern sea and the other half toward the western sea; it will be in summer as well as in winter.

9 And the LORD will be king over all the earth; in that day the LORD will be the only one, and His name the only one.

10 All the land will be changed into a plain from Geba to Rimmon south of Jerusalem; but Jerusalem will rise and remain on its site from Benjamin's Gate as far as the place of the First Gate to the Corner Gate, and from the Tower of Hananel to the king's wine presses.

11 And people will live in it, and there will be no more curse, for Jerusalem will dwell in security.
—Zechariah 14

2 Now it will come about that
   In the last days,
   The mountain of the house of the LORD
   Will be established as the chief of the mountains,
   And will be raised above the hills;
   And all the nations will stream to it.
3 And many peoples will come and say,
   "Come, let us go up to the mountain of the LORD,
   To the house of the God of Jacob;

> That He may teach us concerning His ways,
> And that we may walk in His paths."
> For the law will go forth from Zion,
> And the word of the LORD from Jerusalem.
>
> —Isaiah 2

Isn't that exciting! The land that God promised to our forefather Abraham long ago will be ours. We will inherit that land and dwell there with Jesus as King over all the earth! Hallelujah! I can hardly wait for that day; what a glorious time it will be! We go there with King Jesus in our resurrected bodies, having been transformed to have a body like His, when we see Him (1 John 3:2). Then we, and all the saints from all the ages, will be there to rule and reign with Jesus Christ for a thousand years in that land that is our true inheritance, because God promised it to us.

You might want to pause and let that sink in. The land promised to you, because you are a Christian, will soon be yours. Jesus will be the King over that land, and there will be total peace in it. As I take a deep breath and contemplate that glorious, coming event, a tremendous peace and joy well up from the depths of my soul and permeate my being right down to the soles of my feet! *Thank You, Jesus. Thank You, Father. Thank You, Holy Spirit.*

And, praise God, our Hebrew brothers who receive Jesus Christ as their personal Savior will be there with us, enjoying King Jesus. Equally thrilling is the fact that many Latin brothers, Japanese brothers, Irish brothers and so forth will be there with us singing "Hosanna to the King"! Abraham, Isaac, Jacob, David, Daniel and all of the Old Testament believers will also be right there with us. How exciting that will be! We will all be praising Jesus Christ, and at His name every knee will bow.

I WILL BLESS THOSE WHO BLESS YOU AND CURSE THOSE WHO CURSE YOU

Firstly, we know that we are to bless all people, including our enemies:

> 14 Bless those who persecute you; bless and curse not.
> —Romans 12

Let us look at a promise made to Abraham concerning blessing, that today belongs to Israel:

> 3 "And I will bless those who bless you,
> And the one who curses you I will curse.
> And in you all the families of the earth shall be blessed."
> —Genesis 12

As we saw earlier, the promises to Abraham are passed on to his seed. But his seed, according to Galatians 3:29, reviewed at the start of this chapter, today is everyone who believes in Jesus Christ as his Savior.

Many Christians today erroneously apply this promise made to Abraham to the Jews or the present-day State of Israel. Some may think that this promise has been true of the Jews throughout history. But if you were make a careful study of history, you would find that some nations who "blessed" the Jews did not prosper while, on the other hand, some who persecuted the Jews did prosper. I believe most Christians have almost been brainwashed or duped into applying this promise in that manner. In fact, there is almost a fear among these believers to say anything negative about the State of Israel lest God curse them. Their drive to help and praise the State of Israel approaches paranoia. They want to raise money for them and cheer them on in everything they do, for fear of reprisal from God.

I am 100 percent for helping the State of Israel. They are the only ally in the Middle East that we can count on, and they are admirable people in many respects. However, my reasons for supporting them are totally political and have absolutely nothing to do with this promise made to Abraham in Genesis.

That promise is now the inheritance of Israel (the church). What this means is that those who bless the true believers in Jesus Christ, God will bless, and those who curse the true believers in Jesus Christ, God will curse. It has absolutely nothing to do with the Jews who live on the shores of the Mediterranean, in the land of Canaan.

However, as we pointed out earlier in this book, many Christians are giving away their birthright, just as Esau did. Esau did it with the words of his mouth and many Christians are likewise giving away their inheritance with the words of their mouths. When they say that this promise of blessing belongs to the Jews or the Hebrews, they are giving away their birthright. Remember, at least Esau got a bowl of stew for giving away his birthright! As we said in Chapter 1, so many wonderful, but unfortunately unknowledgeable, Christians are giving away their birthright, and they are not even getting a bowl of stew for it.

Wake up, Christians! Stop emulating Esau—stop giving away your birthright. Realize that today you are God's Israel, and that you alone are inheritors of the promises made to Abraham. Today you alone are Israel.

Through the last one hundred years at least, many Christians have said with their mouths that the Jews were "God's chosen people." This is *absolutely wrong*. Jesus Himself said that those who believed in Him were God's chosen people:

> 16 "You did not choose Me, but I chose you, and appointed you, that you should go and bear fruit, and that your fruit should remain, that whatever you ask of the Father in My name, He may give to you. . . ."
> —John 15

Now if you were to ask Jesus, "Who are God's chosen people?" what would His answer be? He has just told us in this verse: His followers. All those who follow Jesus Christ are God's chosen people, Israel.

Both Paul and Peter took up the theme that the Christians are now the chosen people of God:

> **12** And so, as those who have been chosen of God, holy and beloved, put on a heart of compassion, kindness, humility, gentleness and patience; . . .
> —Colossians 3

> **10** For this reason I endure all things for the sake of those who are chosen, that they also may obtain the salvation which is in Christ Jesus and with it eternal glory.
> —2 Timothy 2

> **9** But you are A CHOSEN RACE, A royal PRIESTHOOD, A HOLY NATION, A PEOPLE FOR God's OWN POSSESSION, that you may proclaim the excellencies of Him who has called you out of darkness into His marvelous light; . . .
> —1 Peter 2

Who are God's chosen people? We have heard what Jesus, Paul and Peter had to say. Who do you say God's chosen people are today? Say it out loud with your mouth, and thus claim your inheritance; do not forfeit it.

Regardless what you have done and said in the past, I believe it is not too late for you to claim your inheritance. I would encourage you to say aloud: "Because Christ Jesus is my Savior and my Lord, I am a Jew, I am part of the seed of Abraham. All the promises made to Abraham are my inheritance. I am part of God's true and only Israel."

God's chosen people have always been and will always be Israel—a group of people based on spiritual criteria. In the Old Testament, as we have seen, Israel was composed of Hebrews (the sons of Abraham) and a whole host of people assimilated from other nations, including such notables as Ruth and Rahab. They were God's chosen people then, and those people are still a part of Israel. But the rules changed about how you become part of Israel, and today the only way to become a part of Israel is to receive Jesus Christ as your personal Savior.

I would say this to my wonderful Hebrew and Jewish friends in America, in the State of Israel and in other places around the world: "God holds out His hands to beckon you to become a part of His true Israel. However, the hands are pierced with nails. How I yearn that you will come to know the peace of being rightly related to God the Father, which can only come as you receive Jesus Christ as your Savior and Lord, and join us in the mighty throng that will be with Christ when He returns and catches up His Israel to meet Him in the clouds. Come go with us. We love you and welcome you, and Jesus loves you even more."

WHAT ABOUT THE UNFULFILLED PROPHECIES?

There are many prophecies concerning Israel in the Old and New Testaments that have not yet been fulfilled. A legitimate question at this point would be whether these apply to the State of Israel or to the real Israel, the one and only Israel, the church. Since I do believe that the State of Israel has absolutely nothing to do with the Israel of God, I believe that any prophecies not fulfilled apply to the church.

How you interpret prophecy is almost totally dependent on your view of who Israel is. For example, if one views Israel as the Hebrews, then the prophecies concerning God collecting Israel together to their own land, to that person would seem to have been fulfilled by the Hebrews returning to the land of Palestine and forming a nation in 1948. He might even assume that this would be the beginning of God's "countdown on the prophetic clock."

I have said for many years that the forming of the State of Israel in 1948 had absolutely nothing to do with Israel returning to the land promised to them in God's promise to Abraham and in that which is prophesied in Ezekiel.

Believing that the State of Israel, formed in 1948, is really Israel, could lead to many errors, such as predicting that there would be a rapture in 1981, 1988 and so forth. All the teachers and writers who stated publicly that the rapture would occur 1981, now have egg on their faces. Unfortunately, people are still listening to these false teachings. When that did not occur, some of them said, "Well, we shouldn't have subtracted the seven years, so Christ will return in 1988."

There are numerous books published to this effect. Christ obviously did not return in 1988, but unfortunately teachers of this false doctrine have beguiled innocent lambs into listening to these theories and following them. Oh, how my heart yearns as a shepherd that these precious little lambs would wake up, listen to the truth of God and stop being deceived.

If one looks at the church as being Israel today, then prophecies about Israel going to the promised land (when Jesus takes them there at His return) become very clear. It becomes obvious that that return to the promised land is something yet in the future.

Since the thesis of this book is that today the church is Israel, at this point I would like to look at some prophecies from the viewpoint of Israel being the church. I think you will see that we will come out with a totally different interpretation of these prophecies—one which I believe is correct and true.

I prayed long and hard about this book, because I did not want to write it. I felt it would be even more controversial than the previous book I wrote concerning the timing of the rapture. There are many outstanding men of God who agree with me that Christians will go through the tribulation, but some who would disagree with me that the church is Israel. As a result, many of them are blowing the trumpet and giving their inheritance to the Hebrews over in the land of Palestine, the State of Israel.

In prayer, I begged God to show me, first, whether this was His truth and, second, if I was to proclaim it. Of course, it could be His truth but still be a subject He might not particularly want me to write about. After much intense prayer, flat on my face, the Lord clearly spoke to me and said:

This is My truth; the church is Israel.
Proclaim My truth and I will bless you.

I have no choice but to write this book. My hope and my prayer is that it will help many Hebrews and Jews become part of true Israel through Jesus Christ and that it will help many precious Christians, who have been inadvertently misled, to wake up and claim their inheritance and realize the true meaning of these prophecies. We will now look at a couple of these prophecies in detail—ones I believe that the church will fulfill in the coming days, months and years.

7

EZEKIEL 36-37—
THE GATHERING OF ISRAEL

There is no system of interpreting prophecy that does not have some problems. If there were one that was totally problem-free, everybody would subscribe to it. However, if one way of looking at prophecy had, say, fifty difficulties with it, and another had only three or four, I would tend to go with the one that had only three or four problems.

If you try to interpret Ezekiel 36, 37, 38 and 39, assuming that the Hebrews or Jews are going to fulfill these prophecies, there are a large number of difficulties. Abusive interpretations of Scripture must be used to force that view to work. However, if you view these prophecies as though Israel (the church today) will be fulfilling them, the vast majority of these problems disappear, as we will see.

We will look at these four chapters of Ezekiel specifically in this chapter and the next, but first we need to say a word about interpreting prophecy.

PROBLEMS WITH PROPHECY

Sometimes a prophet will be prophesying about something in the distant future and then, without taking a breath, he will say something about his current day situation. Then, again without a break, he will talk once more about something in the distant future.

CHAPTER 7

This also occurs in the Scriptures. Simply by writing down what God told them, the prophets may be prophesying something in a single sentence, but there may be a large gap in time between the first half of the sentence and the second half of the sentence, for instance.

Let's take one or two examples. Jesus went to the synagogue one day and read from Isaiah. This is what happened:

> 16 And He came to Nazareth, where He had been brought up; and as was His custom, He entered the synagogue on the Sabbath, and stood up to read.
> 17 And the book of the prophet Isaiah was handed to Him. And He opened the book, and found the place where it was written,
> 18 "THE SPIRIT OF THE LORD IS UPON ME, BECAUSE HE ANOINTED ME TO PREACH THE GOSPEL TO THE POOR. HE HAS SENT ME TO PROCLAIM RELEASE TO THE CAPTIVES, AND RECOVERY OF SIGHT TO THE BLIND, TO SET FREE THOSE WHO ARE DOWN-TRODDEN,
> 19 TO PROCLAIM THE FAVORABLE YEAR OF THE LORD."
> 20 And He closed the book, and gave it back to the attendant, and sat down; and the eyes of all in the synagogue were fixed upon Him.
> 21 And He began to say to them, "Today this Scripture has been fulfilled in your hearing."
> —Luke 4

I particularly want to call your attention to the fact that verse 19 says "To proclaim the favorable year of the Lord." You will notice that this ends with a period.

But now let's go back to Isaiah and read the passage from which Jesus was quoting:

THE GATHERING OF ISRAEL

> 1 The Spirit of the Lord God is upon me,
> Because the Lord has anointed me
> To bring good news to the afflicted;
> He has sent me to bind up the brokenhearted,
> To proclaim liberty to captives,
> And freedom to prisoners;
> 2 To proclaim the favorable year of the Lord,
> And the day of vengeance of our God;
> To comfort all who mourn,
> 3 To grant those who mourn in Zion,
> Giving them a garland instead of ashes,
> The oil of gladness instead of mourning,
> The mantle of praise instead of a spirit of fainting.
> So they will be called oaks of righteousness,
> The planting of the LORD, that He may be glorified.
> —Isaiah 61

You will notice that verse 2 begins a sentence that actually continues into verse 3. We read, "To proclaim the favorable year of the Lord," which ends with a comma, not a period. The rest of verse 2 and all of verse 3 will not occur until Christ's Second Coming. In quoting this in the synagogue, as recorded for us in the New Testament, Jesus gave us the breaking point in this particular prophecy—the "time gap," if you will. But we know that this part of Isaiah 61 is talking about both the First and Second Comings of our Savior.

People in Old Testament times reading these three verses "with their minds" would likely assume that all this was going to happen at the same time, at the First Coming of the Messiah.

A second example is my favorite Psalm, Psalm 91:

> 1 He who dwells in the shelter of the Most High
> Will abide in the shadow of the Almighty.
> 2 I will say to the LORD, "My refuge and my fortress,
> My God, in whom I trust!"

3   For it is He who delivers you from the snare of the trapper,
And from the deadly pestilence.
4   He will cover you with His pinions,
And under His wings you may seek refuge;
His faithfulness is a shield and bulwark.
5   You will not be afraid of the terror by night,
Or of the arrow that flies by day;
6   Of the pestilence that stalks in darkness,
Or of the destruction that lays waste at noon.
7   A thousand may fall at your side,
And ten thousand at your right hand;
But it shall not approach you.
8   You will only look on with your eyes,
And see the recompense of the wicked.
9   For you have made the LORD, my refuge,
Even the Most High, your dwelling place.
10   No evil will befall you,
Nor will any plague come near your tent.
11   For He will give His angels charge concerning you,
To guard you in all your ways.
12   They will bear you up in their hands,
Lest you strike your foot against a stone.
13   You will tread upon the lion and cobra,
The young lion and the serpent you will trample down.
14   "Because he has loved Me, therefore I will deliver him;
I will set him securely on high, because he has known My name.
15   "He will call upon Me, and I will answer him;
I will be with him in trouble;
I will rescue him, and honor him.
16   "With a long life I will satisfy him,
And let him behold My salvation."

—Psalm 91

In much of the Psalm, David is talking about himself and the men following him. Also, I think he is talking about us today, particularly during the tribulation. Then, in verses 11 and 12, he branches off to prophesy about the coming Messiah. Then, without ever breaking stride, in verse 13, he goes right back in to his main thought.

The reason I point out these two examples is to show that only the Holy Spirit can really reveal the true meaning of any passage to a reader or a student of prophecy. I humbly acknowledge that I am not wise enough to interpret these four chapters in Ezekiel, but I ask the Holy Spirit to interpret them for you through me. Some of the parts of these chapters are talking about events in Ezekiel's day, and other parts are prophecies yet to be fulfilled by Israel, the church.

EZEKIEL 36

As we begin looking at Chapter 36 of Ezekiel, we must refresh our memory concerning the fact that, during the great tribulation all of the cities of the world—including those in the State of Israel—will be pulled down. We also need to remember that when Jesus Christ returns in power and glory at the end of the great tribulation, the whole house of Israel (the saints of the Old Testament and the Christians of the New Testament) will be caught up in the air to meet the Lord, and we will go with Him to our land, as He touches down on the Mount of Olives. It does not matter if we are caught up into the air 5 feet or 50 feet or 500 feet; we are all going to go to the Mount of Olives with Christ by "TWA" (of course, *TWA* means "*T*ravel *W*ith *A*ngels").

In the first part of Ezekiel 36, a blessing is pronounced upon Israel. The next portion talks about Israel, which has been scattered among all of the nations, returning to the land promised to Abraham. Again there are some who would view this as having been fulfilled when Israel was formed as a nation back in 1948. As we read these verses, that view presents major problems. A much better interpretation is that it refers to the time when all of the true Israel of God (Christians), which is scattered in all nations, goes to the promised land with Jesus Christ. We will look at verses 22 through 36, with breaks for comments:

> 22 "Therefore, say to the house of Israel, 'Thus says the Lord God, "It is not for your sake, O house of Israel, that I am about to act, but for My holy name, which you have profaned among the nations where you went.
> 23 "And I will vindicate the holiness of My great name which has been profaned among the nations, which you have profaned in their midst. Then the nations will know that I am the LORD," declares the Lord GOD, "when I prove Myself holy among you in their sight.
> 24 "For I will take you from the nations, gather you from all the lands, and bring you into your own land...."
>
> —Ezekiel 36

If you do not think Israel (the church) is profaning God's name among the nations today, just look at some of the major national scandals that we have had, wherein Christians have been shown to be immoral and unethical. Ask any businessman if he would like to do business with a church or a Christian, and almost always the answer will be negative. Ask the average man on the street what he thinks of preachers; very often he will give you a negative answer. Israel (the church) is really not glorifying God out in the nations.

Continuing in Ezekiel 36, we read this:

> 25 "Then I will sprinkle clean water on you, and you will be clean; I will cleanse you from all your filthiness and from all your idols.

> 26 "Moreover, I will give you a new heart and put a new spirit within you; and I will remove the heart of stone from your flesh and give you a heart of flesh.
> 27 "And I will put My Spirit within you and cause you to walk in My statutes, and you will be careful to observe My ordinances. . . ."
> —Ezekiel 36

Have the Hebrews and Jews in the State of Israel been cleansed from all filthiness? The answer is *no*! I have been there, and I can verify this first-hand. Has God put a new heart in them? Again the answer is *no*. You can only get a new heart as you receive Jesus Christ as your Savior. Has He put a new spirit in them? *No*! The only way you can be filled with the Holy Spirit is to receive Jesus Christ as your Savior.

None of these things were fulfilled in 1948, when the Hebrews and Jews formed the State of Israel, as some teachers claim. But they all will be fulfilled when the raptured Israel of God goes to that land, with Jesus at the front of the triumphal parade.

The next several verses talk primarily about the millennium. Then Ezekiel continues with the original thought, as follows here:

> 33 'Thus says the Lord GOD, "On the day that I cleanse you from all your iniquities, I will cause the cities to be inhabited, and the waste places will be rebuilt.
> 34 "And the desolate land will be cultivated instead of being a desolation in the sight of everyone who passed by.
> 35 "And they will say, 'This desolate land has become like the garden of Eden; and the waste, desolate, and ruined cities are fortified and inhabited.'
> 36 "Then the nations that are left round about you will know that I, the LORD, have rebuilt the ruined places and planted that which was desolate; I, the LORD, have spoken and will do it."
> —Ezekiel 36

In 1948, when the Hebrews formed their nation, the cities were inhabited. This is what the Palestinian problem is all about. Many of these people left their homes and businesses, because they did not want to be part of the State of Israel. The place was not desolate ("desolate" means *uninhabited*, as we will discuss further in a later chapter). Certainly, when the Hebrews formed their nation in 1948, that land was not uninhabited (desolate). So, attempting to tie this passage to the Hebrews establishing a nation in 1948 is almost absurd.

On the other hand, it beautifully fits, if you look at the whole house of Israel (Old Testament saints and New Testament Christians) going to that land with King Jesus and the area becoming truly a garden of Eden. The Scriptures tell us that every building on the planet will be in ruins by the end of the great tribulation. We will receive our orders from Jesus, and we will get to rebuild the Mount Zion area. I am looking forward to it!

As a digression, to give you the scriptural basis for this last paragraph, we know that every mountain and island will be moved out of their places:

> **14** And the sky was split apart like a scroll when it is rolled up; and every mountain and island were moved out of their places.
>
> —Revelation 6

> **20** And every island fled away, and the mountains were not found.
>
> —Revelation 16

As we discussed in Chapter 6, Mount Zion, where the Dome of the Rock is today, will be raised up and become the chief (probably the highest) mountain on earth:

> **2** Now it will come about that
> In the last days,

> The mountain of the house of the LORD
> Will be established as the chief of the
> mountains,
> And will be raised above the hills;
> And all the nations will stream to it.
> —Isaiah 2

We also discussed that the Mount of Olives will be split and move in two directions, and the mountainous area around Jerusalem will become a vast plain (Zechariah 14:4-11).

Logic would tell us that, with all of this gigantic earth upheaval, all of the buildings would be destroyed, and we would have to rebuild them during the millennium. However, we do not have to rely on logic, because the Bible tells us that this is what will happen:

> 11 Thus says the LORD, the Holy One of
> Israel, and his Maker:
> "Ask Me about the things to come concerning My sons,
> And you shall commit to Me the work
> of My hands.
> 12 "It is I who made the earth, and created
> man upon it.
> I stretched out the heavens with My hands,
> And I ordained all their host.
> 13 "I have aroused him in righteousness,
> And I will make all his ways smooth;
> He will build My city, and will let My
> exiles go free,
> Without any payment of reward," says the
> LORD of hosts.
> —Isaiah 45

> 18 "But be glad and rejoice forever in what I
> create;
> For behold, I create Jerusalem for rejoicing,
> And her people for gladness.

> 19 "I will also rejoice in Jerusalem, and be glad in My people;
> And there will no longer be heard in her
> The voice of weeping and the sound of crying.
> 20 "No longer will there be in it an infant who lives but a few days,
> Or an old man who does not live out his days;
> For the youth will die at the age of one hundred
> And the one who does not reach the age of one hundred
> Shall be thought accursed.
> 21 "And they shall build houses and inhabit them;
> They shall also plant vineyards and eat their fruit. . . ."
>
> —Isaiah 65

> 13 "Behold, days are coming," declares the LORD,
> "When the plowman will overtake the reaper
> And the treader of grapes him who sows seed;
> When the mountains will drip sweet wine,
> And all the hills will be dissolved.
> 14 "Also I will restore the captivity of My people Israel,
> And they will rebuild the ruined cities and live in them,
> They will also plant vineyards and drink their wine,
> And make gardens and eat their fruit.
> 15 "I will also plant them on their land,
> And they will not again be rooted out from their land
> Which I have given them,"
> Says the LORD your God.
>
> —Amos 9

Most of what we know about the millennium is found in the book of Isaiah. From our previous discussion, we know that Isaiah 61 deals with the First and Second Comings of Jesus Christ. Of course, at His Second Coming we have the rapture, which Ezekiel 37 describes.

EZEKIEL 37

The first half of Ezekiel 37 is the vision of the dry bones. There are some teachers of prophecy who totally distort this picture, claiming it happened in 1948. The reason they do this is that they do not understand who Israel is, and therefore they try to bend, twist and hammer the unfulfilled promises concerning Israel to match the Hebrews.

It is my view that this prophecy will be fulfilled by the Israel of God and that it is the best description of the rapture contained anywhere in the Bible. So without comment, let us read about this part of the rapture—the rapture of those who have died, both the Old Testament saints and the church combined, who are Israel:

> 4 Again He said to me, "Prophesy over these bones, and say to them, 'O dry bones, hear the word of the LORD.'
> 5 "Thus says the Lord GOD to these bones, 'Behold, I will cause breath to enter you that you may come to life.
> 6 'And I will put sinews on you, make flesh grow back on you, cover you with skin, and put breath in you that you may come alive; and you will know that I am the LORD.'"
> 7 So I prophesied as I was commanded; and as I prophesied, there was a noise, and behold, a rattling; and the bones came together, bone to its bone.
> 8 And I looked, and behold, sinews were on them, and flesh grew, and skin covered them; but there was no breath in them.

> 9 Then He said to me, "Prophesy to the breath, prophesy, son of man, and say to the breath, 'Thus says the Lord GOD, "Come from the four winds, O breath, and breathe on these slain, that they come to life."'"
> 10 So I prophesied as He commanded me, and the breath came into them, and they came to life, and stood on their feet, an exceedingly great army.
> 11 Then He said to me, "Son of man, these bones are the whole house of Israel; behold, they say, 'Our bones are dried up, and our hope has perished. We are completely cut off.'
> 12 "Therefore prophesy, and say to them, 'Thus says the Lord GOD, "Behold, I will open your graves and cause you to come up out of your graves, My people; and I will bring you into the land of Israel.
> 13 "Then you will know that I am the LORD, when I have opened your graves and caused you to come up out of your graves, My people.
> 14 "And I will put My Spirit within you, and you will come to life, and I will place you on your own land. Then you will know that I, the LORD, have spoken and done it," declares the LORD.'"
>
> —Ezekiel 37

Obviously, this passage is describing people who were dead and in graves. This is not merely symbolic. The only things left in the graves were bones. God restores new and resurrected bodies to this mighty army, and they are "God's people," a combination of Old Testament saints and New Testament believers in Jesus. This also says that they will not only come to life at the resurrection, but God will place His Spirit within them and He will place them in their own land (verse 14). They will rise from their graves when King Jesus Christ returns and brings them with Him to their land, promised to them so long ago.

Has God placed His Spirit within the Hebrews? Sadly, the answer is *no*, because the only way one can have the Spirit of God within is through Jesus Christ.

THE GATHERING OF ISRAEL 131

The only way one can know the Father today is through Jesus Christ. If you do not know the Father, you are not one of God's people:

> 23 Whoever denies the Son does not have the Father; the one who confesses the Son has the Father also.
> —1 John 2

That is just as plain as the nose on your face. If you deny the Son, Jesus Christ, you do not have the Father and are not part of God's people today.

I would love to examine the entire chapter of Ezekiel 37 verse by verse, but space restrictions will not allow that here. For the sake of this discussion, let us read the last few verses of this chapter to see if they were fulfilled by Israel in 1948 or if they are going to be fulfilled by the Israel of God (spiritual and not physical) when they go to that land with Jesus. In this passage, Jesus is symbolically called "David":

> 24 "And My servant David will be king over them, and they will all have one shepherd; and they will walk in My ordinances, and keep My statutes, and observe them.
> 25 "And they shall live on the land that I gave to Jacob My servant, in which your fathers lived; and they will live on it, they, and their sons, and their sons' sons, forever; and David My servant shall be their prince forever.
> 26 "And I will make a covenant of peace with them; it will be an everlasting covenant with them. And I will place them and multiply them, and will set My sanctuary in their midst forever.
> 27 "My dwelling place also will be with them; and I will be their God, and they will be My people.
> 28 "And the nations will know that I am the LORD who sanctifies Israel, when My sanctuary is in their midst forever.""
> —Ezekiel 37

When we go to the promised land with Jesus (who is from the line of David), and He is King over us and our only Shepherd, we will joyfully walk in His ordinances and keep His statutes. We will live in the land that was promised to Abraham, which is now the inheritance of each and every Christian. The Lord Jesus will be our sanctuary in our midst forever! Hallelujah! Isn't that wonderful?

SUMMARY AND CONCLUSION

Ezekiel 36 and 37 describe some exciting events: the return of Israel (us) to our land; the raising of the portion of Israel who are dead at the rapture; Christ's Kingship over Israel; God putting His Spirit within us; and Israel observing His statutes and ordinances. We have seen that these passages cannot be applied to the Hebrews who went to Israel in 1948, because none of these things are true of them. However, all of these things will be true when the whole house of Israel goes there with Jesus Christ at the rapture, which takes place when He returns in power and glory at the end of the great tribulation.

It is going to be an exciting and wonderful day when our loved ones are raised from their graves to receive their resurrected bodies, and we who are alive and remain are caught up with them and also receive our resurrected bodies. Christ will put a fresh spirit and new heart in each of us, to go with our resurrected bodies. We will go with Him and be part of His team that will rebuild the cities and reign with Him. Jesus Christ will be our King and we will live in peace.

8

EZEKIEL 38-39—
GOG-MAGOG BATTLE

Ezekiel 38 and 39 primarily deal with the Gog-Magog battle. I have heard many Christian teachers and leaders say something like "the next major event on the prophetic calendar will be the Gog-Magog battle, with Russia invading the nation of Israel."

I would like to disagree with this view of prophecy. What has led these good people to what I consider to be an erroneous conclusion? They are still trying to count the Hebrews and Jews of the State of Israel as God's true *Israel* and make the Hebrews fulfill the prophecies of Ezekiel 38 and 39.

To me, it is very clear from the Scriptures that the Israel of God, the spiritual entity, fulfills these prophecies very beautifully. Let me give you a little background, though. I could see a world war occurring either during the time of birth pangs or right at the beginning of the great tribulation. I could also see the battle of Armageddon occurring on the last day of this age, when Christ returns in power and glory and speaks a word, and all the armies are destroyed. But I always had difficulty with the Gog-Magog battle. It did not seem to fit in with either the world war or with the battle of Armageddon.

For eleven years, I asked God if the Gog-Magog war was one of these two wars, or if there was to be a third war. When God finally showed me the truth, it was so obvious that I could not believe I could have missed it all those years.

As we will see, the Gog-Magog war happens after the millennium, during a period of time before the destruction of earth by fire. The Bible gives no idea as to how long that period will be, but it does tell us there will be a minimum of seven years between the millennium and the destruction of the earth.

Now let's take a close look at the Gog-Magog war, as described in Ezekiel 38 and 39.

THE GOG-MAGOG WAR

As we begin to examine the Gog-Magog war, we should first find out why some people think this might be talking about Russia. We must realize that in the Bible, all directions are given from Jerusalem. Thus, if it talks about a king from the east, this would be some place east of Jerusalem. Ezekiel 38:15, which we will read in just a moment, states that the army coming against Israel will come out of "the remotest parts of the north." If you look at a map of the world, you will find that Moscow is almost exactly due north of Jerusalem, and it is certainly remote from Jerusalem.

Thus, it is most likely that the major force in the Gog-Magog war will be from that area. If the Gog-Magog war were to happen in the next few years, that region of course would be Russia. If it happens a thousand years from now, there may be some other group of people or some other nation occupying that territory.

Before discussing this further, let us see what the Bible has to say about Gog and Magog. There are only three chapters in the Bible that mention Gog and Magog. Two of these are Ezekiel 38 and 39. Do you know which other chapter in the Bible talks about Gog and Magog? It is Revelation 20:

GOG-MAGOG BATTLE

> 7 And when the thousand years are completed, Satan will be released from his prison,
>
> 8 and will come out to deceive the nations which are in the four corners of the earth, Gog and Magog, to gather them together for the war; the number of them is like the sand of the seashore.
>
> 9 And they came up on the broad plain of the earth and surrounded the camp of the saints and the beloved city, and fire came down from heaven and devoured them.
>
> 10 And the devil who deceived them was thrown into the lake of fire and brimstone, where the beast and the false prophet are also; and they will be tormented day and night forever and ever.
>
> —Revelation 20

I had taught through the book of Revelation a number of times, and had even authored a book on the subject, but for some reason my spiritual eyes had been blinded to this, until recent years. I had simply skipped over the Gog and Magog of verse 8.

This plainly tells us that the Gog-Magog battle will occur after the millennium. Satan will go out and will deceive the nations, and he will gather together an army. Verse 9 says that they will camp upon the broad plain of the earth and will surround the camp of the saints (the Christians). Then we are told that this is going to happen in the beloved city, which is a biblical way to denote Jerusalem. The area around Jerusalem is not a plain now, but it will be when Mount Zion is raised, as we mentioned in Chapter 6. Verse 9 says that the Gog-Magog war will occur on the broad plain surrounding Jerusalem. Therefore, it must occur after the return of King Jesus Christ. This war will end with fire coming down from heaven and devouring the great army that Satan will have gathered together.

Now let's see if what Ezekiel said about the Gog-Magog war fits with what we just learned about the timing of it from Revelation 20:

CHAPTER 8

2 "Son of man, set your face toward Gog of the land of Magog, the prince of Rosh, Meshech, and Tubal, and prophesy against him,

3 and say, 'Thus says the Lord GOD, "Behold, I am against you, O Gog, prince of Rosh, Meshech, and Tubal.

4 "And I will turn you about, and put hooks into your jaws, and I will bring you out, and all your army, horses and horsemen, all of them splendidly attired, a great company with buckler and shield, all of them wielding swords;

5 Persia, Ethiopia, and Put with them, all of them with shield and helmet;

6 Gomer with all its troops; Beth-togarmah from the remote parts of the north with all its troops—many peoples with you.

7 "Be prepared, and prepare yourself, you and all your companies that are assembled about you, and be a guard for them.

8 "After many days you will be summoned; in the later years you will come into the land that is restored from the sword, whose inhabitants have been gathered from many nations to the mountains of Israel which had been a continual waste; but its people were brought out from the nations, and they are living securely, all of them.

9 "And you will go up, you will come like a storm; you will be like a cloud covering the land, you and all your troops, and many peoples with you."

10 'Thus says the Lord GOD, "It will come about on that day, that thoughts will come into your mind, and you will devise an evil plan,

11 and you will say, 'I will go up against the land of unwalled villages. I will go against those who are at rest, that live securely, all of them living without walls, and having no bars or gates,

12 to capture spoil and to seize plunder, to turn your hand against the waste places which are now inhabited, and against the people who are gathered

from the nations, who have acquired cattle and goods, who live at the center of the world.'

13 "Sheba, and Dedan, and the merchants of Tarshish, with all its villages, will say to you, 'Have you come to capture spoil? Have you assembled your company to seize plunder, to carry away silver and gold, to take away cattle and goods, to capture great spoil?'"

14 "Therefore, prophesy, son of man, and say to Gog, 'Thus says the Lord GOD, "On that day when My people Israel are living securely, will you not know it?

15 "And you will come from your place out of the remote parts of the north, you and many peoples with you, all of them riding on horses, a great assembly and a mighty army;

16 and you will come up against My people Israel like a cloud to cover the land. It will come about in the last days that I shall bring you against My land, in order that the nations may know Me when I shall be sanctified through you before their eyes, O Gog."

—Ezekiel 38

If you read this passage carefully, you will see in verse 8 that the people living in the land of Israel at that time have been gathered from many nations and are living securely. (This is certainly not true of the State of Israel today.)

Verse 11 says that the villages in the reconstructed promised land will not have walls. Verse 12 tells us that these people, gathered from all of the nations, live at the center of the world (where Christ reigns) and they have acquired cattle and goods.

In verse 15, we see that the enemy comes from the remotest parts of the north with a great and mighty army. Remember, Revelation 20:8 said that the army was numbered like the sand of the seashore. All of these things will be true when Israel goes to Mount Zion with Jesus at His Second Coming and reigns with

Him for one thousand years, but they are not true about the Hebrew nation today.

Now let's read how this Gog-Magog war will end:

1 "And you, son of man, prophesy against Gog, and say, 'Thus says the Lord GOD, "Behold, I am against you, O Gog, prince of Rosh, Meshech, and Tubal;

2 and I shall turn you around, drive you on, take you up from the remotest parts of the north, and bring you against the mountains of Israel.

3 "And I shall strike your bow from your left hand, and dash down your arrows from your right hand.

4 "You shall fall on the mountains of Israel, you and all your troops, and the peoples who are with you; I shall give you as food to every kind of predatory bird and beast of the field.

5 "You will fall on the open field; for it is I who have spoken," declares the Lord GOD.

6 "And I shall send fire upon Magog and those who inhabit the coastlands in safety; and they will know that I am the LORD.

7 "And My holy name I shall make known in the midst of My people Israel; and I shall not let My holy name be profaned anymore. And the nations will know that I am the Lord, the Holy One in Israel.

8 "Behold, it is coming and it shall be done," declares the Lord GOD. "That is the day of which I have spoken.

9 "Then those who inhabit the cities of Israel will go out, and make fires with the weapons and burn them, both shields and bucklers, bows and arrows, war clubs and spears and for seven years they will make fires of them.

10 "And they will not take wood from the field or gather firewood from the forests, for they will make fires with the weapons; and they will take the spoil of

those who despoiled them, and seize the plunder of those who plundered them," declares the Lord GOD.

11 "And it will come about on that day that I shall give Gog a burial ground there in Israel, the valley of those who pass by east of the sea, and it will block off the passers-by. So they will bury Gog there with all his multitude, and they will call it the valley of Hamon-gog.

12 "For seven months the house of Israel will be burying them in order to cleanse the land. . . ."
—Ezekiel 39

In verse 6 of this chapter of Ezekiel, we see fire coming down upon Magog. Revelation 20:9 also spoke of fire that came down from heaven and ended the war. Another very interesting thing we learn here is that the weapons will be made out of wood. We know this from verse 9 of Ezekiel 39, which tells us that it will take seven years for them to burn all of the weapons. If Russia were to invade the State of Israel today, they certainly would not be using wooden weapons. However, during the millennium, without any foundries and factories (which pollute), there will not be a source of metal available. So, any weapons would, of necessity, have to be made of wood. We also see in this passage that it will take seven months to bury the dead. Some of them will be consumed by the fire and some of them will be eaten by predatory birds and beasts, but the remainder will require seven months to bury.

Thus, we have seen that, after the millennium, Satan will be loosed for a little while and will gather up an army. Then there will be the Gog-Magog war. We know that the earth will exist at least an additional seven years after that Gog-Magog war (because Ezekiel says that it will take seven years to burn all of the weapons). Incidentally, this is another reason why Russia invading the State of Israel does not seem likely to fulfill this prophecy. The great tribulation is only three and a half years, and yet it will take seven years to burn the wooden weapons after this war. (For further discussion on why I believe the Bible teaches that the great tribulation will be three and a half years in duration, I would refer you to Chapter 2 of my book entitled *The Rapture Book* or Chapter 6 of *The Future Revealed*.)

The real key is the identity of Israel. If one were considering the State of Israel to be *Israel*, then I could see where one would fall into the trap of thinking that Russia might invade. However, if one looks at Israel as who it really is, the Christians and Old Testament saints, then this all makes sense. At the end of the tribulation, the Christians and the saints from the Old Testament are gathered to their promised land and are living securely. When Satan is released at the end of the millennium, he comes against God's people (Israel) with the great army he has gathered. This army is destroyed by fire from heaven and Satan is cast into the lake of fire for eternity.

When you view it this way, the prophecies of Gog and Magog are no longer a mystery, but they are clearly fulfilled at the end of the millennium.

THE GREAT PLAIN OF THE EARTH

I would like to repeat the four verses that we read from Revelation 20:

7 And when the thousand years are completed, Satan will be released from his prison,
8 and will come out to deceive the nations which are in the four corners of the earth, Gog and Magog, to gather them together for the war; the number of them is like the sand of the seashore.
9 And they came up on the broad plain of the earth and surrounded the camp of the saints and the beloved city, and fire came down from heaven and devoured them.

10 And the devil who deceived them was thrown into the lake of fire and brimstone, where the beast and the false prophet are also; and they will be tormented day and night forever and ever.
—Revelation 20

Around the Jerusalem of the millennium, as we noted earlier, verse 9 says that there will be "the broad plain of the earth." Today the area around Jerusalem is anything but a "broad plain." It is very hilly, so obviously something is wrong. Gog-Magog cannot happen until that area becomes a great plain.

We find the answer to this dilemma in a passage from the writings of the prophet Zechariah, from which we quoted in Chapter 6. In light of our discussion of the Gog-Magog war, it bears repeating here.

3 Then the LORD will go forth and fight against those nations, as when He fights on a day of battle.

4 And in that day His feet will stand on the Mount of Olives, which is in front of Jerusalem on the east; and the Mount of Olives will be split in its middle from east to west by a very large valley, so that half of the mountain will move toward the north and the other half toward the south. . . .

9 And the LORD will be king over all the earth; in that day the LORD will be the only one, and His name the only one.

10 All the land will be changed into a plain from Geba to Rimmon south of Jerusalem; but Jerusalem will rise and remain on its site from Benjamin's Gate as far as the place of the First Gate to the Corner Gate, and from the Tower of Hananel to the king's wine presses.

11 And people will live in it, and there will be no more curse, for Jerusalem will dwell in security.
—Zechariah 14

This describes the time when King Jesus Christ comes, with all of the saints (Israel), and touches down on the Mount of Olives. To review what we have mentioned in previous chapters, it is split open at that time, and we know from other Scriptures that the Mount Zion area will be lifted up and will be chief of the mountains. Zechariah also tells us that the entire area around Jerusalem will be changed into a plain.

Thus, you can see that it is impossible for the Gog-Magog battle to occur now. It must happen after these geologic changes prophesied by Zechariah take place. Since these things occur on the last day of this age, when Jesus Christ returns, it could not happen before the great tribulation or even during it. As we consider the passage from Revelation 20, with the clues that it gives us, we see that the battle of Gog-Magog must occur after the millennium.

To help you crystallize your understanding of these coming geological changes, I will also repeat here the passage we quoted in an earlier chapter about the Mount Zion area being raised up:

> 2 Now it will come about that
> In the last days,
> The mountain of the house of the LORD
> Will be established as the chief of the mountains,
> And will be raised above the hills;
> And all the nations will stream to it.
> 3 And many peoples will come and say,
> "Come, let us go up to the mountain of the LORD,
> To the house of the God of Jacob;
> That He may teach us concerning His ways,
> And that we may walk in His paths."
> For the law will go forth from Zion,
> And the word of the LORD from Jerusalem.
> 4 And He will judge between the nations,

And will render decisions for many peoples;
And they will hammer their swords into plowshares, and their spears into pruning hooks.
Nation will not lift up sword against nation,
And never again will they learn war.
—Isaiah 2

As discussed earlier, we learn here that the mountain of the house of the Lord will be raised up and become the chief mountain in the entire world. We know from Zechariah and Revelation that all the area around it will become a broad plain.

It is on this broad plain that surrounds the mountain of the Lord that Satan will muster the forces of Gog and Magog, after the millennium. This is where the fire of God will come down and destroy all of those soldiers who have pledged an allegiance to Satan. Greater is He, who is in us (Jesus Christ) than he who is in the world (1 John 4:4)! King Jesus wins again!

SUMMARY AND CONCLUSION

Do you see how simply and clearly all the prophecies begin to fit together, when we accept who Israel really is? The living part of Israel on the earth today is everyone who believes in Jesus Christ, whether he be Hebrew, Chinese, Irish or any other nationality. The prophecies concerning Israel that will be fulfilled before the return of Jesus Christ in power and glory (when the rapture occurs) will be fulfilled by the church.

Once all of Israel—which includes the Old Testament saints—is resurrected at the rapture when Jesus Christ comes in power and glory, then the whole house of Israel will be the inheritor of the promises made to Abraham and the fulfillment of prophecies yet ahead, such as the Gog-Magog battle.

Praise God! When He totally rids us of our brainwashing, and we can see who the true Israel is, the interpretation of prophecy becomes easy, under the guidance of the Holy Spirit. And it really glorifies Jesus Christ, our soon-coming King.

9

JERUSALEM MADE DESOLATE

Like most people, I prefer to talk about positive and uplifting subjects. However, the prophecies concerning the end of this age (not the end of the world) inform us that there are some major negative events that will occur. These things were put in the Bible for a reason—God wants us to know what is coming and to understand it.

There is a major event coming involving the State of Israel that very few teachers of prophecy have addressed or seem to be willing to address. That event is the coming desolation of Jerusalem.

RECENT MIDEAST EVENTS

As long as Iran and Iraq were fighting, they kept each other occupied so that neither of them could concentrate on their common enemy, the State of Israel. However, those two warring nations have signed a cease-fire and are working on a peace treaty, so it looks as though that war is over.

Lieutenant General Dan Shomorn, Chief-of-Staff of Israeli military forces, said that Israel was safer while Iran and Iraq were fighting each other. Now he is worried about Israel becoming an eventual target for the buildup of Iraqi forces who are now better-trained as a result of the war. He pointed out that Iraq has sent ground forces to fight against Israel in three of the five Arab wars with the Jewish state.

Shomorn was also concerned about Syria, because they have significantly improved both the quality and the quantity of their military equipment in recent years. He noted that Syria has also developed chemical warheads for its surface-to-surface missiles and has doubled its ground force, increasing the number of tanks from 1,700 to 4,000 since the 1973 Yom Kippur War.

Another major event occurring in the Middle East is that King Hussein of Jordan has given up all claims to the West Bank, which the State of Israel has occupied since the 1973 war. By doing this, he not only gave up the claim but also the financial responsibility. He has had, for example, over 1,800 teachers in the West Bank on his payroll since 1973. He has dumped all the financial responsibilities for the West Bank on the PLO and has called for a separate Palestinian state.

With all of this activity, it is very likely that these Arab nations—all of whom have vowed to destroy the State of Israel—may band together within the next few years and once again attack the State of Israel. Before we proceed to look at the potential outcome of that war, we first need to define "desolation," since that is what the Bible says will be the result of some war or catastrophe.

WHAT IS DESOLATION?

I always find it safest to get my definitions from the Bible. As you will see presently, in the Scriptures "desolation" means *uninhabited*, as we mentioned in passing in Chapter 7. When Jesus went out to a desolate place, He went out to a place where there were no people. Here are a few Scriptures that help you see the biblical definition of desolation:

> 25 May their camp be desolate;
> May none dwell in their tents.
> —Psalm 69

JERUSALEM MADE DESOLATE

> 9 In my ears the LORD of hosts has sworn,
> "Surely, many houses shall become desolate,
> Even great and fine ones, without occupants.
> —Isaiah 5

> 11 Then I said, "Lord, how long?" And He answered,
> "Until cities are devasted and without inhabitant,
> Houses are without people,
> And the land is utterly desolate, . . .
> —Isaiah 6

> 9 "Why have you prophesied in the name of the LORD saying,
> 'This house will be like Shiloh, and this city will be desolate, without inhabitant'?". . .
> —Jeremiah 26

> 11 "And I will make Jerusalem a heap of ruins,
> A haunt of jackals;
> And I will make the cities of Judah a desolation, without inhabitant."
> —Jeremiah 9

We could examine many additional verses, but throughout the Scriptures, desolation means "uninhabited" or with a tremendous reduction in the number of inhabitants.

When asked to tell about what things would be like right before He came back and right before this age would end, Jesus Himself had this to say:

> 3 And as He was sitting on the Mount of Olives, the disciples came to Him privately, saying, "Tell us, when will these things be, and what will be the sign of Your coming, and of the end of the age?". . .
>
> 15 "Therefore when you see the ABOMINATION OF DESOLATION which was spoken of through Daniel

> the prophet, standing in the holy place (let the reader understand),
> 16 then let those who are in Judea flee to the mountains; . . .
>
> —Matthew 24

In these verses, Jesus said that at the end of the age, which contained His coming, we were going to see an abomination which would make the holy place desolate (without inhabitants).

I have asked some prophecy teachers if they believed in the coming abomination of desolation and they said, "Oh, yes!" I asked them then if they thought that we would see Jerusalem uninhabited, and they said, "Oh, no!" This is inconsistent, because the "abomination of desolation" means that there is an abomination coming which is going to cause Jerusalem to be uninhabited.

When that does occur, many of those who think the State of Israel is the Israel of God are going to lose faith. They will think God has abandoned "His people." God may abandon the Hebrews who do not believe in Jesus Christ, but He will not abandon His true people, who are all those of every nationality who believe in Jesus Christ.

THE TIMES OF THE GENTILES

One of the questions that naturally arises is this: "How long will Jerusalem be desolate, essentially uninhabited or with few occupants?" The Bible tells us:

> 1 And there was given me a measuring rod like a staff; and someone said, "Rise and measure the temple of God, and the altar, and those who worship in it.
> 2 "And leave out the court which is outside the temple, and do not measure it, for it has been given to the nations; and they will tread under foot the holy city for forty-two months. . . ."
>
> —Revelation 11

JERUSALEM MADE DESOLATE

This says that Jerusalem will be trampled underfoot by the Gentiles for forty-two months, which is three and a half years. In searching the Scriptures, I find that they consistently indicate that the great tribulation will last three and a half years, but also that God will mercifully cut that time short (Matthew 24:22).

How will we know when Jerusalem is about to become desolate? Let's read what the book of Luke has to say about this:

> 20 "But when you see Jerusalem surrounded by armies, then recognize that her desolation is at hand.
> 21 "Then let those who are in Judea flee to the mountains, and let those who are in the midst of the city depart, and let not those who are in the country enter the city;
> 22 because these are days of vengeance, in order that all things which are written may be fulfilled.
> 23 "Woe to those who are with child and to those who nurse babes in those days; for there will be great distress upon the land, and wrath to this people,
> 24 and they will fall by the edge of the sword, and will be led captive into all the nations; and Jerusalem will be trampled under foot by the Gentiles until the times of the Gentiles be fulfilled.
> 25 "And there will be signs in sun and moon and stars, and upon the earth dismay among nations, in perplexity at the roaring of the sea and the waves,
> 26 men fainting from fear and the expectation of the things which are coming upon the world; for the powers of the heavens will be shaken.
> 27 "And then they will see THE SON OF MAN COMING IN A CLOUD with power and great glory.
> 28 "But when these things begin to take place, straighten up and lift up your heads, because your redemption is drawing near."
>
> —Luke 21

This passage tells us that when we see Jerusalem surrounded by *armies* (note that "armies" is plural, which means it is not just one army, such as the Roman army), then we will know that her desolation is at hand (verse 20).

There are some who feel that this passage in Luke 21 (and the corresponding one in Matthew 24) deal with the destruction of Jerusalem in 70 A.D. However, that is not a conclusion that the Scriptures allow us, if we read this in context. Immediately following the discussion of Jerusalem becoming desolate, in verse 27, we see Jesus Christ returning in great power and glory. So the "Jerusalem becoming desolate" that is being discussed here is the one that immediately precedes the return of our Lord and Savior, Jesus Christ.

In fact, if you study history, Jerusalem was not made desolate in 70 A.D. by any means. There were still large numbers of Jews living in Jerusalem after that period in time, up until the second major Jewish revolt against Rome, which was ultimately squelched by Rome in 135 A.D. It was after that second revolution that Rome flattened Jerusalem, but immediately built a Roman city there. You can see the chariot ways, the arches, the shops and so forth from that Roman city underneath the present Jewish sector of old Jerusalem. But even during the squelching of the second revolt and the building of a Roman city on top of Jerusalem, there was no point in time that Jerusalem was desolate. However, there will be a time that it will become desolate and that, according to Jesus Christ, will be after another Mideast war.

THE NEXT MIDEAST WAR

The Bible says that there will be yet another Mideast war and that Jerusalem will be surrounded by armies and will become essentially uninhabited or desolate.

JERUSALEM MADE DESOLATE 151

Those who think that the State of Israel is the Israel of God would point out that since the State of Israel was formed in 1948, Arab nations in various combinations have come against it in war five times, and all five times the State of Israel has come out victorious. Obviously, this is a true statement. However, they proceed to assume that, in the next war, Israel will once again be victorious.

This is human reasoning. The Bible says that there will come a war (probably the next such confrontation) wherein the opposite will occur. When I have to choose between human reasoning and what the Bible has prophesied, I will *always* go with what the Scriptures have to say. The Scriptures say that the State of Israel will lose in an upcoming war.

I have been to the top of Masada. This is the place where the Jewish patriots all committed suicide in order not to be captured by the Roman army. But the Israeli leaders and army will tell you today that they no longer have the "Masada Complex"; they now have the "Samson Complex."

The "Samson Complex" means, "I'm willing to die, but I'm going to take as many of you with me as possible." Since the Israelis have nuclear weapons, it could even be that they, by design or by accident, will set off a nuclear bomb in Jerusalem thinking that if they cannot have that sacred city, no one else can. It could be that the surrounding armies will simply level Jerusalem with a vengeance. However it occurs, the Bible says that Jerusalem is going to become uninhabited.

In all of history, when has man invented weapons that he did not use? The Israelis have nuclear weapons and, I believe, the will to use them, if backed to the wall. The Arabs have the technology and the will to use chemical/biological weapons. Either of these could make Jerusalem desolate.

This desolation was not fulfilled in 70 A.D., by any stretch of the imagination. In Matthew 24, Christ is not talking about what will happen in 70 A.D. He is talking about what will happen at the end of the age that contains His coming, what will happen right before He comes back. He says clearly that right before He comes back, Jerusalem is going to become desolate (uninhabited).

However, it is my finding and understanding that this destruction of Jerusalem and its coming desolation is *not* the Gog-Magog war, as some teach. As we saw this in the last chapter, the Gog-Magog war occurs at the end of the millennium.

THE WORLD DESTROYED BY FIRE

Let's review briefly what the Bible says will occur after the millennium. Satan will be released and will deceive many, but he and the great army he has gathered will be destroyed by fire from heaven in the Gog-Magog war (the final war). After some unknown amount of time (a minimum of seven years), at the very end of all this, the earth will be destroyed by fire and the existing heavens will also melt. After the existing heaven and earth melt, God is going to create a new heaven and a new earth. Let's look at what Peter has to say about this:

> 7 But the present heavens and earth by His word are being reserved for fire, kept for the day of judgment and destruction of ungodly men. . . .
>
> 10 But the day of the Lord will come like a thief, in which the heavens will pass away with a roar and the elements will be destroyed with intense heat, and the earth and its works will be burned up.
>
> 11 since all these things are to be destroyed in this way, what sort of people ought you to be in holy conduct and godliness,
>
> 12 looking for and hastening the coming of the day of God, on account of which the heavens will be destroyed by burning, and the elements will melt with intense heat!

13 But according to His promise we are looking for new heavens and a new earth, in which righteousness dwells.

—2 Peter 3

These are tremendous verses. I would encourage you to go back and read them one more time before proceeding. This passage says that the earth and the heavens will pass away with a roar and will be melted with intense heat. That will be an awesome day, wouldn't you agree? This will be the end of this world (*cosmos* in Greek).

But look at the hope in verse 13! There will be a new heaven and a new earth, in which righteousness will dwell. How marvelous that will be!

Returning to the subject at hand, let us continue our prayerful consideration of Israel by proceeding to examine what became of the "ten lost tribes" of the Old Testament.

10

THE TEN LOST TRIBES

When discussing Israel, the subject of the ten lost tribes inevitably comes up. Before we discuss that specifically, we need to look at the population of Israel at various points in time. Let's start at the beginning. We know that when Jacob and his sons and their direct descendants went to Egypt, there was a total of seventy people:

> 26 All the persons belonging to Jacob, who came to Egypt, his direct descendants, not including the wives of Jacob's sons, were sixty-six persons in all,
> 27 and the sons of Joseph, who were born to him in Egypt were two; all the persons of the house of Jacob, who came to Egypt, were seventy.
> —Genesis 46

So we see that there were seventy people who were direct descendants from Jacob, plus his son's wives and servants. So perhaps there were about two hundred people who went to Egypt as part of Israel.

Now let's take a look at how many came out of Egypt.

> 1 Then the LORD spoke to Moses in the wilderness of Sinai, in the tent of meeting, on the first of the

CHAPTER 10

> second month, in the second year after they had come out of the land of Egypt, saying,
>
> 2 "Take a census of all the congregation of the sons of Israel, by their families, by their fathers' households, according to the number of names, every male, head by head
>
> 3 from twenty years old and upward, whoever is able to go out to war in Israel, you and Aaron shall number them by their armies. . . .
>
> 44 These are the ones who were numbered, whom Moses and Aaron numbered, with the leaders of Israel, twelve men, each of whom was of his father's household.
>
> 45 So all the numbered men of the sons of Israel by their fathers' households, from twenty years old and upward, whoever was able to go out to war in Israel,
>
> 46 even all the numbered men were 603,550.
>
> 47 The Levites, however, were not numbered among them by their fathers' tribe.
>
> 48 For the LORD had spoken to Moses, saying,
>
> 49 "Only the tribe of Levi you shall not number, nor shall you take their census among the sons of Israel. . . ."
>
> —Numbers 1

Here we see that, out of the eleven tribes (counting Ephraim and Manasseh as one, and excluding Levi), we have 603,550 men, above the age of twenty who were able to go to war. The tribe of Levi had 22,000 males, but these were numbered from one month old and up (Numbers 3:39). Assuming one-third of these were below twenty years old, we come up with approximately 620,000 men over the age of twenty.

Making a reasonable assumption that, on the average, each of these men over twenty had a wife and two children, that would mean that there were about 2,500,000 who came out of the land of Egypt with Moses.

We know that a number of Jacob's descendants must have married Egyptians, because the Bible says

THE TEN LOST TRIBES 157

that a "mixed multitude" came up out of Egypt. It is also likely that some Egyptian families believed in the God of Israel, and joined them. Yet they were all *Israel*:

> 36 and the LORD had given the people favor in the sight of the Egyptians, so that they let them have their request. Thus they plundered the Egyptians.
> 37 Now the sons of Israel journeyed from Rameses to Succoth, about six hundred thousand men on foot, aside from children.
> 38 And a mixed multitude also went up with them, along with flocks and herds, a very large number of livestock.
> 39 And they baked the dough which they had brought out of Egypt into cakes of unleavened bread. For it had not become leavened, since they were driven out of Egypt and could not delay, nor had they prepared any provisions for themselves.
> 40 Now the time that the sons of Israel lived in Egypt was four hundred and thirty years.
> —Exodus 12

So we see that in 430 years, Israel had grown from 200 people to over 2,000,000. In other words, they had grown by 10,000-fold—that is, for every one person who went to Egypt, 10,000 left! And all this increase took place in 430 years.

Let us look at the period of time after they left Egypt. There were the 40 years of wandering in the wilderness and 356 years under judges, before King Saul. Then there were 120 years of kings up through Solomon. This totals 516 years. If Israel had grown from just 200 to 2,500,000 in 430 years, to what number did the 2,500,000 grow in the next 516 years? They certainly did not grow by another factor of 10,000, but would it be reasonable to assume a factor of 1,000? Or, if that is too high, would a growth factor of 100 be reasonable to assume? If that still seems high, how about a factor of 10?

Growing by a factor of 10 in 516 years is a minimal assumption. They wanted big families in Old Testament times. They also did not have the availability of the numerous birth control methods that we have today. But calculating the population increase, using just the low figure of a growth factor of 10, this would mean that there would have been 25,000,000 Jews in the promised land by the year 721 B.C., when the Assyrians came down and conquered the northern kingdom and all of the southern kingdom, except Jerusalem.

A study of history tells us that approximately 700,000 Israelites went into the Assyrian captivity and, of these, about 200,000 were from the tribe of Judah. Where did the other 20 million or so from the ten northern tribes go? Of course, some of them surely were killed in the battle, but that does not nearly account for all of them. I believe the answer is that most of them had already left, especially those of the tribe of Dan.

THE DISPERSAL OF THE TRIBE OF DAN

The tribe of Dan had an interesting history in the promised land. The Scriptures tell us that they were promised an inheritance (Joshua 19:47,48), yet they never really did possess it. Even though they had been promised an inheritance on or near the Mediterranean (but squeezed between it and the Philistines), they evidently never occupied it:

> **1 In those days there was no king of Israel; and in those days the tribe of the Danites was seeking an inheritance for themselves to live in, for until that day an inheritance had not been allotted to them as a possession among the tribes of Israel.**
>
> **—Judges 18**

THE TEN LOST TRIBES

Chapter 18 of Judges goes on to tell us about a small part of the tribe of Dan conquering a city and changing its name to the city of Dan; evidently they liked to name things.

From the Scriptures, we also know that at least a goodly portion of Dan dwelt in ships:

> 17 "Gilead remained across the Jordan;
> And why did Dan stay in ships?
> Asher sat at the seashore,
> And remained by its landings.
> —Judges 5

Most likely the reason for the battle over just one city in Judges 18 was the portion of the tribe of Dan who did not want to be seafaring people. Since the Bible does not tell us what happened to the tribe of Dan beyond this, we have to turn to history.

History tells us that out of the tribe of Dan came a Semitic group of Phoenicians (our alphabet came down through them). These Danite Phoenicians went through the Mediterranean to Spain, which they called *Iberia*. Even today it is called the "Iberian peninsula." (*Iberia* comes from the Hebrew word *Heber*.)

They went around Spain and up the coast and to the British Isles. There was tin being mined in the Welsh areas 700-800 years before Christ. The British Isles are called "the tin islands." In fact, Ireland—apparently the first one they landed on—was called Hibernia.

Another interesting thing is the phrase "*Tuatha de Danaan*" which means "tribe of Dan." The *Tuatha de Danaan* is spoken of in Irish history; it does not come from the Bible. In Irish history, the *Tuatha de Danaan* came to Ireland around 800 B.C. This is prior to the time the Assyrians came down and conquered the northern kingdoms and much of the southern kingdom of Israel.

The Danite Phoenicians had gone throughout the Mediterranean and had named many places. Many of these names are still in use in Europe today: for example, the "*Dan*ube River," the country "*Dan*mark" (Denmark), "Lon*dan*" (London), and even "Scan*dan*avia" (Scandinavia)—(the vowels are interchangeable). We could go on with many other examples. There must be well over a hundred "Dan" names of rivers, towns and mountains in that region. The tribe of Dan evidently settled this area and named a vast number of locales.

Jim Spillman, an outstanding evangelist and teacher, has helped me with much of this background. I hope that he puts his findings into a book, because it would be very interesting and helpful. He says that he has a book that starts out with the kings of Israel and goes on through the kings of Ireland, the kings of Scotland, on up to the kings and queens of today, stopping with Queen Elizabeth II. He feels that the names show us they came from the tribes of Israel.

Jim Spillman feels that the tribe of Dan had much influence in Greece. There is a Greek cruise ship named "*Danae*," which is a Greek word. In Greece that is a common name which is used today; and, of course, *Dan* is part of it. In Greek mythology, we have the story of Hercules, the strong man. Jim Spillman says this is simply a retelling of the story of Sampson, who was a Danite. It is interesting that the Greeks never called themselves "Greeks"; they called themselves "*Macedanians*" (Macedonians), *Danaes* or *Dorians*. There were names for different tribes, but they never called themselves Greeks. The Romans were the ones who called them Greeks.

We have discussed the pre-exile wanderings of the tribe of Dan for a reason. Unlike a nuclear war today, which could happen instantly, in the time of the divided kingdom, it took the Assyrians months or perhaps years to get down to Israel and Jerusalem. They brought huge armies; they were on horses; they had wagons for food, and so forth. Thus, anyone who wanted to leave before

THE TEN LOST TRIBES 161

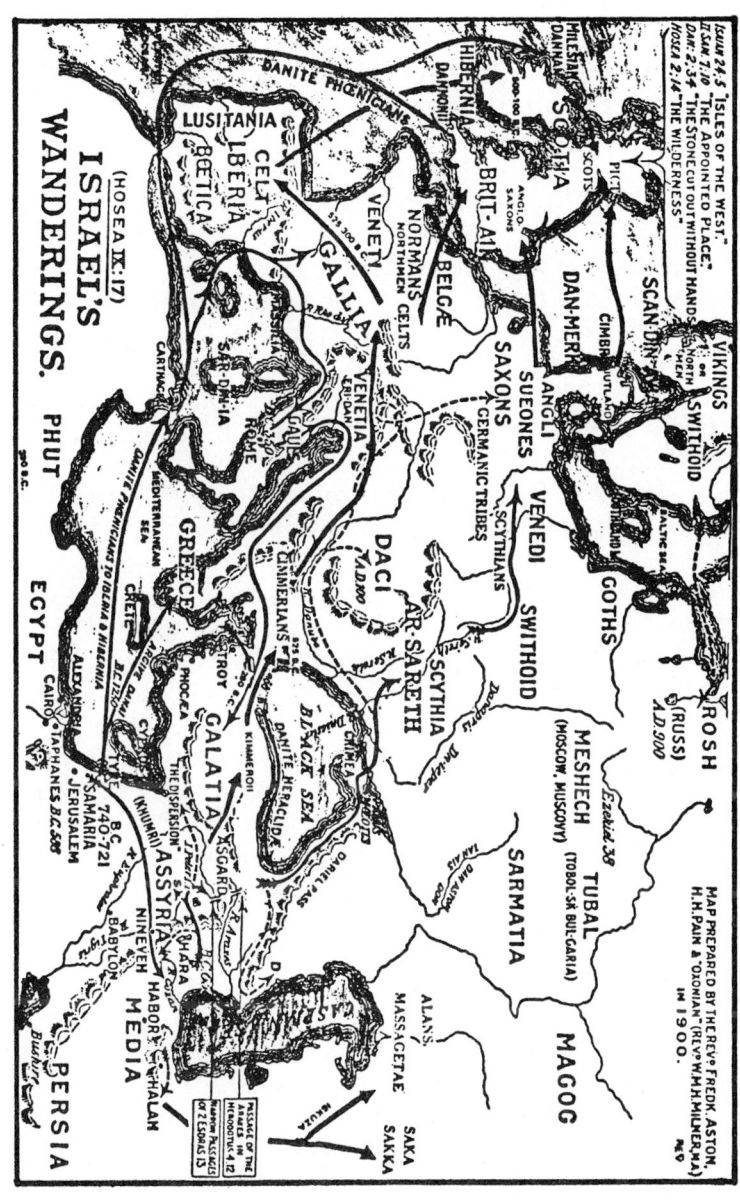

the war began had ample time to do so. We have used the tribe of Dan here as an example, but there is historical evidence that vast numbers of the other tribes also migrated, primarily to Europe (which includes Britain), prior to the Assyrian invasion.

THE TEN TRIBES
WHO WENT INTO CAPTIVITY

Really it was the ten tribes, plus most of Judah, who went into the first captivity (Assyrian) in 721 B.C. As we mentioned earlier, there were 200,000 Jews from Judah who went into Assyria at that time, and only about 100,000 went into Babylonian captivity later, in 586 B.C. The Assyrians conquered all of Judah, except Jerusalem.

My good friend and historian, Jim Spillman, describes the Assyrian captivity as follows:

> When Assyria came down and took Israel captive, as well as taking the 10 tribes, they also took 200,000 Judahites captive. They probably did not take very many Danites, since most of the tribe of Dan had already departed by ship. The good strong ones left with their families. When the Assyrians returned to Assyria with their captives, they went north from Israel, and when they got up to a little above Heron, they had to turn east. Assyria is a little southwest of the Caspian Sea, which is due north of Babylon.
>
> The portion of Israel taken in this captivity then became *Gamera*, which is not far from the shores of the Caspian Sea, just a little southwest. Gamera then changed their name as they migrated west and north. They came to a point just below the Black Sea, and there changed their name to *Gimera*. All of this time they were wandering and migrating, trying to fight their way through, much like our western pioneers did. They then moved up to the shores of the Black Sea. When they got there, they began to call themselves the *Kim-*

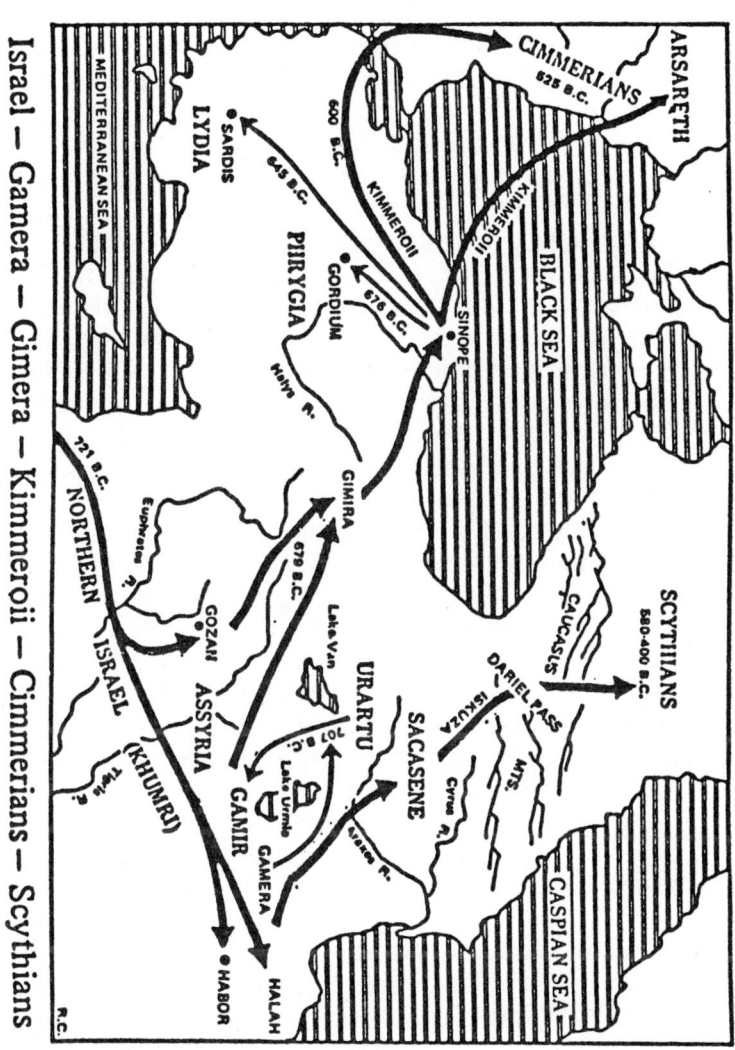

Israel – Gamera – Gimera – Kimmeroii – Cimmerians – Scythians

merolii (a translation from Gimera to Kimmeroii). The "oii" is a Hellenization of the Greek meaning "plural." They spent some time there, just south of the Black Sea, and then began to move west again. By the time they moved to the western side of the Black Sea, and then north up the western side, they called themselves the *Cimmerians*. This is all the same group: Israel, Gamera, Gimera, Kimmeroii and Cimmerians.

They then moved further north and joined with another portion of the tribes who had moved up north from Gamera, and they were then called Scythians. The Scythians were the first ones to use bows and arrows on horseback, and they were employed by the Babylonians and the Chaldeans. When Babylon came against Assyria, they used the Scythians. But to review, we have this progression: Israel, Gamera, Gimera, Kimmeroii, Cimmerians and the Scythians. They then started to move again, and their wanderings and migrations took them north and west.

At that point, a very interesting thing occurred. They moved into the great land mass of Europe, and carried on as tribes. Then a wonderful group sort of appeared in history, the *Celts* (pronounced "Kelts," although Boston's basketball team, "the Celtics," is pronounced with a soft "c"). We know that the Celts went into Germany and up into the British Isles. We believe that the Celts also went into France, where they were called the *Gauls*. All of these were of the ten tribes as well.

They came to Europe by the Caspian Sea, the Black Sea, and through a pass that is called the "Pass of Israel" to this day.

There are many Christian writers confirming these facts—biblical scholars, archaeologists and historians. These are not just from the movement of "British Israelism." The British Israel people got their information from credible sources, but I believe they have distorted the conclusion, and claim that Britain and the U. S. are the ten lost tribes, and thus are "Israel."

They are right when they conclude that a portion of the population of Europe—including the British Isles—are descendants of the ten tribes and that a portion of these came to America. In that, we would have to agree. However, it does not matter whether they are descendants of the ten tribes or not. If they know Christ as their personal Savior, they are a part of Israel, whether or not they can trace their ancestry back to Abraham. Even if somebody can trace his lineage back to Abraham, but does not know Christ as his personal Savior, then according to Scripture, he is not a part of *Israel.* Remember, the Israel of God always has been and always will be a spiritual entity. It never was and never will be an entity hooked to a genealogical chain. I am so glad that I am a part of Israel, and I could care less whether or not I came from Abraham, in the physical sense. If I did, it would make me no more or no less a part of true Israel. We are all total and complete *in Christ*, and I, for one, claim my birthright as part of Israel. I am an Israelite (not an Israeli).

Now let us turn to study the tribe of Judah, the Jews, to see where they fit into the scheme of things. In the next chapter, we will basically be looking at history, and not the current State of Israel, which we will examine in Chapter 12.

11

THE ONE "FOUND TRIBE"

We just discussed the ten lost tribes. Now let us turn our attention to the one tribe with whom we are all familiar: the Hebrews, commonly called the "Jews" today. There are some who claim that many of the Jews living on the shores of the Mediterranean in the land of Palestine today are not descendants of Abraham. Rather, they say that these are "Ashkenazic Jews" who descended from Ashkenaz, the son of Gomer, who was the son of Japheth (Genesis 10:2-3). The "Semitic Jews," on the other hand, were the descendants of Shem ("Shemitic"), who was Abraham's forefather. (If you recall, Shem and Japheth were two of Noah's three sons, who survived the flood—Genesis 9:18,19).

To me, it doesn't matter a bit whether or not the "Jews" living in Palestine are descended from Abraham. If they know Christ as their Savior, they are a part of Israel, regardless who their forefathers were. If they do not know Jesus as their Savior, they are not part of Israel, regardless who their forefathers were.

We have already discussed the fact that there are Japanese Jews, black Jews from Ethiopia, and Jews from many other nationalities. Remember that "Jew" today means one who is a believer in the religion of Judaism.

However, among those who actually "look Jewish," many people may not realize that there are actually two major types of Jews which have different genealogical roots. One would think that in the State of Israel there would be one chief rabbi, but there is not; there are two. There is one for the Sephardic Jews and another for the Ashkenazic Jews. These two are not only vying with each other for power, but between the two of them, they feel that they should be running Israel, not the politically-elected Knesset.

The Sephardic Jews trace their lineage back through Abraham, Isaac and Jacob, all the way back to Shem, one of the sons of Noah. Thus, we get the Shemitic (Semitic) people. On the other hand, by their own writings, the Ashkenazic Jews trace their lineage back to Gomer and Japheth (not Abraham and Shem).

In Figure 11.1, we see Noah's three sons listed, and then their sons (following their sons, we show the nations that came from them). Of course, the main lineage of interest in this figure is the one that came from Shem down through Abraham and ultimately spiritually to Christ. This figure does show graphically that it is possible that many of the Jews living in Palestine are not biologically from Abraham. To me, this is not an important issue, since today being part of Israel does not require one to be biologically from Abraham. However, this is a subject that we need to touch on in order to help you to understand some of the things going on in the State of Israel today.

In order to be more complete in our coverage of the subject of Israel, we would like to quote extensively from Chapter 4 of the book *Hear, O Israel*, by Pat Brooks (reprinted by permission from New Puritan Library, 91 Lytle Road, Fletcher, NC 28732). Most of the remainder of this chapter will be a quote from her book, although we will not use quote marks. If you find the remainder of this chapter difficult reading and too technical, then I would suggest that you simply skip to the next chapter.

THE ONE "FOUND TRIBE"

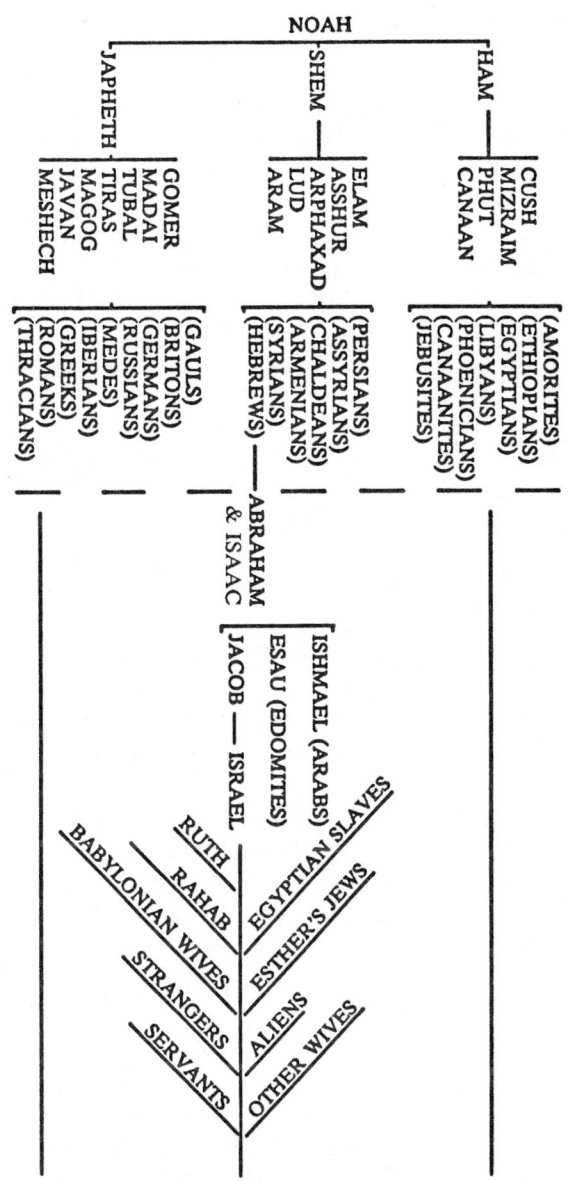

Figure 11.1

We are to love the "Jews" as well as the Arabs, both of whom came from Abraham. We should have no prejudice against either group. But it is interesting to note that there is at least a good likelihood that many of the "Jews" living in Palestine today actually did not descend from Abraham, even according to Israeli sources and literature. I do not necessarily agree with everything Pat says on every subject, but in this area, I think she has done an excellent job of research. The following portion of this chapter inset from the left margin is quoted from the evidence that Pat Brooks presents in her book on the subject:

WILL THE REAL JEWS PLEASE STAND UP?

Some puzzling facts confront any honest investigator into modern Jewry. Official estimates of world Jewish population range from 17 million to 18 million. Yet it is difficult to get accurate figures on where they are.

Israel has 3.8 million. Of these there are three distinct types: Sabras (native-born Israelis); Ashkenazim (Eastern European Jews); and Sephardim (Jews from Spain, Portugal, or North Africa). Although the Zionist state was originally planned as an Ashkenazi homeland, two-thirds are Oriental Jews: primarily Sabras and Sephardim. Presumably the term "Oriental Jews" refers to the Semitic origins of these people, since it is obvious that the Sephardim, at any rate, have not come from the Orient. However, there are Jews in the Far East. These immigrants to Israel must be included in these figures. Since Jews have come to Israel from over 100 nations, doubtless these general forms of categorizing are simply for convenience in a rather confusing situation.

The United States has a Jewish population of 5.4 million, according to official estimates in 1980. Some informal estimates run twice that high, but there is no way to find out, since Jews are classified as a "religion," and this category was removed from the U.S. census after 1950.

THE ONE "FOUND TRIBE"   171

Regarding the Jews as a particular religious group is thoroughly misleading. Within Judaism itself there are three major divisions: Orthodox, Conservative, and Reform. In addition, many Jews have no affiliation with a synagogue and frankly describe themselves as atheists or agnostics. Then there are the Messianic Jews—born again Christians—who certainly would not want to be classified as Jewish in religion, yet have a real appreciation for their Jewish heritage.

An authority on Jewish immigration to the United States is Joseph R. Rosenbloom, author of the *Biographical Dictionary of Early American Jews.* He divides American Jewish settlements into three waves of immigration: the Sephardic period (1654-1840); the German (1841-1880); Eastern European (1881-1920). He categorizes the period from 1921 as a "National" period, since immigration has been more restricted since then, and most Jews here have been born here.

Rosenbloom says that "from 1654 through 1800 it is unlikely that the number of Jews ever exceeded 2,000." He also states that these early Sephardic Jews integrated into their communities and were active in the Freemasonry movement in America.

The German period began the mass migrations to America in the mid-nineteenth century. Actually, the fact that this period is dealt with *separately* from either the Sephardic or Eastern European periods has led this author into some exciting speculations. Since there are differences between German Jews and those from Eastern Europe, it may well be that the German Jewish group, although termed Ashkenazic, may have come from the original Diaspora (i.e., Dispersion) in 70 A.D. (The roots of the Ashkenazim will be dealt with later.)

There were two basic reasons for the German wave of Jewish immigration to America. Persecution of Jews in Germany led to this move because of such problems as special taxes and quota laws. Rosenbloom also gives another, very significant factor: "the failure of the liberal revolutions of 1830 and 1848." He refers, of course, to the Marxist uprisings of the 19th century and gives powerful documentation to a little-known fact in America today. Most of the prime movers of liberal, socialist movements, like Karl Marx himself, have been Jews. Rosenbloom verifies that these German Jews brought Reform Judaism to America, a Jewish liberalism very similar to Unitarianism.

A fascinating book by Rabbi Marvin Antelman, *To Eliminate the Opiate*, documents the roots of Reform Judaism as spawned from Adam Weishaupt's Bavarian *Illuminati*. He points out that Moses Mendelssohn, father of the "Haskala" movement (Jewish "Enlightenment"), was close to Count Mirabeau, notorious leader of the French Revolution.

Antelman, an Orthodox rabbi and Zionist, verifies that "the conspirators undermined Judaism by attempting to radicalize Zionism. Unfortunately, the radical side of Zionism has won out in terms of the Socialist Histradut Party that has dominated the State of Israel to this very day. ... Israeli bureaucracy, spawned by socialism, has given birth to a disgraceful, stultifying status quo which permeates the government, manifested by a *sachevet*, 'red tape,' which saps the very life blood of the state."

These words were written in 1974. In 1977 Menachem Begin ousted the Labor Party with his Likud alignment, but socialism has only grown worse in Israel. Now with Begin's reelection in 1981 in a cliff-hanger, inflation is soaring at 140% [this book by Pat Brooks was published in 1981]. According to *U.S. News & World Report*, "The campaign, the most violent in Israel's 33-year history, was marred by clashes between dark-skinned Jews—from North Africa and Asia—who lined up behind Begin, and lighter-skinned Jews—of American or European descent—who backed Peres."

That news item points up what sometimes is called a secret civil war between Sephardic and Ashkenazic Jews. Since the Ashkenazim dominate the leadership of Israel, the Zionist movement, and world finance, it is well worth giving this people some careful scrutiny. They consistently get better housing and jobs than the Sephardim in Israel, and they pay lower interest rates, according to travelers who have spent time in Israel. Who are they?

Pushing and shoving, these are the self-assertive people who throng the theaters (and subways) of New York, the beaches of Miami, and the streets of Tel Aviv and Jerusalem. With a constant drive to make money, to come out on top, they consummate endless business deals at the synagogue or Cahilla meetings. . . .

An interesting tract published by The American Board of Missions to the Jews says, "The 'Ashkenazim' are generally admitted by the Jews to be their own people, who speak Yiddish. Those Jews lived for centuries in Russia, Poland, Germany and Southeastern Europe. Yiddish is based on archaic German, with words of other languages, especially Hebrew, included." In the same paragraph the author notes that Ashkenaz was the son of Gomer, son of Japheth, as noted in Genesis 10:3 and 4.

This is very surprising information for the average Christian, who knows that the word "Semitic" refers to descendants of Shem. Both the Hebrew and the Arabic peoples came from the line of Shem, through Abraham.

We shall examine the evidence of Jewish scholars on the origin of the Ashkenazim, in this chapter. However, before we embark on that study, here is the description of the ancient people of Ashkenaz, in Biblical times, as recorded in *Unger's Bible Dictionary*: "In the time of Jeremiah they dwelt in the neighborhood of Ararat and Minni (the Minnai of the Assyrian inscriptions) S.E. of Lake Van. They were rude and retarded in civilization and periodically overran extensive territory, so that their name came to be tantamount to barbarians."

Now for the fascinating account of the roots of Ashkenazic Jewry, we call our first witness, Arthur Koestler, author of *The Thirteenth Tribe:*

CHAPTER 11

"About the time when Charlemagne was crowned Emperor of the West, the eastern confines of Europe between the Caucasus and the Volga were ruled by a Jewish state, known as the Khazar Empire. . . . The country of the Khazars, a people of Turkish stock, occupied a strategic key position at the vital gateway between the Black Sea and the Caspian, where the great eastern powers of the period confronted each other. . . ."

"What is in dispute is the fate of the Jewish Khazars after the destruction of their empire, in the twelfth or thirteenth century. On this problem the sources are scant, but various late medieval Khazar settlements are mentioned in the Crimea, in the Ukraine, in Hungary, Poland, and Lithuania. The general picture that emerges . . . is that of a migration of Khazar tribes and communities into those regions of Eastern Europe— mainly Russia and Poland—where, at the dawn of the Modern Age, the greatest concentrations of Jews were found. This has led several historians to conjecture that a substantial part, and perhaps the majority of eastern Jews—and hence of world Jewry—might be of Khazar, and not of Semitic origin. . . . If so, this would mean that their ancestors came not from the Jordan but from the Volga, not from Canaan but from the Caucasus, once believed to be the cradle of the Aryan race; and that genetically they are more closely related to the Hun, Uigar and Magyar tribes than to the seed of Abraham, Isaac, and Jacob. Should this turn out to be the case, then the term 'anti-Semitism' would become void of meaning, based on a misapprehension. . ."

Koestler then makes a mighty case for this thesis. He traces the Khazars from their appearance in Eastern Europe during the fifth century, to their mass conversion to Judaism in the eight century, down to the period of their westward migrations. His documentation is impressive, embracing a wide range of viewpoints from Jewish, Christian, and Muslim scholars. Most fascinating of all, however, is his story of the Khazar conversion to Judaism.

THE ONE "FOUND TRIBE"   175

"At the beginning of the eighth century the world was polarized between the two super-powers representing Christianity and Islam. . . . The Khazar Empire represented a Third Force. . . . But it could only maintain its independence by accepting neither Christianity nor Islam—for either choice would have automatically subordinated it to the authority of the Roman Emperor or the Caliph of Baghdad. . . . What could have been more logical than to embrace a third creed, which was uncommitted towards either of the two, yet represented the venerable foundation of both?"

Several accounts of the Kagan (king) of Khazaria being converted to Judaism and proselytizing his entire nation with him occur in ancient history. However, the tenth century "Khazar correspondence" between two Jews is most fascinating.

A brilliant Sephardic Jew in Spain, Hasdai Ibn Shaprut, initiated the correspondence. He had heard of a Jewish national homeland in Khazaria, and wrote the Kagan, Joseph, to ask him about it. Shaprut especially wanted to know to which of the twelve tribes the monarch belonged. Joseph's reply decimates the myth of Semitic heritage for his people. He traces his ancestry not to Shem, but to Japheth, Noah's third son. However, he claims *Togarmah* rather than Ashkenaz, as his ancestor—the third son of Gomer, rather than the first. Koestler quotes Joseph as follows:

"We have found in the family registers of our fathers that Togarmah had ten sons, and the names of their offspring are as follows: Uigar, Dursu, Avars, Huns, Basilii, Tarniakh, Khazars, Zagora, Bulgars, Sabir. We are the sons of Khazar, the seventh . . ."

Joseph's reply raises more questions. If Jews today are known as Ashkenazic, could they not represent a broader background even than that—as this reference to another son of Gomer shows?

It is only fair to include, here, the argument that many Jewish historians advance, claiming their European lineage back to the twelve tribes from the original

Diaspora. (Actually, as we have seen from the Biblical evidence, they would only be able to trace some from the House of Judah, or three tribes.) These scholars say "true Jews" lived in France and the Rhine area of Germany, later emigrating east into Poland.

Koestler systematically destroys this argument by showing how these tribes became extinct during the Black Plague. Jews who did not die in the plague were killed in the persecution afterward, since the people of that area blamed the plague on the Jews. History also records the decimation of these peoples, but no migration to Eastern Europe. However, the final, most convincing argument comes from the work of the great expert on the Yiddish language, Mathias Mieses. He wrote two authoritative works in German (1915 and 1924) on Yiddish origins.

Mieses said, "No linguistic components derived from the parts of Germany bordering on France are found in the Yiddish language.... Even the more central regions of Western Germany, around Frankfurt, have not contributed to the Yiddish language.... The history of the German Jews, of Ashkenazi Jewry, must be revised. The errors of history are often rectified by linguistic research. The conventional view of the erstwhile immigration of Ashkenazi Jews from France belongs to the category of historic errors which are awaiting correction."

Koestler's own summary of the rest of Mieses' research is that "the dominant influence in it (Yiddish) are the so-called 'East-Middle German' dialects which were spoken in the Alpine regions of Austria and Bavaria roughly up to the 15th century. In other words, the German component which went into the hybrid Jewish language originated in the eastern regions of Germany, adjacent to the Slavonic belt of Eastern Europe."

Our second witness in our examination of those "who say they are Jews, and are not . . ." is Benjamin Freedman. Of a distinguished Jewish background in New York, this man became a Christian at the age of 25, along with his wife. His is a staunch American patriot who has strong words of warning and advice for U.S. Christians. He is quoted here from a speech he gave to a military organization in Washington, D.C., in 1974.

Freedman bought a copy of the first English dictionary of Dr. Samuel Johnson, published in 1797. In that rare edition, he says, "the word, Jew, does not appear!" A British friend says the word *did* exist, however and was in the King James Bible of 1611. A political backlash against Jewish financial practices was responsible for this deliberate omission, according to him.

The word, *Jew*, does have an interesting etymology, however. *Young's Concordance* lists it for the first time in 2 Kings 16:6. It is listed in the plural, giving first the Hebrew characters and then its equivalent phonetically, using our English alphabet: *Yehudim.* The Greek word follows, used in the New Testament passages: *Ioudaioi.* The meaning of both words is the same: Judeans, or those from the southern kingdom. This fascinating note occurs after the singular word, Jew, in *Young's:* "A descendant of Judah; in later times, also an Israelite. In 2 Kings 16:6 this appellation is applied to the *two* tribes (i.e., Judah and Benjamin); in later days the *twelve* tribes. *Strictly speaking, the name is appropriate only to the subjects of the kingdom of the two tribes after the separation of the ten tribes, B.C. 975*" (italics added).

There is a wealth of information in the above lines. First, since the Bible term is really "Judean," to apply the term to the descendants of the Khazars is absurd. Second, the Bible only uses the word to refer to members of the tribes of Judah and Benjamin. We can safely assume that in the later days Young refers to modern usage, apparently to mean anyone ever associated with Judaism, even if he happens to be an atheist!

Freedman says flatly, "The word, 'Jew,' has been used for a purpose by the people who got us into two wars, who laid a trap to get us into a third one, and who have practically taken over the control of the world, especially the control of this country.... I am certain that, unless something is done to change the thinking of the 200,000,000 U.S.A. Christians, that this country is headed for disaster. . . . You have been told that it is your Christian duty to help repatriate God's Chosen People to their promised land. You have been told that by every media of mass information, including the pulpit, including every other means by which they can shape your thinking. . . .

"Now, I'll tell you what a lie that is! I can cite the sources here that I've consulted, maybe 234 official documents, maps, books, and other records, but the best is one that I found in the last few years, *The Encyclopedia Britannica*, the 1911 Edition, Volume 15, three pages define the word 'Khazar.' . . . The Khazars were an Asian nation; they were a Mongoloid, Turko-Finn tribal nation in Asia. And they had so much trouble with the other nations there, who finally succeeded in driving them out of Asia, across the border, into what is known today as Russia, in the area of the Ukraine. They found there a lot of peaceful agricultural people, mostly Slavic, and they conquered them. They did the same thing then as they are still doing in the Middle East! They took them, for no reason at all, except the people weren't trained to fight! They established there the Khazar kingdom."

Freeman's message is too lengthy to quote here in great detail, but he tells how a Swede named Rurik, a Varengian, organized the principality of Rokh into the Russian Empire and drove the Khazars into Europe. Ever since the 11th century the Khazars were intent on overthrowing the Russian regime, and out of this came Bolshevism. Possibly one of the best kept secrets in the West today is that communism is overwhelmingly a Jewish movement. We shall have more to say about that, later.

Right now it is time to call our third Jewish witness to the stand, Dr. Alfred M. Lilienthal, author of *The Zionist Connection*. Recently I spoke with Dr. Lilienthal on the phone, and he told me that he was being branded

THE ONE "FOUND TRIBE" 179

"anti-Semitic" by such leftist organizations as the A.D.L. (Anti-Defamation League of B'nai B'rith) and the A.C.L.U. (American Civil Liberties Union).

"The genetic derivation of most Jews—only the Sephardic may be accounted Hebrews by blood—has been long if not *widely* known. Dunlap at Columbia, Bury in England, and Poliak at Tel Aviv University have researched this 'cruelest of jokes' and won research acceptance over the past half-century. . . .

"*What Price, Israel?*, published 23 years before the Koestler work, pointed out that the lineal ancestors of Eastern and Western Jewry were these 8th-century Khazar converts, and noted how this was being kept a dark secret because it tended to vitiate the principal prop of the Zionist claim to Israel."

Now we are getting down to some basic information which world Zionists have done their best to keep quiet.

There are in the world today only two groups of people who are considered Jews: the *Ashkenazim* and the *Sephardim*. Webster's *New World Dictionary* defines *Ashkenazim* this way: "a German Jew, earlier, a German after *Ashkenaz*, second of Gomer . . . the Jews who settled in middle and northern Europe after the Diaspora, or their descendants; distinguished from the *Sephardim*."

The documented research of the past few pages indicates just how contradictory a statement, under the editing hand of David B. Guralnik, this is. Clearly a Japhetic people who proselyted to Judaism in the 8th century cannot be described as Semitic Jews who came out of the Diaspora following the destruction of Jerusalem in 70 A.D.!

It is interesting that the second edition of *Webster's Unabridged Dictionary* has no such comment. After *Ashkenazim* it says simply, "The Jews of middle and northern Europe as opposed to the Sephardim, or Jews of Spain and Portugal." This edition was published in 1950 by apparently non-Jewish editors, just two years after the Zionist state of Israel was founded.

This same unabridged dictionary defines *Sephardim* as follows: "Jews who are the descendants of the former Jews of Spain and Portugal. They are as a rule darker than the Ashkenazim, or northern Jews. They are chiefly settled in North Africa, Greece, the Balkans, the Levant, Holland, England, and America."

The *New World Dictionary* is similar, but eliminates the references to racial characteristics. However, both dictionaries include material in brackets before the definition that is an eye-opener: "Heb. *Sepharadhim*, fr. *Sepharadh*, prob. a region in Asia Minor, but later identified with Spain." . . .

. . . the Dispensational teaching that all the Jews are from the original tribes of Israel cannot be supported by the facts concerning the Ashkenazim. As we have seen, they are of Gentile origin. Obviously, many Christians and Jews are in for many surprises when the Lord comes back.

Perhaps some readers will still wonder what the real answer to our question is: *Will the real Jews please stand up?* For them, the Bible has an answer which cannot be controverted.

The Lord Jesus, in speaking to the Jews of His own day who bragged about being Abraham's seed, gave this startling assessment of their situation: "I know that ye are Abraham's *seed*, but ye seek to kill me, because my word hath no place in you. . . . If ye were Abraham's *children*, ye would do the works of Abraham. But now ye seek to kill me, a man that told you the truth. . . . Ye are of your father the devil, and the lusts of your father ye will do. He was a murderer from the beginning, and abode not in the truth, because there is no truth in him. When he speaketh a lie, he speaketh of his own: for he is a liar and the father of it" (John 8: 37,39,40,44, KJV).

The apostle Paul uses the same argument in Romans and Galatians.

"For he is not a Jew, which is one outwardly; neither is that circumcision, which is outward in the flesh: But he is a Jew, which is one inwardly; and circumcision is that of the heart, in the spirit, and not in the letter;

whose praise is not of men, but of God" (Romans 2: 28,29, KJV).

"So then they which be of faith are blessed with faithful Abraham. . . . Now to Abraham and his seed were the promises made. He saith not, And to seeds, as of many; but as of *one*, And to thy seed, *which is Christ*. . . . For ye are all the children of God by faith in Christ Jesus. . . . There is neither Jew nor Greek, there is neither bond nor free, there is neither male nor female: for ye all are one in Christ Jesus. And if ye be Christ's then are ye Abraham's seed, and heirs according to the promise" (Galatians 3: 9,16,26,28,29, KJV).

Some years ago, when I had first learned of the differences between the Ashkenazic and Sephardic Jews, I remember discussing these things with a young Jewish man who was a missionary to the Jews. At the end of our talk, he made a comment which I have never forgotten:

"Pat, I don't see what difference it really makes. They are all lost without Jesus."

Amen. And so are all members of all the twelve tribes, and all Gentiles.

SUMMARY AND CONCLUSION

The above ends the quote from Pat Brooks' book *Hear, O Israel*. In a recent census, it was found that the majority of the Jews living in the State of Israel are "Ashkenazic," and thus not biologically descended from Abraham. It is from the Ashkenazic Jews that we have the Yiddish language, which is primarily based on the German language, since many of them originated in that part of Europe. Not being descended from Abraham, they are not part of the "one found tribe." However, today they are certainly Israelis (citizens of the State of Israel). Some of them are Jews by religion, and others— even though they have a Jewish cultural background—are atheists, and thus spit in God's face.

When the Jews were exiled to Babylon, there had to be a change in the way they practiced Judaism. Prior to that, it was centered around the temple and the sacrifices. With the exile, they had to come up with a new set of rules by which they could practice Judaism in a foreign country, without a temple. The Talmud is the document the Jewish elders produced to offer guidelines or rules for a Jew to live by in a foreign country. This document today is still their "law," and it is almost on a par with the Scriptures.

By law, the State of Israel is an anti-Christian nation. For example, if you were to hand a New Testament to someone on the street, you could be subject to a large fine and up to five years in prison. Thus, in a sense, they continue to reject Jesus Christ, their Messiah.

With this incredible mixture of people in the country of Israel today, the question arises as to how the current State of Israel fits into the entire scenario, particularly as this age ends.

12

WHAT ABOUT THE STATE OF ISRAEL?

As we begin to look at the present day State of Israel, let me first repeat something that I said earlier in this book: I love the Hebrews and the Jews who live in the State of Israel. I am all for them. If our government is going to give foreign aid to any nation, I think that the State of Israel should be at or near the top of the list. If we did not have them as an ally in the Mideast, the United States would be in trouble.

It is obvious that some amazing things occurred as they became a nation and struggled to continue as a nation—things that could be considered miraculous. However, there were also some marvelous miracles as the United States became a nation and continued as a nation. The mere fact that we see things which could be miracles of God in the forming of these two nations (and other nations as well) is not a reason to claim that the State of Israel is the *Israel* of the Bible and the inheritor of the promises made to Abraham.

When looking at the State of Israel, one must realize that he is looking at a very diverse group of people, as we have seen in preceding chapters. As we have discussed, living there are black Jews from Ethiopia and other African countries, Japanese Jews, Jews from Russia and Germany, and even some Jews who have biologically descended from Abraham, the Hebrew Jews. All of the Jews have the religion of Judaism.

In addition, also living in the State of Israel are many Hebrews—genealogically descended from Abraham—who are either atheists or agnostics and either hate God or totally ignore Him. In addition, there are a few Hebrews who have become Christians. These Hebrew Christians, as far as we can tell from the Scriptures, are the only Hebrews who truly belong to Israel.

Therefore, when someone tells me that the present-day "State of Israel" is "God's chosen people," I genuinely do not know what he means. Does he mean all of the Jews living there, including the Japanese Jews, the black Jews, the Ashkenazic Jews and other Jews who are not biologically from Abraham? Or does he mean all of the Hebrews who are biologically from Abraham whether they be Jewish, agnostic or atheistic?

Some would say that the Jews or the "State of Israel" is God's "physical Israel." I would have the same question for them as to what they mean. Are they talking about all the Jews, regardless of their racial background (of course, this would not match with physical Israel) or are they talking about all the Hebrews—even those who laugh at God and spit in His face? I think that to say that the present day "State of Israel" is either "God's chosen people" or "God's physical Israel" is not in keeping with the truth and the Scriptures.

THE ZIONIST MOVEMENT

One cannot understand the State of Israel without understanding at least a little bit about the Zionist movement. Rather than give my opinion, I would like to quote from *Jews, God and History*, by a Jewish author, Max I. Dimont, (pages 393-409, a Signet book published by The New American Library of World Literature, Inc., 501 Madison Avenue, New York, NY

10022). This little book, written by a liberal Jew, beautifully defines Zionism for us:

> Actually, "Zionism" was a new name for an old ideology; it simply signifies "a return to Zion"—that is, a return to Jerusalem. The idea of such a return has permeated Jewish thinking ever since the earliest days of the Diaspora. Though the Jews had lost physical possession of Palestine, they had never given up their hope of someday again establishing their capital in Zion. Modern Zionism differed in one important respect from this old aspiration. Until modern Zionism, most Jews had always thought that a messiah would lead them back to the Promised Land. The Zionists shifted this responsibility from the shoulders of the Jews. Having saddled themselves with this responsibility, the Zionists reappraised this "Zion," this future homeland of the Jews. . . .
>
> The Zionists decided to redeem Palestine by buying land on a grand scale for all Jewish settlers. Suddenly, the scraggy soil of Palestine, neglected for fifteen centuries by its alien custodians, acquired value. Though prices asked by Arab and Turkish landholders were outrageous, the Zionist Jewish National Fund paid them. By 1948, when the State of Israel was founded, the Jews had paid millions of dollars for 250,000 acres of desert land, had settled 83,000 Jews on the land, had founded 233 villages, and had planted 5,000,000 trees on soil which but fifty years previous had been barren. Before 1880 there had been about 12,000 Jews in Palestine, mostly the pious and orthodox who had come to live out their days and be buried in the Holy Land. From 1880 until World War I, Hess' *Rome and Jerusalem*, Smolenskin's *The Eternal People*, Pinsker's *Auto-Emancipation*, and Herzl's *The Jewish State* motivated 115,000 Jews to settle in Palestine. The "intellectuals" and the "motivators" had done their work. After World War I the "politicals" took over. . . .

CHAPTER 12

With the ascent of Hitler to power, a new type of Jew began immigrating to Palestine, propitiously timed with the country's economic development. By 1936 there were 60,000 German Jews in Palestine, providing her with much-needed scientists, engineers, managers, chemists, and research men to increase her productive capacity and to improve the quality of her goods. But even more importantly, eminent scholars now staffed Palestine's educational institutions, and financial experts and government career men provided her with the framework of self-government even while she remained ostensibly a mandated territory under Britain. . . .

When Britain became embroiled in World War II, 130,000 Jews clamored for enlistment in the British Africa Corps. The wary British feared to arm so many Jews. Nevertheless, out of sheer necessity, Britain did accept 30,000 who fought as independent companies. Grudgingly the British admired the courage of these Jewish soldiers; ruefully Rommel's Afrika Korps found out that against Jews armed with guns they were not supermen.

As the British had suspected, the Jews fought not only for the pleasure of meeting the Nazis in combat, but also to train themselves for the inevitable showdown in Palestine. Once the war was over, everybody jockeyed for position. When the curtain rose again in 1945 on the Palestinian drama, the actors sprang to life, taking the same parts they had in 1941; British policy was still the White Paper; Arab policy was still to oppose all Jewish immigration; and Jewish policy remained that of unrestricted immigration.

Terror again erupted in 1946 when the British refused to admit 100,000 Jews from Germany, as proposed by United States President Harry S. Truman. Enraged by the British policy of barring Jewish refugees from Palestine and by the detention of refugee Jews on the island of Cyprus, Irgun leaders determined to force a showdown on the issue. Irgunists dynamited the King David Hotel, the Jerusalem headquarters of

WHAT ABOUT THE STATE OF ISRAEL? 187

the British, killing eighty British officers and men, and wounding seventy others. Goaded into reprisals, the British ordered a boycott of all Jewish shops. Far from shattering Jewish unity, however, this solidified Jewish sentiment against British rule. . . .

The United Nations, meanwhile, had sent a special committee to Palestine to investigate the situation. It came back with basically the same recommendations made by the Peel Commission in 1939—that the British Mandate be terminated and that Palestine be partitioned into an Arab and a Jewish state. In September 1947, the General Assembly voted for such partition. The Jews accepted the decision; the Arabs defied it. After twenty-six turbulent years, the British Mandate had come to an end.

In spite of what happened, in spite of the White Paper and the reprisals, the British must elicit our admiration. Under the most trying circumstances, they had behaved like civilized soldiers representing a civilized nation. They fought hard, and lost courageously. They were not animated by evil intent or inhuman policies, but by affairs of state and the will to preserve their empire. The fact that friendly relations exist today between Israel and Britain testifies to the realization of the Israelis themselves that Britain had been a formidable foe, not an anti-Semitic enemy, and that Israel had won, not because she was mightier, but because Britain was beset with other, more pressing problems. On May 14, 1948, the day the British departed, the Jews listened to David Ben-Gurion proclaim the independence of the State of Israel. That evening the Israelis toasted their new homeland. The next morning they manned the front lines to defend it. . . .

The moment the Israeli state was proclaimed, Ben-Gurion shed his role as a Zionist political, realizing this phase of the revolution had become an anachronism the moment victory had been achieved. He became the statesman bureaucrat. Boldly he declared the Zionist party defunct, its mission over, having "committed suicide" by success. It was time for the bureaucrats to take over to solidify gains, institutionalize new mores, and domesticate revolutionary tempers into normal activity. A new democracy, based on "liberty and groceries," had to be secured.

There was to be no second-class citizenship for anyone in Israel. No Jew needed to pass tests to become an Israeli. All he had to do was to land on Israeli soil and proclaim himself a citizen. Citizenship was also extended to every Arab living in Israel. The franchise, universal education, and the right to hold jobs according to ability were granted to all, regardless of religion, sex, or previous condition of servitude. For the first time in history, Arab women could vote.

It is interesting to note that the Orthodox Jews were against forming the State of Israel. They felt that the Zionists were trying to do by man's effort that which could be done by God alone. The Orthodox Jews felt that the Zionists were trying to establish a socialist democracy. They felt that the messiah should take them to Palestine, and it should be a Theocracy instead. In fact, the Orthodox Jews in the State of Israel today are still demanding a Theocracy, while the rest of the Jews want a secular state. It was only after it was definite that there would be a State of Israel that the Orthodox Jews jumped on the band wagon in significant proportions.

As we mentioned in the last chapter, even today in the State of Israel, there is a battle going on as to whether the rabbis should be the highest authority in the nation and run the nation or whether the politically-elected Knesset should be the highest authority and run the nation. They are even having major debates about "who is a Jew." Some of the most strict Orthodox Jews feel that those like the Ethiopian Jews, who perhaps were not strictly following all of the 613 Orthodox rules, should have to be recertified as Jews. The outcome of that debate will be very significant.

WHAT ABOUT THE STATE OF ISRAEL? 189

When a movement is not one of the Holy Spirit, things can become very tangled and confused.

The Hebrews and Jews are doing a beautiful job of building up that country. However, even though they are raising crops in areas that formerly were deserts and so forth, I am not persuaded that that is "prophecy being fulfilled today," as some Christian leaders would say. This is simply a nation doing what we did here in America—claiming wastelands and turning them into agriculturally-productive areas. That is wonderful, but it is not fulfilling biblical prophecy any more than what we did in America fulfilled biblical prophecy.

I do not in any way want to make light of the significant political event of the State of Israel being formed in 1948. The Zionists did a magnificent job of developing a plan and carrying it out. The Israelis should be glad that we support them on a solid basis of political self-interest, national security and global strategic considerations. That is far better than supporting them on a religious inclination which could change as easily as the wind changes direction.

Unfortunately, all that the Israelis (citizens of the State of Israel) are building today is going to be wiped out during the great tribulation, as we discussed in Chapter 7. You and I will have the privilege of rebuilding that area during the millennium. If you are interested in further study on this subject, I have discussed this in more depth in Chapter 11 of the book, *The Future Revealed* (formerly *The Coming Climax of History*).

THE STATE OF ISRAEL

I cannot say enough good things about the State of Israel, although nonetheless I see some negatives about that nation. Israel is a stable democracy surrounded by brutal, military regimes and fragile monarchs. No matter who wins an Israeli election, the Israeli government has remained pro-American.

The State of Israel is an invaluable strategic partner in that unstable region. American interests in the Mideast are protected at a fraction of the cost of defending East Asia or Europe. More importantly, Israeli soldiers bear their own defense burden without the U.S. having to send American troops.

Frankly, I envy the patrotic dedication of the Israelis to the State of Israel (to reiterate, an *Israeli* is a citizen of the State of Israel, and I use the term *Israelite* to be someone who belongs to the *Israel* of God). How I wish that Americans had even one-tenth the patriotism that Israelis have. They would gladly fight and die for their country, without even a second thought. They are proud of their country and their heritage. Unfortunately, as I discovered on my last trip to that country, the State of Israel has almost become the "god" of many Israelis. It is the entity for which they are willing to die, they are dedicated to it, and they are evangelistic about it. Many of them only talk about their nation and never mention God.

We flew *El Al,* the Israeli airline, over to the State of Israel. The Israeli security was extremely tight and the flight crew looked very capable of handling anyone who might even think about hijacking the plane. I felt far safer on *El Al* than I would on any of the United States airliners.

Israelis are an inventive and creative people. They are "plastic farming" and exporting that technique to other countries, including countries in the Middle East, such as Jordan. When the queen of England needed extra electronic security, she came to the State of Israel, because they were the experts in that area.

I also appreciate the way the State of Israel is preserving many of the archaeological sites, including sites where Jesus performed different miracles and where major events in the life of Jesus Christ occurred. We owe them a tremendous debt of gratitude for this.

WHAT ABOUT THE STATE OF ISRAEL?

Man for man, I believe the Israeli army is the best in the world. If I had to have a platoon of soldiers to protect me, and I could pick that platoon from any nation in the world, a platoon of Israeli soldiers would be at (or very near) the top of the list. In fact, when we had hostages taken by the Ayatollah Khomeini in Tehran during President Carter's administration, we probably should have hired the Israeli army to go in and get them; I believe they would have done it, and successfully.

One negative factor is that the State of Israel tends to lean heavily towards the collectivism or socialistic side of the spectrum, but—even with that—it does remain a democracy. This aspect, along with their defense needs, is what has caused the economic crises and double- and triple-digit inflation.

The question relevant to our discussion in this book is whether the formation of this outstanding nation in 1948 fulfilled the prophecies of Ezekiel 36 and 37 or whether it is in the same category as the formation of the United States, for example. As we mentioned at the start of this chapter, many things occurred in the forming of both of these nations which could almost be considered miraculous. But does that alone make either nation the fulfillment of biblical prophecies?

WHAT ABOUT THE RETURN OF THE STATE OF ISRAEL TO THAT LAND?

There is one major reason why the Hebrews or Jews had to go back to land of Palestine: to build a place of worship. We know that this place of worship must be rebuilt because, in Matthew 24, Christ referred to the "abomination of desolation" appearing in the "holy place." Some think that this "holy place" will be a temple that is built on top of the Temple Mount, either adjacent to the Dome of the Rock or replacing the Dome of the Rock. I personally doubt this very seriously. This "holy place" could be referring to a specific area of the tabernacle or temple, or it could be referring to Jerusalem as a whole. I think it is referring to Jerusalem as a whole, much as most Christians refer to the land of Palestine as "the holy land."

Another alternative is the Great Synagogue in Jerusalem. I was there with the architect and builder during its construction. As of the writing of this book, I have just returned from the State of Israel and have seen that beautiful, completed structure. Daniel says that the beast will declare himself to be God in a "fortified sanctuary." Either a rebuilt temple or a synagogue could be considered a sanctuary. Whichever one it turns out to be, it will be well fortified. Believe me, this Great Synagogue in Jerusalem is indeed a fortified sanctuary. There are many parking levels below it which are well fortified and stocked with supplies to withstand siege for a long period of time. I do not know whether or not this will prove to be the "sanctuary fortress" of which Daniel prophesied, but it is a possible candidate.

So the main reason the Hebrews had to go back to the land of Palestine was to build a place of worship, a fortified sanctuary, where the abomination of desolation would take place and where the beast would announce himself and declare himself to be God. Let's read about this coming abomination:

> 29 "At the appointed time he will return and come into the South, but this last time it will not turn out the way it did before.
>
> 30 "For ships of Kittim will come against him; therefore he will be disheartened, and will return and become enraged at the holy covenant and take action; so he will come back and show regard for those who forsake the holy covenant.
>
> 31 "And forces from him will arise, desecrate the sanctuary fortress, and do away with the regular

WHAT ABOUT THE STATE OF ISRAEL? 193

sacrifice. And they will set up the abomination of desolation.

32 "And by smooth words he will turn to godlessness those who act wickedly toward the covenant, but the people who know their God will display strength and take action.

33 "And those who have insight among the people will give understanding to the many; yet they will fall by sword and by flame, by captivity and by plunder, for many days.

34 "Now when they fall they will be granted a little help, and many will join with them in hypocrisy.

35 "And some of those who have insight will fall, in order to refine, purge, and make them pure, until the end time, because it is still to come at the appointed time...."

—Daniel 11

1 "Now at that time Michael, the great prince who stands guard over the sons of your people, will arise. And there will be a time of distress such as never occurred since there was a nation until that time; and at that time your people, everyone who is found written in the book, will be rescued.

2 "And many of those who sleep in the dust of the ground will awake, these to everlasting life, but the others to disgrace and everlasting contempt.

3 "And those who have insight will shine brightly like the brightness of the expanse of heaven, and those who lead the many to righteousness, like the stars forever and ever...."

—Daniel 12

As you can see in these passages, when the sanctuary fortress is desecrated and the abomination which will make Jerusalem desolate occurs, then there will be a time of great distress (the great tribulation). The major reason why the State of Israel needed to be formed was to establish a sanctuary fortress. As far as

I can tell from Bible prophecy, this is the only place they fit in.

WHAT IS THE SIGNIFICANCE OF THE FORMATION OF THE STATE OF ISRAEL IN 1948?

I am praying that the Lord will help me deal with this next topic completely in His will. It is a ticklish subject, because so many Bible scholars today look at the establishment of the State of Israel in 1948 as the beginning of the countdown on the prophetic clock. These teachers attach much significance to the biological Hebrews.

Once the Hebrews rejected Jesus Christ, God's very own Son, and the old covenant was replaced by the new covenant, the Hebrews lost their unique spiritual status with God (their status as God's chosen people). After that they could only come to God like everyone else—through Jesus Christ. The language they speak is Hebrew. It is unfortunate, in some ways, that they called their state "Israel"; it would have avoided much confusion if it had been called some name relating to the word "Hebrew." Possibly a good name for the country would have been "Judea."

It is interesting to consider that, while the Hebrews lost their status as God's chosen people, they may not have lost the genetic and cultural gifts God gave them. As a rule, God does not rescind His gifts. The gifts of scholarship and intellectual rigor that were expressed in the scribes were necessary for God's word to be handed down, and for Jesus to be seen as the fulfillment of hundreds of prophecies. In a sense, one can still see those gifts evidenced among Hebrews over the last four thousand years. The extraordinarily disproportionate impact they have had on the world (Marx, Freud, Einstein) and their seminal influence in Western culture (arts, humanities, sciences) are testimony of this.

WHAT ABOUT THE STATE OF ISRAEL?

We have already seen that the church is Israel. Therefore, prophetic passages—such as Ezekiel 36 and 37—which deal with the return of Israel to the promised land, I believe refer to when Christ will take all Christians to that land.

Historically, the Hebrews were never allowed to return to the land of Palestine in a state of unbelief. They had to wander in the wilderness for forty years, until all of the generation of unbelievers had died. Then those who did believe were allowed to enter. Over and over again, Israel was warned that it would be dispersed if it entered in a state of unbelief. When they became unfaithful to God, they were exiled. In past times, Israel was only allowed to return to the land of Palestine when they repented and turned back to God. God would not allow them to be gathered back in unbelief.

Let us now look at the Scriptures which prophesy the end-time return of Israel to the promised land. We have already looked at some of these verses from Ezekiel 36 in Chapter 7, but let us take a closer look as to how this pertains to the formation of the State of Israel.

> 24 "For I will take you from the nations, gather you from all the lands, and bring you into your own land.
>
> 25 "Then I will sprinkle clean water on you, and you will be clean; I will cleanse you from all your filthiness and from all your idols.
>
> 26 "Moreover, I will give you a new heart and put a new spirit within you; and I will remove the heart of stone from your flesh and give you a heart of flesh.
>
> 27 "And I will put My Spirit within you and cause you to walk in My statutes, and you will be careful to observe My ordinances.
>
> 28 "And you will live in the land that I gave to your forefathers; so you will be My people, and I will be your God.

CHAPTER 12

> 29 "Moreover, I will save you from all your uncleanness; and I will call for the grain and multiply it, and I will not bring a famine on you.
>
> 30 "And I will multiply the fruit of the tree and the produce of the field, that you may not receive again the disgrace of famine among the nations.
>
> 31 "Then you will remember your evil ways and your deeds that were not good, and you will loathe yourselves in your own sight for your iniquities and your abominations.
>
> 32 "I am not doing this for your sake," declares the Lord GOD, "let it be known to you. Be ashamed and confounded for your ways, O house of Israel!"
>
> 33 'Thus says the Lord GOD, "On the day that I cleanse you from all your iniquities, I will cause the cities to be inhabited, and the waste places will be rebuilt.
>
> 34 "And the desolate land will be cultivated instead of being a desolation in the sight of everyone who passed by. . . ."
>
> —Ezekiel 36

As we have seen, the biological Hebrews of today do not spiritually qualify as the "house of Israel." One of the key verses in this passage is verse 33. It says: "On the day that I cleanse you from all your iniquities, I will cause the cities to be inhabited, and the waste places will be rebuilt." In other words, when Israel (true Israel) is gathered from all nations, on that day God will "cleanse them from all their iniquities." Do you believe that the Hebrews living in Palestine today have been cleansed from all their iniquities? The only way people can be cleansed from their iniquities today is through the blood of Jesus Christ. In my opinion, this prophecy could not have been fulfilled by the Hebrews in 1948, since they returned to the land of Palestine in unbelief and without being cleansed.

Another such prophecy is found three chapters later in Ezekiel:

WHAT ABOUT THE STATE OF ISRAEL?

> **25** Therefore thus says the Lord GOD, "Now I shall restore the fortunes of Jacob, and have mercy on the whole house of Israel; and I shall be jealous for My holy name.
> **26** "And they shall forget their disgrace and all their treachery which they perpetrated against Me, when they live securely on their own land with no one to make them afraid.
> **27** "When I bring them back from the peoples and gather them from the lands of their enemies, then I shall be sanctified through them in the sight of the many nations.
> **28** "Then they will know that I am the LORD their God because I made them go into exile among the nations, and then gathered them again to their own land; and I will leave none of them there any longer.
> **29** "And I will not hide My face from them any longer, for I shall have poured out My Spirit on the house of Israel," declares the Lord GOD.
> —Ezekiel 39

Here we see that when the "whole house of Israel" (true Israel) is gathered back to the promised land, God will have poured out His Spirit on the house of Israel (verse 29). The only way the Spirit of God is poured out on anyone today is after he has received Jesus Christ as his Savior. Has the Holy Spirit been poured out upon the non-Christian Hebrews living in Palestine (the State of Israel) today? No. Again, I do not feel that there is any way that the Hebrews fulfilled this prophecy in 1948; rather, I feel it will be fulfilled when the church is taken en masse to Palestine at the end of the tribulation.

The return of Israel to the promised land is also prophesied in Jeremiah:

> **13** 'And you will seek Me and find Me, when you search for Me with all your heart.

> 14 'And I will be found by you,' declares the LORD, 'and I will restore your fortunes and will gather you from all the nations and from all the places where I have driven you,' declares the LORD, 'and I will bring you back to the place from where I sent you into exile.'
>
> —Jeremiah 29

It is evident when you read this passage in context that it was talking specifically about the return of Israel from the Assyrian-Babylonian captivity, but it serves to show the sequence in which things must happen. Verse 13 says that Israel must seek God; they must search for Him with their whole heart. When they do this, they will find Him, and then He will restore them to their land. Today, the only way that anyone can find God is through Jesus Christ, for He said: "I am the way, and the truth, and the life; no one comes to the Father, but through Me...." (John 14:6). The Hebrews returning to Palestine in 1948 did not follow this pattern of first seeking God with all of their heart.

These are but a sampling of the Scriptures we could present. The return of the Jews and Hebrews to Palestine in 1948 does not fulfill the prophecies. These prophecies were either referring to earlier returns, when the Hebrews did return in belief, or to a future return of Israel (Christians) in belief, in righteousness, and having been cleansed by the blood of Christ.

If the Hebrews' return to Palestine did not fulfill these prophecies, what will? I do not claim to have all of the answers, but in my spirit I sense that those who comprise true Israel today (all those who believe in Jesus Christ, and this excludes anyone who does not believe in Him) are the ones who will return in belief and in cleanliness. It is likely that, at the end of the tribulation, true Israel (Christians and Old Testament saints) will return to Palestine to rule and reign with Christ from Mount Zion for a thousand years. So when we, as Christians, look forward to "marching to Zion,"

WHAT ABOUT THE STATE OF ISRAEL? 199

as the song says, those are not empty words; we will indeed go to Zion. What a day of rejoicing that is going to be, when we see Jesus and we learn from Him directly!

SUMMARY ON ISRAEL AND THE COVENANTS

I have tried to help you see clearly from the Bible that Israel today is composed of all those who believe in Jesus Christ, regardless of racial background. All those who do not believe in Jesus Christ as Lord and Savior are not part of Israel, even if they are of a Hebrew lineage.

We have also seen that all Christians will inherit all of the promises made to Abraham, Isaac, and Jacob (whose spiritual name was *Israel*). This means that the land that God promised to Abraham (Palestine) is our land. We should be looking forward to ruling and reigning with Christ from there for a thousand years.

I believe that Christians should support the Hebrews and Jews in Palestine. They are going to build (or have already built) a place of worship, which we see involved in the time of birth pangs and the great tribulation. It is possible that the "fortified sanctuary" spoken of in Scripture is the Great Synagogue which was dedicated in Jerusalem in 1982.

As we have mentioned, there are sincere men of God who attach prophetic significance to the Hebrews and Jews forming the "State of Israel" in 1948. There are entire ministries that are dedicated to evangelizing those Hebrews. The evangelical world, in general, still looks at the Hebrews and Jews in Palestine as "God's chosen people," and as Israel. I am casting no stones at any of these people. They know Christ as their Savior and they are preaching Jesus as the only way to eternal life. Therefore, I praise God for their ministries, and I would encourage them to continue in any effort to reach the Hebrews with the good news that even though they are lost, that they can be saved through

Jesus Christ, God's only begotten Son and the *only* way to the Father.

However, I cannot reconcile to the Scriptures any teaching other than the fact that, as the Bible declares, all those who believe in Christ are Israel and are heirs to the promises made to Abraham. As such, the Christians are now God's chosen people. I'm sure Satan would like to keep us blind to our true identity and our birthright, and all that it implies. He would love to convince us that our inheritance belongs to someone else.

I am not asking you to agree with me, but I am asking you to prayerfully consider it. You can see that if one Bible teacher felt that the Hebrews were Israel and another Bible teacher felt that the born-again Christians were Israel, they would view the gathering of Israel to the land of Palestine, as prophesied in the Bible, in two totally different ways.

As I said earlier, when the Hebrews returned to Palestine in 1948, I do not believe that they fulfilled the prophecies of Ezekiel 36 and 37 concerning Israel returning to their promised land. That will be fulfilled when we Christians are caught up by Christ's gathering angels, at the end of the tribulation, and are taken to our land, to the Mount of Olives, right outside of Jerusalem.

There, on Mount Zion and in our promised land, for a thousand years, Christ will teach us His ways and we will walk in His paths.

I would suggest that you pause and pray right now; settle the question in your own mind as to who Israel is. I realize that, for many, this view of Israel is not the standard "party line," and that sincere men and women of God may not agree. (However, if they claim that they love the Hebrews and Jews more than I do, that is not true.) It is exciting that, in these end times, God is giving new light on many things, and we must be open to changing some of our old thinking.

WHAT ABOUT THE STATE OF ISRAEL? 201

To reiterate, if you know Christ as your personal Savior and Lord, I strongly believe the Bible declares that you are part of Israel. I believe that the Bible says you are an heir to the promises made to Abraham. If someone were to walk up to you and ask whether you were of Israel, you would have to answer "Yes," according to the New Testament. You are an Israelite.

Another key topic in understanding what the Bible teaches about Israel, and from which arise some misconceptions about the State of Israel, is the subject of the fig tree. Let's now move on to examine this.

THE FIG TREE AND ISRAEL

As we have said, there are many Bible teachers, and especially those who teach about prophecy, who say that "God's prophetic clock started its countdown in 1948 when the State of Israel was formed" and that Christ will return or the tribulation will start within one generation of that time. I say that this is nonsense.

They base their belief on the teachings of Jesus in Matthew 24, where He gives a parable about a fig tree. They claim that the fig tree is the newly-formed State of Israel. I feel that this is fantasy, with no biblical basis.

I believe that God would have me lovingly caution the teachers and authors who are propagating this teaching that "enough is enough." I ask that you would be prayerful as you read this, asking God to show you what He would wish to say to you personally and to the body of Christ. Also, please pray that He will protect you from misunderstanding my heart and my motives, which are to help the body of Christ and to obey Him.

According to most of the teachers who claim that the fig tree is the State of Israel, a generation is forty years. Thus, if you add forty years to 1948, then you have the tribulation beginning in 1988 and Christ's return in 1988, if you believe in a pre-tribulation rapture. 1988 has come and gone, and neither event occurred. Still, it is important to understand the foundations relied on by those teachers, so as to discern the biblical truths they failed to see.

THE TRIBULATION DID NOT START IN 1981

The June, 1980 issue of *End-Times News Digest* had the following as the title of the main article:

"WILL THE TRIBULATION START IN 1981?"

The reason we discussed that subject in 1980, well ahead of time, was that many were teaching that the prophetic countdown clock started on May 14, 1948. If one added forty years to that, one would come up to 1988. If one then subtracted seven years for the tribulation, the great tribulation would begin in 1981. Since all these people believed in a pre-tribulation rapture, in essence they were teaching that Christ would return in 1981.

Most of these teachers did not explicitly state that that was what they were teaching, but that indeed was the essence of their teaching.

In fact, my wife, Jeani, and I went to hear a prominent Christian leader speak here in Medford on April 29 and 30, 1980. Accompanying us was a couple, the wife of which was then the President of the Women's Aglow chapter. After hearing him talk on April 30, her comment was, "He is really teaching that Christ is coming back next year!" And we all agreed. The speaker did not state this in his talk, but this was the teaching that he gave.

Also, in that issue of the newsletter, I quoted from a book written by another well-known pre-tribulationist, and it was evident that this was what he believed as well. I wrote that issue early in 1980, so that if any of these teachers disagreed concerning my perception of what they were teaching, they had plenty

WHAT ABOUT THE STATE OF ISRAEL?

of time to reply (and I would have been happy to have printed their response). However, none of them responded. Later in 1982, some began to deny that they ever taught that. They would sidestep the issue by saying, "I never said that Christ was going to return in 1981." That is true. They may never have said it explicitly, yet that is what they were teaching.

A wonderful Christian, who formerly attended a church in the Rogue Valley of Oregon, told me that in her church they were clearly teaching that Christ would return in 1981. However, after that year nothing was said about it and no admission of error was ever made.

Let me hasten to add that I love the brothers who believe in and teach the pre-tribulation rapture. They are my brothers in Christ and I praise the Lord for their lives and service to God. I hope they reach more and more people for Jesus. However, I think that in some major areas of prophecy they are misleading people by teaching false doctrine. In 1981, when Christ didn't come as they had taught, they were able to soft-shoe dance around the issue and start claiming that they were wrong in subtracting the seven years, and that the tribulation would start in 1988.

In February of 1987, in real love and concern, I wrote in *End-Times News Digest* saying that if Christ did not return in 1988, these teachers would have some public recanting and changing to do. There is just so long that one can hold to an old theory after it has proven false. Since the rapture did not occur in 1988, either their teaching about the prophetic clock and the State of Israel is wrong, or their pre-tribulation rapture theory is wrong, or both. Of course, by now you have realized that I think both are false. Anyone who continues to listen to their teachings on prophecy now deserves the misleading that he will get. I suggest that you stop listening to them, unless these brothers repent of past errors and turn to a more biblical position concerning the end times of the age.

You may wonder why I include these comments in a book. The reason is certainly not to belittle or speak evil against any brother. Rather, I feel that this issue is important enough to the body of Christ today that someone needs to address it head on. At times, it is human nature to let slide something that we have believed and perhaps even taught for years, because it is "comfortable" or more convenient to do so. I believe the identity of Israel is significant enough that truth-seeking Christians should spend the time and energy to rethink the issue in view of what the Bible has to say and not just based on what is commonly expounded.

WHERE DID THIS 1988 TEACHING GET ITS START?

To discuss Jesus' teaching on the fig tree, from which this "rapture in 1988" theory was ultimately derived, it is necessary to read it in the context in which it appears. For that reason, we will get a running start by first walking through the end-time events as Jesus Christ Himself outlined them for His disciples.

> 3 And as He was sitting on the Mount of Olives, the disciples came to Him privately, saying, "Tell us, when will these things be, and what will be the sign of Your coming, and of the end of the age?"
> —Matthew 24

Evidently our Savior had taught the disciples much about the age ending and about His return. Here they asked Him plainly what it was going to be like right before He came back and right before the age ended.

The age that they were talking about was obviously the age that contained His return. They did not ask, "What will the end of the next age be like?" Therefore, the age that we are living in had already started as they were sitting on the Mount of Olives that day.

I do not know when it started—whether it was at Christ's conception, at His birth, when He was eight days old, when He was twelve, when He was baptized by John in the river Jordan, or at the Mount of Transfiguration. However, at some point in time, prior to this verse, the age that you and I are now living in had begun.

Since Jesus was going to be crucified in just a few days, I believe that He gave them a very straightforward answer to their question about what things would be like right before He came back and right before this age ended. Here is His answer:

> 4 And Jesus answered and said to them, "See to it that no one misleads you.
>
> 5 "For many will come in My name, saying, 'I am the Christ,' and will mislead many.
>
> 6 "And you will be hearing of wars and rumors of wars; see that you are not frightened, for those things must take place, but that is not yet the end.
>
> 7 "For nation will rise against nation, and kingdom against kingdom, and in various places there will be famines and earthquakes.
>
> 8 "But all of these are merely the beginning of birth pangs.
>
> 9 "Then they will deliver you to tribulation, and will kill you, and you will be hated by all nations on account of My name.
>
> 10 "And at that time many will fall away and will deliver up one another and will hate one another.
>
> 11 "And many false prophets will arise, and will mislead many.
>
> 12 "And because lawlessness is increased, most people's love will grow cold.
>
> 13 "But the one who endures to the end, he shall be saved.
>
> 14 "And this gospel of the kingdom shall be preached in the whole world for a witness to all the nations, and then the end shall come.

> 15 "Therefore when you see the ABOMINATION OF DESOLATION which is spoken of through Daniel the prophet, standing in the holy place (let the reader understand),
> 16 then let those who are in Judea flee to the mountains;
> 17 let him who is on the housetop not go down to get the things out that are in his house;
> 18 and let him who is in the field not turn back to get his cloak.
> 19 "But woe to those who are with child and to those who nurse babes in those days!
> 20 "But pray that your flight may not be in the winter, or on a Sabbath;
> 21 for then there will be a great tribulation, such as has not occurred since the beginning of the world until now, nor ever shall. . . ."
>
> —Matthew 24

We see here that the great tribulation begins in verse 21, but Jesus says that preceding that will be a time that He calls the "time of birth pangs." In the time of birth pangs, there will be wars, famine, earth upheavals, persecution and the gospel of the Kingdom will be preached in all nations.

Also before the great tribulation begins, as we saw in Chapter 9, Jesus said there would be the abomination of desolation standing in the holy place. In that chapter, we discussed the word *desolate* which means "devoid of people" or "uninhabited" (Isaiah 6:11, Jeremiah 33:10, Jeremiah 50:13). Another verse that gives a good definition of desolate is:

> 8 "Be warned, O Jerusalem,
>   Lest I be alienated from you;
>   Lest I make you a desolation,
>   A land not inhabited."
>
> —Jeremiah 6

WHAT ABOUT THE STATE OF ISRAEL?

So, in review, something is going to happen in Jerusalem that is going to make it uninhabited before the great tribulation begins.

Let us continue reading the description that Jesus gave of the end of this age. As we noted, the great tribulation begins in verse 21, and we read about it as follows:

21 for then there will be a great tribulation, such as has not occurred since the beginning of the world until now, nor ever shall.

22 "And unless those days had been cut short, no life would have been saved; but for the sake of the elect those days shall be cut short.

23 "Then if anyone says to you, 'Behold, here is Christ,' or 'There He is,' do not believe him.

24 "For false Christs and false prophets will arise and will show great signs and wonders, so as to mislead, if possible, even the elect.

25 "Behold, I have told you in advance.

26 "If therefore they say to you, 'Behold, He is in the wilderness,' do not go forth, or, 'Behold, He is in the inner rooms' do not believe them.

27 "For just as the lightning comes from the east, and flashes even to the west, so shall the coming of the Son of Man be.

28 "Wherever the corpse is, there the vultures will gather.

29 "But immediately after the tribulation of those days THE SUN WILL BE DARKENED, AND THE MOON WILL NOT GIVE ITS LIGHT, AND THE STARS WILL FALL from the sky, and the powers of the heavens will be shaken,

30 and then the sign of the Son of Man will appear in the sky, and then all the tribes of the earth will mourn, and they will see the SON OF MAN COMING ON THE CLOUDS OF THE SKY with power and great glory.

31 "And He will send forth His angels with A GREAT TRUMPET and THEY WILL GATHER

TOGETHER His elect from the four winds, from one end of the sky to the other. ..."

—Matthew 24

In this passage, we not only see the great tribulation, but also what is going to happen immediately after it. Immediately after the tribulation, the angels will go out to collect the living Christians from the four winds and the dead Christians from one end of the sky to the other. This is talking about the time of the rapture.

A Close Look At The Fig Tree

Jesus continued with His answer to the disciples' question this way:

> 32 "Now learn the parable from the fig tree: when its branch has already become tender, and puts forth its leaves, you know that summer is near;
> 32 even so you too, when you see all these things, recognize that He is near, right at the door.
> 34 "Truly I say to you, this generation will not pass away until all these things take place. ..."

—Matthew 24

Jesus says here that we should take a lesson from nature: when we see a tree—in this case He used a fig tree—and its branch becomes tender and it puts forth leaves, we should know that it is spring and that summer is coming. Jesus then points out that when we begin to see all the things happen that He talked about in the early part of the chapter, we should recognize that His return is near. Then He says that the generation that sees these things begin to happen will not pass away until *all* of the things that He mentioned in verses 4 through 31 take place.

Jesus' mentioning of the fig tree example had absolutely nothing to do with the Hebrews forming a nation. He simply and plainly taught that the genera-

WHAT ABOUT THE STATE OF ISRAEL?

tion that began to see the earth upheavals, the famines and so forth was going to be the generation that would see His return, and that generation would see all of the things that He had mentioned from verses 4 through 31.

There is no biblical evidence that Christ intended the fig tree mentioned here to be anything but simply a fig tree. There are those who try to make out the fig tree to represent Israel. I see no justification for arbitrarily applying the Matthew 24 passage about the fig tree to Israel and not the following passage about a fig tree, for example:

> **12** And on the next day, when they had departed from Bethany, He became hungry.
>
> **13** And seeing at a distance a fig tree in leaf, He went to see if perhaps He would find anything on it; and when He came to it, He found nothing but leaves, for it was not the season for figs. . . .
>
> **20** And as they were passing by in the morning, they saw the fig tree withered from the roots up.
>
> **21** And being reminded, Peter said to Him, "Rabbi, behold, the fig tree which You cursed has withered."
> —Mark 11

If you ask proponents of the fig tree theory if this fig tree that Jesus cursed, and caused to dry up and die, represents Israel, they would say, "Absolutely not." I would encourage them to endeavor to be consistent in interpreting the Scriptures. I try to be consistent but do not always make it. However, when someone points out an inconsistency in something I have been teaching, I try to correct it and acknowledge it publicly.

I have read every verse that mentions fig, figs, or fig tree, and I cannot find a single Scripture that equates the State of Israel to a fig tree. I will give you some of the key verses that these people use to try to come up with this:

CHAPTER 12

> 7 Now when they told Jotham, he went and stood on the top of Mount Gerizim, and lifted his voice and called out. Thus he said to them, "Listen to me, O men of Shechem, that God may listen to you.
> 8 "Once the trees went forth to anoint a king over them, and they said to the olive tree, 'Reign over us!'
> 9 "But the olive tree said to them, 'Shall I leave my fatness with which God and men are honored, and go to wave over the trees?
> 10 "Then the trees said to the fig tree, 'You come, reign over us!'
> 11 "But the fig tree said to them, 'Shall I leave my sweetness and my good fruit, and go to wave over the trees?'
> 12 "Then the trees said to the vine, 'You come, reign over us?'
> 13 "But the vine said to them, 'Shall I leave my new wine, which cheers God and men, and go to wave over the trees?'
> 14 "Finally all the trees said to the bramble, 'You come, reign over us!'
> 15 "And the bramble said to the trees, 'If in truth you are anointing me as king over you, come and take refuge in my shade; but if not, may fire come out from the bramble and consume the cedars of Lebanon.'..."
> —Judges 9

There is nothing here in Judges 9 that equates Israel to the fig tree. Another Scripture that some teachers try to use is found in Deuteronomy:

> 7 "For the LORD your God is bringing you into a good land, a land of brooks of water, of fountains and springs, flowing forth in valleys and hills;
> 8 a land of wheat and barley, of vines and fig trees and pomegranates, a land of olive oil and honey; ..."
> —Deuteronomy 8

WHAT ABOUT THE STATE OF ISRAEL? 211

Here again, there is no way you can stretch that to say that Israel is represented by a fig tree. You could just as well say that pomegranates or barley represent Israel.

I have checked out all of the Scriptures concerning the fig tree, and nowhere does it represent Israel. I would have to say that the statement of many of these people that "Israel is always represented by the fig tree in the Scriptures" is simply a false statement.

I would welcome anyone to show me from the Scriptures where the State of Israel is ever described as a fig tree. In Jeremiah 24:5, some of the Jews were compared to figs, and in Hosea 9:10, some of the fathers were compared to the first fruit on a fig tree, but I cannot find anywhere in the Scriptures that the State of Israel is referred to as a fig tree. I would appreciate being enlightened on the subject. I am open to learning.

A tree that does represent Israel, at least in one instance in the Scriptures, is the olive tree. You can read Romans 11:17-24 and see this very clearly.

If we examine Luke 21, which is a parallel passage to Matthew 24, we see even more clearly that the fig tree does not represent Israel in Christ's Olivet discourse. This is a long passage, but please read it carefully.

> 5 And while some were talking about the temple, that it was adorned with beautiful stones and votive gifts, He said,
>
> 6 "As for these things which you are looking at, the days will come in which there will not be left one stone upon another which will not be torn down."
>
> 7 And they questioned Him, saying, "Teacher, when therefore will these things be? And what will be the sign when these things are about to take place?"
>
> 8 And He said, "See to it that you be not misled; for many will come in My name, saying, 'I am He,' and, 'The time is at hand'; do not go after them.

9 "And when you hear of wars and disturbances, do not be terrified; for these things must take place first, but the end does not follow immediately."

10 Then He continued by saying to them, "Nation will rise against nation, and kingdom against kingdom,

11 and there will be great earthquakes, and in various places plagues and famines; and there will be terrors and great signs from heaven.

12 "But before all these things, they will lay their hands on you and will persecute you, delivering you to the synagogues and prisons, bringing you before kings and governors for My name's sake.

13 "It will lead to an opportunity for your testimony.

14 "So make up your minds not to prepare beforehand to defend yourselves;

15 for I will give you utterance and wisdom which none of your opponents will be able to resist or refute.

16 "But you will be delivered up even by parents and brothers and relatives and friends, and they will put some of you to death,

17 and you will be hated by all on account of My name.

18 "Yet not a hair of your head will perish.

19 "By your endurance you will gain your lives.

20 "But when you see Jerusalem surrounded by armies, then recognize that her desolation is at hand.

21 "Then let those who are in Judea flee to the mountains, and let those who are in the midst of the city depart, and let not those who are in the country enter the city;

22 because these are days of vengeance, in order that all things which are written may be fulfilled.

23 "Woe to those who are with child and to those who nurse babes in those days; for there will be great distress upon the land, and wrath to this people,

24 and they will fall by the edge of the sword, and will be led captive into all the nations; and Jerusalem

WHAT ABOUT THE STATE OF ISRAEL? 213

will be trampled under foot by the Gentiles until the times of the Gentiles be fulfilled.

25 "And there will be signs in sun and moon and stars, and upon the earth dismay among nations, in perplexity at the roaring of the sea and the waves,

26 men fainting from fear and the expectation of the things which are coming upon the world; for the powers of the heavens will be shaken.

27 "And then they will see THE SON OF MAN COMING IN A CLOUD with power and great glory...."

—Luke 21

One thing to note in this passage is that, in the end times of this age, Jerusalem will be surrounded by armies (verse 20). It is at that point that she is about to become uninhabited ("her desolation is at hand").

As a conclusion to His teaching about the end of the age, Christ shares this parable:

28 "But when these things begin to take place, straighten up and lift up your heads, because your redemption is drawing near."

29 And He told them a parable: "Behold the fig tree and all the trees;

30 as soon as they put forth leaves, you see it and know for yourselves that summer is now near.

31 "Even so you, too, when you see these things happening, recognize that the kingdom of God is near.

32 "Truly I say to you, this generation will not pass away until all things take place...."

—Luke 21

In verse 29, we see that when the fig tree *and all the other trees* put forth leaves, we know that summer is near. Thus, obviously this illustration has nothing to do with establishing a Hebrew nation. Jesus is simply taking an example out of nature about all the trees putting forth their leaves as a signal that summer is near. If the fig tree represents the State of Israel being formed in 1948, what do all of the other trees represent? The answer is that they are not meant to represent anything but trees, and neither is the fig tree.

In the same way, Jesus tells us that if we see the things beginning to happen that He described earlier in the chapter, then we would know that we are that generation. Within the length of that generation, all of it will happen. This includes His return in power and glory to rule and reign on the earth for a thousand years! Even so, come King Jesus!

A QUICK REVIEW

Let us briefly review what we have covered concerning the fig tree and how it relates to Israel. We have seen that the fig tree does not represent Israel in the first place. If it did, we would also have to take into account passages such as the one in which Christ cursed the fig tree and caused it to die.

We have also seen that Christ was not talking about a fig tree being "planted," such as those would imply who teach the 1948-prophetic-clock theory, which is obviously false. Christ taught a simple parable from nature about an existing fig tree and other trees that were already planted and were in place. He simply said that when you see them put out leaves, you know it is spring. And just as surely, when you see the things begin to happen that are in the time of birth pangs, then you know that Jesus is at the door and that the generation which sees these things will see His return.

It is exciting that we are most likely the generation which is going to see all these things begin to happen and come to full fruition with the return of our glorious Savior, Jesus Christ, here on the earth. How I am looking forward to His return!

BEWARE OF FALSE TEACHINGS

You notice that I said, "Beware of false teachings," not "Beware of false teachers." There are many good

WHAT ABOUT THE STATE OF ISRAEL? 215

Christian brothers who teach that the fig tree is the State of Israel. I believe they are wrong on that particular subject, but much of what they teach about Jesus is very good and really glorifies Jesus Christ. Therefore, I would not classify them as false teachers but rather as giving false teachings. They are precious brothers of mine in Jesus Christ. As a watchman, however, I would encourage you to stop listening to them on things concerning prophecy, unless they turn away from these false teachings.

It is becoming more critical with each passing day that you weigh very carefully all that you are taught, to be sure that it conforms to the Scriptures. If someone tells you, "Israel is always referred to as a fig tree," then you are going to need to take your concordance and look up under "fig" to see if this is so. If it is not so, that gives you reason to discard that teaching and certainly to be more cautious regarding other things that particular teacher might proclaim to you.

There are many false teachings about the end times of this age going around today. All of us can fall into error; that is one of the reasons that we need one another—no man is all-sufficient and has all the answers. I encourage you to check out my writings and teachings also. You still must be sure yourself that they match the Scriptures.

WHY ARE THESE THINGS IMPORTANT?

Some people think that we as Christians should concentrate on becoming more like Jesus and witnessing, and not on things concerning the end of this age. However, it is interesting to note that one-third of the Bible is prophecy. If we disregard it, are we not really saying that God made a mistake by including that one-third of the Bible? God put it there for a reason, and the reason is for us to read it and understand it.

In the end times of this age, many Christians are going to be misled and deceived. Remember, we read this in Matthew 24:

> 11 "And many false prophets will arise, and will mislead many...."

Here Christ is talking about many Christians being misled at the end of this age. This misleading can go a long way to damaging their faith.

For example, when Jerusalem is surrounded by armies and then some abomination in it causes Jerusalem to become uninhabited, some Christians are likely to lose faith in God. The reason is that they are convinced that God would never let down the State of Israel.

In order that things like that do not shake your faith, you need to know clearly what the Bible has to say about the end of this age. I do not want your faith to be shaken. I want you to know the truth. Among other things, the truth will set you free from fear. It will set you free from fear of the future and of the unknown.

WE MUST BE WILLING TO CHANGE

Perhaps in the past you have believed that the prophetic clock started in 1948 with the establishment of the State of Israel; that the State of Israel was the fig tree; and that forty years after her establishment, this whole thing would wrap up. Maybe you have even taught these things to others.

The tribulation did not begin in 1988 (and, for those who believe in a pre-tribulation rapture, Christ obviously did not return in 1988). Thus, I would challenge those of you to whom this applies to recant a false teaching and to declare God's truth. The quicker you let go of the old, when God shows you that you are in error, and embrace what He shows you is truth, the more He can use you.

Just as an example, I used to believe that the rapture would occur before the tribulation, because that was what I had been taught. But when God showed me otherwise, from the Scriptures and the counsel of a brother in Christ, I did not hang on to what I had previously believed, but gladly changed. I also once believed that the fig tree was Israel, because that was what I had heard others say. Then I checked it out in the Scriptures for myself, asking the Holy Spirit to teach me, and I learned that there was no basis for that belief.

Therefore, I cannot fault someone who believes that way today. The difficulty comes when one refuses to check the Scriptures and then change his belief to conform to the word of God.

There may be Christians of varied persuasions reading this book—pastors, authors, teachers, and laymen alike—who need to make a personal examination of the Scriptures, asking the Holy Spirit to teach them the truth concerning some of the subjects raised herein, regardless what their prior beliefs might have been. If the Lord shows them something different, they need to have the courage (guts) to acknowledge it. If they are "truth seekers," this will be a joy and not something to be dreaded.

Jim Hylton, pastor of the Lake County Baptist Church in Ft. Worth, Texas, once said this:

> There are no graduates from the school of Christ. No alumni are listed as achievers who have gone out to make their mark on the world. What would approach graduation is not going out from Christ but going to be with Him in heaven. Marks are made by those who talk with Him. Those who make such marks are not graduates but students who are learning. Leaders are disciples. Unlike so-called old soldiers, who never die

but just fade away, old disciples never die or fade away. Old disciples go on learning.

Hopefully, our discussion of what I consider to be widespread false teachings concerning the State of Israel, will serve to encourage you to do your own study, in order to verify the truth of what you are being taught. If I have caused you to run and get your Bible, I praise God, because you will be the richer for it.

13

WILL ALL OF ISRAEL BE SAVED?

Will all of Israel be saved? The answer is definitely *yes*. However, what is meant by that question and the answer to it depends on your definition of who Israel is. Most people who ask the question are talking about the Hebrews, the physical descendants of Abraham. The question usually stems from Paul's discourse in Chapters 8-11 of his letter to the Christians in Rome.

If Romans 8-11 are not a problem for you, you may want to skip on to Chapter 14. However, we will discuss these chapters here to try to give more of a complete coverage to the entire subject matter of Israel. In order to do so, we will have to refer back to several passages of Scripture that we have already discussed, in previous chapters, from different perspectives.

We will deal with those chapters in Romans specifically, but for the sake of clarity, we first need to define a little better the question that we are addressing here.

WILL ALL OF THE HEBREWS BE SAVED?

When one asks, "Will all of Israel be saved," he is usually asking whether all of the Hebrews will be saved. When I am asked this question, I immediately ask, "Do you mean the Hebrews who died yesterday or last year or a hundred years ago, who did not know Christ as their Savior, or are you just asking about those who are alive today?" Of course, the inquirer often will mumble that those who have died without Christ will not be saved.

Then I ask, "What about the Hebrews who will die tomorrow without knowing Jesus Christ as their personal Savior? Are you asking, will they be saved?" Again I get a similar answer—that, of course, if they die without Christ they won't be saved. I then point out that we are saying exactly the same thing: that all of those who die believing in Jesus Christ will be saved, and all of those who die without knowing Jesus Christ will not be saved. I share with them a verse that we referred to earlier, which I would like to repeat here:

> 23 Whoever denies the Son does not have the Father; the one who confesses the Son has the Father also.
>
> —1 John 2

This says plainly that if someone denies Jesus Christ as the Son of God, and does not believe in Him, he absolutely does not have the Father, regardless of his racial background or whether he goes to a synagogue every Saturday.

Of course, Jesus Himself put it even stronger:

> 6 Jesus said to him, "I am the way, and the truth, and the life; no one comes to the Father, but through Me...."
>
> —John 14

Either what Jesus said here was truth or it was a lie! I personally believe it was the truth. When He said *no one* can come to God except through Him, He meant exactly that. No one, not even a Hebrew, can come to God and be saved (can come into a right

WILL ALL OF ISRAEL BE SAVED? 221

relationship with the Father), except by coming through Jesus Christ Himself.

The Muslims worship the God of Abraham, but sadly they are trying to get to God through an invalid means. They can never get to God the Father through Mohammed. In reality, they can only get to Him through Jesus Christ.

The Hebrews and other nationalities who practice Judaism as their religion, who are thus "Jews," are trying to get to God the Father through Abraham. Sadly they too are trying to get to God through an invalid method, because—according to the Son of God Himself—absolutely the *only* way to God is through the Son of God, Jesus Christ.

Jesus loves the Jews, just as He did when He was here on earth. He would still love to "gather them under His wings" (Matthew 23:37). But the choice is still theirs. They can come to Him and have eternal life or they can refuse to accept Him and have the wrath of God:

> 36 "He who believes in the Son has eternal life; but he who does not obey the Son shall not see life, but the wrath of God abides on him."
>
> —John 3

It is not that Christians got together and decided they would have an exclusive club. This is something that Jesus Christ Himself claimed and, as the Son of God and One who cannot lie, it is true. As I said earlier, some Christians are delighted when Hebrews who embrace Judaism go to the synagogue on the Sabbath. I think it is sad, because they absolutely can not get to God without Jesus Christ. Some Christians try to reach out to be friends with them, which is good, yet they are afraid to tell them that they are absolutely wrong and that they are headed down a dead-end street. They need to know what the truth is: without Jesus Christ, they are doomed to an eternity in hell.

> **15** "Woe to you, scribes and Pharisees, hypocrites, because you travel about on sea and land to make one proselyte; and when he becomes one, you make him twice as much a son of hell as yourselves. . . .
>
> **33** "You serpents, you brood of vipers, how shall you escape the sentence of hell? . . ."
> —Matthew 23

Christ repeatedly made it clear that it was necessary to come to God the Father through Himself; He stated it in different ways. Once He said:

> **23** "He who hates Me hates My Father also. . . ."
> —John 15

Here Jesus is saying that anyone who does not love Him, does not love the Father. The only way to the Father is through Jesus Christ, His only begotten Son.

If you ask me, "Will all Israel be saved?" my answer is, "*Yes*," but I mean *true Israel*. For all those in the Old Testament who believed God, such as Abraham, their belief would be counted unto them as righteousness, and they will be saved and resurrected at the rapture. This is true whether they were biologically from Abraham or not. Certainly Ruth and Rahab were among those who believed God and it was accounted to them as righteousness and they too will be saved, not because of genealogical heritage, but because they were in a proper relationship with God the Father; they were part of Israel.

Similarly today, all those who believe in Jesus Christ, whether they are Hebrew or not, will be saved, and all those who do not believe in Jesus Christ as the Son of God will not be saved, even if they are Hebrew and biologically from Abraham. It's very simple.

Now let's turn and look at the passage in Romans that tends to confuse so many.

WILL ALL OF ISRAEL BE SAVED? 223

ROMANS 9 & 10

The trouble in looking at these three passages is that if one comes to them with a presupposition—an assumption that the Hebrews living in the land of Palestine are Israel—he will interpret these Scriptures one way. On the other hand, if one comes looking at Israel as a combination of Old Testament saints and New Testament believers, he will look at these chapters very differently.

Another problem is that, at times, Paul is almost mathematical in his precise use of logic and language, whereas at other times he is very ambiguous. For example, the last two verses in Romans 2 tell us this:

> **28 For he is not a Jew who is one outwardly; neither is circumcision that which is outward in the flesh.**
> **29 But he is a Jew who is one inwardly; and circumcision is that which is of the heart, by the Spirit, not by the letter; and his praise is not from men, but from God.**
> —Romans 2

Here we see Paul saying that one is not a Jew who is one outwardly, in the flesh (biologically), but he is a Jew who is one inwardly and who has his heart circumcised by the Holy Spirit. He knew full well at that point in time that the only way to have one's heart circumcised by the Holy Spirit was to receive Jesus Christ as one's Savior.

Then Paul turns around and says this in the next two verses:

> **1 Then what advantage has the Jew? Or what is the benefit of circumcision?**
> **2 Great in every respect. First of all, that they were entrusted with the oracles of God.**
> —Romans 3

Paul has then used the same word "Jew" to mean something very different—the Hebrews of the Old Testament. He also uses it this way in a number of other places, such as in this passage:

> 9 There will be tribulation and distress for every soul of man who does evil, of the Jew first and also of the Greek,
> 10 but glory and honor and peace to every man who does good, to the Jew first and also to the Greek.
> 11 For there is no partiality with God.
> —Romans 2

Incidentally, these are three very interesting verses, because they say that there will be tribulation and distress for everyone who does evil, and honor, peace and glory for everyone who does good. Paul says that, with respect to the Hebrew or the Gentile, there is no difference. There is no partiality with God. He is not partial to the Hebrews; He treats them like everyone else.

Paul repeats this even more strongly in Romans, in Chapter 10:

> 12 For there is no distinction between Jew and Greek; for the same Lord is Lord of all, abounding in riches for all who call upon Him;
> 13 for "WHOEVER WILL CALL UPON THE NAME OF THE LORD WILL BE SAVED."
> —Romans 10

Here Paul points out that there is absolutely no distinction, no difference between Jew and Greek, now that we are under the new covenant. The only way to God is by calling upon the name of the Lord Jesus, and whoever does that will be saved. The only way for a Jew to be saved is to call upon the name of the Lord Jesus Christ. Without Him, they are doomed, just as anyone else is likewise doomed apart from Christ.

WILL ALL OF ISRAEL BE SAVED?

Three verses from Romans 9, which we quoted in an earlier chapter, should settle this question in anyone's heart and mind:

> 6 But it is not as though the word of God has failed. For they are not all Israel who are descended from Israel;
> 7 neither are they all children because they are Abraham's descendants, but: "THROUGH ISAAC YOUR DESCENDANTS WILL BE NAMED."
> 8 That is, it is not the children of the flesh who are children of God, but the children of the promise are regarded as descendants.
> —Romans 9

If we analyze these verses prayerfully, asking the Holy Spirit to show us truth, we will find some incredible things. First, in verse 6, we see that not everyone who is a descendant of Jacob is part of Israel. This simply means that being a Hebrew biologically does not make one a part of Israel.

Verse 7 then tells us that not all of Abraham's descendants are children of God, only those who come down through Isaac spiritually.

Verse 8 is the clincher. It says plainly that it is not the children of the flesh (biological children) who are the children of God, but the children of the spiritual promise who are the descendants of Abraham and the children of God, the inheritors of the promises made to Abraham. Today, Hebrews are not the children of God, but believers in Jesus Christ are.

Later in that same chapter of Romans, Paul says this:

> 22 What if God, although willing to demonstrate His wrath and to make His power known, endured with much patience vessels of wrath prepared for destruction?

> 23 And He did so in order that He might make known the riches of His glory upon vessels of mercy, which He prepared beforehand for glory,
> 24 even us, whom He also called, not from among Jews only, but also from among Gentiles.
> 25 As He says also in Hosea,
> "I WILL CALL THOSE WHO WERE NOT MY PEOPLE, 'MY PEOPLE,' AND HER WHO WAS NOT BELOVED, 'BELOVED.'"
> 26 "AND IT SHALL BE THAT IN THE PLACE WHERE IT WAS SAID TO THEM, 'YOU ARE NOT MY PEOPLE,' THERE THEY SHALL BE CALLED SONS OF THE LIVING GOD."
> —Romans 9

Here the Lord plainly says, through the prophet Hosea, that those people who were not initially His people are going to become His people, and that those who were not part of His beloved are going to become His beloved. Those who were not initially His people are the ones who are going to be called the "sons of the living God." This shows clearly that the people whom God calls, whether Hebrew or not, are going to be the ones called the sons of the living God—they are God's *Israel*. Verse 24 tells us that Jews and Gentiles alike are called. If we answer that call, we will be called sons of the living God:

> 12 But as many as received Him, to them He gave the right to become children of God, even to those who believe in His name, . . .
> —John 1

From Chapters 9 and 10 of Romans, it should be abundantly clear at this point that Israel is not biological (of the flesh) but spiritual (from the promise), and

WILL ALL OF ISRAEL BE SAVED?

that it includes all those who believe in God through Jesus Christ.

ROMANS 11

Now we go to the passage that causes some people difficulty with regard to all of Israel being saved. Remember that in the book of Romans, Paul was writing to both Hebrew and Gentile Christians who lived in Rome:

> 13 But I am speaking to you who are Gentiles. Inasmuch then as I am an apostle of Gentiles, I magnify my ministry,
> 14 if somehow I might move to jealousy my fellow countrymen and save some of them.
> —Romans 11

Here Paul says that Gentiles coming to know Christ and having their own apostle will, he hopes, move to jealousy his fellow Hebrews so that *"some of them"* might be saved. Paul himself recognized, at this point, that *not all of them were going to be saved*, only those who received Jesus Christ. He then goes into the example of the olive tree:

> 17 But if some of the branches were broken off, and you, being a wild olive, were grafted in among them and became partaker with them of the rich root of the olive tree,
> 18 do not be arrogant toward the branches; but if you are arrogant, remember that it is not you who supports the root, but the root supports you.
> 19 You will say then, "Branches were broken off so that I might be grafted in."
> 20 Quite right, they were broken off for their unbelief, but you stand by your faith. Do not be conceited, but fear;
> 21 for if God did not spare the natural branches, neither will He spare you.

228 CHAPTER 13

> 22 Behold then the kindness and severity of God; to those who fell, severity, but to you, God's kindness, if you continue in His kindness; otherwise you also will be cut off.
>
> 23 And they also, if they do not continue in their unbelief, will be grafted in; for God is able to graft them in again.
>
> 24 For if you were cut off from what is by nature a wild olive tree, and were grafted contrary to nature into a cultivated olive tree, how much more shall these who are the natural branches be grafted into their own olive tree?
>
> —Romans 11

In this example, Israel is the olive tree. There are *not* two olive trees: there is not a physical olive tree and a spiritual olive tree. There is only one olive tree, and that olive tree is Israel. There is only one Israel of God, not two.

As we discussed earlier in this book, the rules changed with the advent of Jesus Christ on how one becomes part of Israel. Jesus is now the means to become part of that olive tree—to get into a right relationship with God. You can no longer come by the old covenant; you must come through Jesus Christ and through Him alone.

The branches on the olive tree that were in existence before the coming of Christ are still there; but, at some time after Christ's life, death, resurrection and ascension into heaven, the branches of the olive tree who did not believe in Jesus Christ were broken off, and Gentile branches who believed in Jesus Christ were grafted in. Verse 23 says that if some of these broken off Hebrew branches come to believe in Jesus Christ, they are going to be grafted back in again. Here again, Paul clearly stated that some of the Hebrew branches would remain broken off from Israel, because of lack of belief in Jesus Christ, and some of

WILL ALL OF ISRAEL BE SAVED? 229

them who did believe in Jesus Christ would be grafted back in and become part of Israel.

We need to keep all that has gone before in mind, as we read the next few verses, lest we become confused and arrive at some very erroneous conclusions:

> 25 For I do not want you, brethren, to be uninformed of this mystery, lest you be wise in your own estimation, that a partial hardening has happened to Israel until the fulness of the Gentiles has come in;
> 26 and thus all Israel will be saved; just as it is written,
> "THE DELIVERER WILL COME FROM ZION,
> HE WILL REMOVE UNGODLINESS FROM JACOB."
> 27 AND THIS IS MY COVENANT WITH THEM,
> WHEN I TAKE AWAY THEIR SINS."
> 28 From the standpoint of the gospel they are enemies for your sake, but from the standpoint of God's choice they are beloved for the sake of the fathers; . . .
> —Romans 11

There is hardly any Christian doctrine (belief) that does not have some difficulties, such as "once saved, always saved versus falling from grace" or "predestination versus free will." Whatever you believe on either of these issues, there are verses of Scripture that appear to teach the opposite. Frankly, Romans 11:26 is somewhat of a problem, but I think the Lord has shown me how it could fit in.

When Paul talks about the deliverer who will come from Zion, he is talking about the return of Jesus Christ in power and glory. At that time, He is going to remove all ungodliness from Israel. I believe this is the whole house of Israel and that, at that time, all of Israel will be saved. The problem is that in verses 25 and 26, Paul uses the word "Israel" in two different meanings, just as we saw earlier that he used the word "Jew" with two different meanings. In verse 25, Israel is referring to the Hebrews of his day. But in verse 26, I believe Paul uses "Israel" with a different meaning. He says that when the "fulness of the Gentiles has come" (which will be culminated at the end of the great tribulation), all of Israel will be saved. So, in verse 26, Paul is saying that all of the Israel of God will be saved.

I praise the Lord that you and I are part of the Israel that will be saved! Every person who believes in Jesus Christ as his Savior and Lord is a part of that Israel and will be saved. Unfortunately, "when the fulness of the Gentiles has come," every Hebrew who does not believe in Jesus Christ at that point will not be saved. There is no back door or side door—the only door to God is Jesus Christ.

In writing to the Gentile Christians at Galatia, Paul called them "children of promise, like Isaac," as we discussed earlier in this book. Please note verse 28, as we reread this passage:

21 Tell me, you who want to be under law, do you not listen to the law?
22 For it is written that Abraham had two sons, one by the bondwoman and one by the free woman.
23 But the son by the bondwoman was born according to the flesh, and the son by the free woman through the promise.
24 This is allegorically speaking: for these women are two covenants, one proceeding from Mount Sinai bearing children who are to be slaves; she is Hagar.
25 Now this Hagar is Mount Sinai in Arabia, and corresponds to the present Jerusalem, for she is in slavery with her children.
26 But the Jerusalem above is free; she is our mother.
27 For it is written,

> "REJOICE, BARREN WOMAN WHO DOES NOT BEAR;
> BREAK FORTH AND SHOUT, YOU WHO ARE NOT IN LABOR;
> FOR MORE ARE THE CHILDREN OF THE DESOLATE
> THAN OF THE ONE WHO HAS A HUSBAND."
>
> 28 And you brethren, like Isaac, are children of promise.
>
> 29 But as at that time he who was born according to the flesh persecuted him who was born according to the Spirit, so it is now also.
>
> 30 But what does the Scripture say?
> "CAST OUT THE BONDWOMAN AND HER SON,
> FOR THE SON OF THE BONDWOMAN SHALL NOT BE AN HEIR WITH THE SON OF THE FREE WOMAN."
>
> 31 So then, brethren, we are not children of a bondwoman, but of the free woman.
>
> —Galatians 4

Paul tells the "brethren" (those who believe in Jesus Christ) that they are children of promise—they are children of Sarah and not of Hagar. This means that you and I and all "brethren in Jesus" are the children of promise, the children who are to inherit all the promises made to Abraham, Isaac and Jacob.

WILL ALL ISRAEL BE SAVED?

My answer to the question, "Will all Israel be saved?" is a resounding, *"Yes!"* Every branch on the olive tree will be saved. Since the time of Christ, to be a branch of the olive tree, one must believe in Jesus Christ as one's Savior. It does not matter if a person is 1,000 percent Hebrew—today he is not a branch on the olive tree, unless he knows Christ as his personal Savior.

The Hebrews and other nationalities who practice Judaism are dead wrong. God is not pleased with them. He has taken His Spirit from them. In true biblical terms, a rabbi is not a rabbi of Israel. He is truly a rabbi of Judaism, because Israel is a special group of people—a spiritual group.

Some would say, "But the Jews are so sincere." Believe me, the Muslims are also sincere. Even the witch doctor is sincere. But he is sincerely wrong. Sincerity is of no value, if it is focused on the wrong thing.

While we are on the subject, as we mentioned in Chapter 5, there are some people who think a "completed Jew or Hebrew" has a special status with God that a "completed Japanese" or a "completed Mexican" can never obtain. That is absolutely false. With God there is no Greek nor Jew. He has made the two into one new person:

> 11 Therefore remember, that formerly you, the Gentiles in the flesh, who are called "Uncircumcision" by the so-called "Circumcision," which is performed in the flesh by human hands—
> 12 remember that you were at that time separate from Christ, excluded from the commonwealth of Israel, and strangers to the covenants of promise, having no hope and without God in the world.
> 13 But now in Christ Jesus you who formerly were far off have been brought near by the blood of Christ.
> 14 For He Himself is our peace, who made both groups into one, and broke down the barrier of the dividing wall,
> 15 by abolishing in His flesh the enmity, which is the Law of commandments contained in ordinances, that in Himself He might make the two into one new man, thus establishing peace,
> 16 and might reconcile them both in one body to God through the cross, by it having put to death the enmity.

WILL ALL OF ISRAEL BE SAVED?

17 AND HE CAME AND PREACHED PEACE TO YOU WHO WERE FAR AWAY, AND PEACE TO THOSE WHO WERE NEAR;

18 for through Him we both have our access in one Spirit to the Father.

19 So then you are no longer strangers and aliens, but you are fellow citizens with the saints, and are of God's household, . . .

—Ephesians 2

There are some who would try to pull apart this one new man that Christ created (which is composed of all those who believe in Him, whether Hebrew or Gentile) and split it back into two groups. That is an abomination before God. They are trying to undo what Jesus did. A completed Hebrew or a completed Jew does not have any better status than other believers. We are all complete in Christ and being complete in Him leaves absolutely nothing to be desired. Jesus Christ loves us all and treats us all equally.

Now with the understanding that we have gained from these chapters, how should this affect our lives?

14

CLAIM YOUR BIRTHRIGHT

In this concluding chapter, I would like to touch briefly on the highlights of the book and then look specifically at how to claim your birthright, an inheritance that is rightfully yours in Christ Jesus.

THE COVENANTS AND OLD TESTAMENT ISRAEL

We have seen that the Scriptures solidly teach that Jesus Christ completed and finished the Old Testament covenant (the Old Testament law or the old contract) and that the new covenant (the new contract) replaced it. This new contract was sealed and validated by His precious blood.

> 14 how much more will the blood of Christ, who through the eternal Spirit offered Himself without blemish to God, cleanse your conscience from dead works to serve the living God?
> 15 And for this reason He is the mediator of a new covenant, in order that since a death has taken place for the redemption of the transgressions that were committed under the first covenant, those who had been called may receive the promise of the eternal inheritance.

16 For where a covenant is, there must of necessity be the death of the one who made it.

17 For a covenant is valid only when men are dead, for it is never in force while the one who made it lives.

18 Therefore even the first covenant was not inaugurated without blood.

—Hebrews 9

We saw that the first covenant was a conditional one, and that one of the conditions required for it to apply to a man was that he be circumcised. We then saw, in in the New Testament, that the early disciples did not require new believers to be circumcised, because they realized that they were no longer under the old covenant.

One of the ways we know that the old covenant is finished, and that only the new covenant is valid, is from the words of Jesus Himself:

6 Jesus said to him, "I am the way, and the truth, and the life; no one comes to the Father, but through Me. . . ."

—John 14

Jesus does not leave any exceptions here. He said that the only way to come to God is through Him, through the new covenant. John also tells us the same truth very plainly when he shares the fact that if anyone denies Jesus as the Son of God, he does not have the Father:

23 Whoever denies the Son does not have the Father; the one who confesses the Son has the Father also.

—1 John 2

It doesn't matter if you are trying to reach Father God through Judaism, the Muslim faith or any other religion—you can never make it that way. The *only way* to reach God today is through Jesus Christ, *period*.

One very interesting and important thing that we discovered is that Old Testament Israel was a spiritual entity and not a physical entity. There were many who came out of Egypt who were not biologically from Abraham. Ruth and Rahab, the harlot from Jericho, were included in Israel, and they were not biologically from Abraham. There were many wives who came back from the Babylonian captivity, who were not genealogically from Abraham, but were part of Israel.

In fact, even today there are "Jews," who worship in synagogues, who are from many different races. There is an entire wing in the Great Synagogue in Jerusalem that is dedicated to the Japanese Jews, and, of course, there are black Jews from Africa, and so forth. So even today, being a Jew is not based on genealogy, even by Jews. Jews are considered to be those who embrace Judaism as their religion, or perhaps those raised in a "Jewish" culture.

We saw that in the Old Testament, there were many Hebrews excluded from the congregation of Israel. Since you cannot change a person's genealogy, to exclude them from Israel proves that Israel was a spiritual entity, even in the Old Testament. In New Testament times, even Jesus Himself told the scribes and the Pharisees (who were "Hebrews") that they were going to hell and would not see the kingdom of God (Matthew 23:13,14,33). He also told some Hebrews that they were not the children of Abraham:

> **39** They answered and said unto him, Abraham is our father. Jesus saith unto them, If ye were Abraham's children, ye would do the works of Abraham.
> —John 8, KJV

If the Hebrews and Jews who live in the State of Israel are not the Israel of God, then who is? In looking further, we saw that the Bible teaches that all believers in Jesus Christ, regardless of race or nationality, are a part of the Israel of God today. They are Abraham's seed:

> **29 And if you belong to Christ, then you are Abraham's offspring, heirs according to promise.**
> —Galatians 3

We also saw that even if a person could trace his lineage right back to Abraham, if he does not know Jesus Christ as his personal Savior, he is not part of God's Israel today. The church—that is, regenerated followers of Jesus Christ—is Israel today. The whole house of Israel is thus comprised of all the Old Testament saints who believed God for righteousness and all the New Testament believers in Jesus Christ.

UNFULFILLED PROMISES AND PROPHECIES

The question that naturally arises is this: "Who are the inheritors of the promises made to Abraham, Isaac and Jacob?" As we saw in Galatians 3:29, all those who belong to Christ are Abraham's seed and heirs to the promises made to Abraham. Those promises belong to the Israel of God, which today is equated to believers in Jesus Christ.

Those promises include a piece of land that goes from the Euphrates all the way down to the river of Egypt. We will possess that land as Christians, when we go there with Jesus Christ and His foot touches down on the Mount of Olives. God also promises Abraham and his seed that He will bless those who bless them and curse those who curse them. That does not apply to the Hebrews over in the State of Israel or the Hebrews living in any other nation. This is a promise that applies to the church today, and we need to claim that promise as part of our birthright.

One of the major keys to understanding unfulfilled prophecies is to realize that the church today *is*

Israel. Thus, the prophecies in Ezekiel 36 and 37 concerning the return of Israel to its land can only be properly understood when you see that Israel means the believers in Jesus Christ who are caught up alive with the resurrected Christians and resurrected Old Testament saints, gathered together from all nations by our Commander in Chief at the rapture, and taken to that land. The "dry bones" can only be correctly understood as describing the rapture.

The Gog and Magog war, as described in Ezekiel 38 and 39, seems to be a major cause of confusion for many Christian teachers and leaders, because they say that it is the next major event to occur in prophecy. The Bible clearly tells us that this war is not going to happen any time soon, but it will happen *after the millennium.* Those who are looking for Russia to come down and invade Israel any day are wrong. That will not be the "Gog and Magog" spoken of in Ezekiel 38 and 39 and Revelation 20. The armies that will invade Israel before the millennium will not be destroyed by fire.

Those armies will come, but they are going to make Jerusalem desolate, just as Jesus said. When those armies come, from whatever source (possibly the Arab nations and possibly the Soviet Union) and they make Jerusalem desolate, many Christians' faith will be shaken, because they do not understand who Israel is. They are expecting an invasion of the State of Israel to be the Gog and Magog battle, and they expect the State of Israel to win. But, according to the Bible, the State of Israel will lose and Jerusalem is going to become uninhabited for approximately three and a half years.

We need to realize that any other unfulfilled prophecy concerning Israel is going to be fulfilled by the church.

BIOLOGICAL DESCENDANTS OF ABRAHAM

One of the things that we discussed in this book was that the ten lost tribes most likely migrated to Europe, including Britain, and possibly over America.

This is where the "British-Israelism" teaching came from. However, I believe that proponents of this teaching used some good facts but came to some erroneous conclusions. Ultimately, it does not matter whether or not the people in Europe or America are biologically descended from some of the ten lost tribes; that does not make them part of Israel. The only thing that makes one part of Israel today is receiving Jesus Christ as one's Savior and Master.

We also looked at some evidence that possibly some of the Jews living in the State of Israel today are not descendants from Abraham. Abraham, forefather of Jacob and the twelve tribes of Israel, was a descendant of Shem, one of Noah's three sons. But the "Ashkenazic Jews" of today came down through another son of Noah, Japheth. There is significant historical question as to whether or not this group is genealogically from Abraham. Here again, my conclusion is the same: it does not matter if they are or they are not. Lineage does not make them part of Israel. The only thing that will exclude a person from Israel is not having received Jesus Christ as his Savior.

In Old Testament days, if you met a Jew, he would rattle off his genealogy back to Abraham. But Paul, a Jew, urged Timothy not to pay any attention to genealogies:

> **3** As I urged you upon my departure for Macedonia, remain on at Ephesus, in order that you may instruct certain men not to teach strange doctrines,
> **4** nor to pay attention to myths and endless genealogies, which give rise to mere speculation rather than furthering the administration of God which is by faith.
> —1 Timothy 1

Paul was saying that genealogies do not matter. They are of no importance. He was saying that it did not matter whether or not one's ancestral line went back to Abraham. Forget genealogies, forget ancestry, and concentrate on Jesus. Your lineage will not—in fact, cannot—make you part of God's one and only Israel.

CLAIM YOUR BIRTHRIGHT!

Wake up, church! You *alone* are Israel today. You *alone* are the inheritors of the promises made to Abraham, Isaac and Jacob. You are the eventual inheritors of the piece of real estate on the shores of the Mediterranean. You alone inherit the protection of God's promise to Abraham to bless those who bless you and curse those who curse you. Church, you alone have as your birthright these blessings, and so many more that space does not allow us to delve into in this book. This is your birthright, your inheritance. Today you alone are God's chosen people. As Jesus said:

> 16 Ye have not chosen me, but I have chosen you. . . .
> —John 15, KJV

Now, you can take this birthright and give it away, as Esau did, by the words of your mouth. If you make the following statements, that is essentially what you are doing:

"The Israelis are God's chosen people today."
"God will bless us, if we bless the State of Israel."

At least Esau received a bowl of lentil stew for his birthright! You could be giving yours away and getting absolutely nothing in return.

Many Christians today will put their "rubber stamp of approval" on anything that the State of Israel does. No matter what type of atrocities they might commit, so many Christians would shake in their boots at the thought of condemning them for something, for fear that they might come under the curse of God.

Much of what the State of Israel does *is* good, but some of it is bad. They are a nation run by human beings who make mistakes. They are a nation of human beings who do some things contrary to the will of God. Should we applaud them for this? *No.* The church must stop rubber stamping everything that the State of Israel does and marking it *"Good."* We must start looking at them through spiritual eyes and using spiritual discernment. We should applaud what they do that is good and not approve what they do that is bad.

Having the wrong belief about who Israel is can lead one to some very serious errors. For example, there are some Christian organizations dedicated to getting the Jews out of the U.S.S.R. They are raising funds for the effort and establishing places for emigrants to stay when they exit the Soviet Union. This is a good work, and I certainly have nothing against it. However, I must ask, "Where are the Christian organizations whose emphasis is to get the persecuted *Christians* out of the U.S.S.R.?" We have many books containing accounts of Christians who want to leave and have not been able to. There were the seven Pentecostals who lived in the basement of the U.S. Embassy for many, many months, trying to get out of the Soviet Union to escape the persecution. There are at least as many born-again believers in Jesus Christ who are being persecuted in the Soviet Union as there are Jews.

I believe it is a shame to put so much effort into helping those who have rejected our Lord and Savior, Jesus Christ, while seeming to ignore the plight of those who have been bold enough to receive Jesus Christ as their Savior, who are being persecuted for that faith. A wrong theology about Israel can cause one to place the emphasis in the wrong place.

I challenge the church to put at least as much emphasis, if not more, on helping the persecuted Christians get out of the U.S.S.R. as they do in helping the Jews get out. The church should encourage the

President not just to stand up for freedom for the Jews, in talks with the Soviets, but at least to stand up equally for the persecuted Christians.

As I have stated before, we should be thankful for the State of Israel. They are our only ally in the Mideast. They have developed military technology that we need, and I am for supporting the State of Israel more than we do. But they are not the Israel of God. They are not *Israel* in any sense, except in name only. All through the Old Testament and right up to today, the Israel of God has always been a spiritual entity comprised of all those who believe in God and obey Him. Today the only way one can have eternal life with God is by accepting His Son, Jesus Christ.

Perhaps you are a Christian who has inadvertently been giving away your birthright, and you have now decided that you want to claim it. In order to claim what is rightfully yours as an offspring and seed of Abraham, you might want to pray a prayer that goes something like this:

> *"Father God, I come to You through the only way possible today—through Jesus Christ, your only begotten Son. I acknowledge Him as Your Son and I ask you to wipe away my sins by His blood, something that the blood of bulls and goats cannot do. I commit my life to follow Jesus as my Lord and Master.*
>
> *"Thank You, Father, that I am of the seed of Abraham, the offspring of Abraham, and I am a child of promise just as much as Isaac. Thank You that I am part of Your one and only Israel. Thank You that I am an Israelite. Thank you for choosing me and that I am now a part of Your chosen people. Right now I claim back my birthright that I may have given away. I claim that all of the promises made to Abraham flow through to me as my inheritance. I claim my portion of the land of promise, where I will*

rule and reign with Jesus Christ for a thousand years, and I claim Your promise that those who bless me will be blessed and those who curse me will be cursed. I claim all the other promises made to our forefathers, and I gladly join with the portion of Israel that existed in the Old Testament.

"I further thank You, Father God, that I am a joint heir with Jesus Christ of everything in the universe. Thank You for the power that He gives me through the Holy Spirit, who guides me, teaches me and gives me the gifts that He chooses. Father in heaven, I recognize that I deserve hell and everything bad. Thank You for Your mercy that washed away that penalty and set me in a neutral condition. Yet I rejoice even more in your GRACE that allows me to be one of Your chosen people, an inheritor of the promises made to Abraham, and a joint heir with your only begotten Son, Jesus Christ. How rich is Your grace, how deep is Your love, and how wonderful is Your mercy!

"I pray this prayer, claiming the full portion of my birthright and the full portion of my inheritance through Jesus Christ my Lord and Savior. Amen."

Praise God! You now have roots, you now have an inheritance. You have now claimed your birthright. You, along with every other believer in Jesus Christ, are a vital part of Israel.

Jesus is so good to us! Praise His holy name. To Him be all power and glory and honor forever.

In the name of Jesus, I say to His church:

Wake up, Church! You alone are Israel.
Claim your birthright.
Jesus loves you and wants you to have what is rightfully yours.

I love the Hebrews and Jews and those of other religions, and I pray earnestly that they might become part of Israel by receiving Jesus Christ as their personal Savior and Master.

I love all Christians and praise God for you, even if you disagree with me on this or other issues. Remember, our fellowship is around Jesus Christ, not around some doctrine or teaching. I earnestly pray that each individual Christian will wake up and realize that he or she is part of Israel, and claim his birthright.

I do pray that this book may bless and help all who read it and that it may glorify Jesus Christ.

Appendix A

HOW TO BECOME A CHRISTIAN

If you are reading this, I am assuming that you are not sure that you have received Jesus Christ as your personal Savior. Not only is it possible to know this for sure, but God wants you to know.

> 11 And the witness is this, that God has given us eternal life, and this life is in His Son.
> 12 He who has the Son has the life; he who does not have the Son does not have the life.
> 13 These things I have written to you who believe in the name of the Son of God, in order that you may know that you have eternal life.
> —1 John 5

These things are written to us who believe in the name of the Son of God, so that we can know that we have eternal life. It is not a "guess so," or "hope so" or "maybe so" situation. It is so that we can know for certain that we have eternal life. If you do not have this confidence, please read on.

In order to get the point of knowing that we have eternal life, we first need to review some basic principles. It is important to note that all things that God created (the stars, trees, animals, and so on) are doing exactly what they were created to do, except man. Isaiah 43 indicates why God created us:

> 7 "... Everyone who is called by My name,
> And whom I have created for My glory,
> Whom I have formed even whom I have made."
> —Isaiah 43

This says that humans were created to glorify God. I am sure that neither you nor I have glorified God all of our lives in everything that we have done. This gives us our first clue as to what "sin" is. We find more about it in Romans:

> 23 for all have sinned and fall short of the glory of God, ...
> —Romans 3

This says that we have all sinned and we all fall short of the purpose for which we were created—to glorify God. I have an even simpler definition of sin. I believe that sin is "living independent of God." A young person out of high school can choose which college to attend. If he makes this decision apart from God, it is "sin." This was the basic problem in the garden of Eden. Satan tempted Eve to eat the fruit of the tree of "the knowledge of good and evil." He said that if she would do this, she would know good from evil and would be wise like God. This would mean that she could make her own decisions and would not have to rely on God's wisdom and guidance. Since you and I fit in the category of living independent of God and not glorifying Him in everything we do, we need to look at what the results of this sin are.

First let me ask you what "wages" are. After thinking about it, because you probably receive wages from your job, you will probably come up with a definition something like "wages are what you get paid for what you do." That is a good answer. Now let's see what the Bible has to say concerning this:

23 For the wages of sin is death, but the free gift of God is eternal life in Christ Jesus our Lord.
—Romans 6

Here we see that the wages of sin is death—spiritual, eternal death. Death is what we get paid for the sin that we do. Yet this passage also gives us the other side of the coin: that is, that through Jesus Christ we can freely have eternal life, instead of eternal death. Isn't that wonderful!

But let's return for a moment to this death penalty that the people without Christ have hanging over their heads, because of the sin that they live in. In the Old Testament, God made a rule: "The soul who sins will die" (Ezekiel 18:4). If we were able to live a perfect, sinless life, we could make it to heaven on our own. If we live anything less than a perfect life, according to God's rule, we will not make it to heaven, but instead will be sentenced to death. All through the Bible, we find no one living a good enough life to make it to heaven.

This brings us to the place where Jesus Christ fits into this whole picture. His place was beautifully illustrated to me when I was considering receiving Christ as my Savior, by a story about a judge in a small town.

In this small town, the newspapermen were against the judge and wanted to get him out of office. A case was coming up before the judge concerning a vagrant—a drunken bum—who happened to have been a fraternity brother of the judge when they were at college. The newspapermen thought that this was their chance. If the judge let the vagrant off easy, the headlines would read, "Judge Shows Favoritism to Old Fraternity Brother." If the judge gave the vagrant the maximum penalty, the headlines would read, "Hardhearted Judge Shows No Mercy to Old Fraternity Brother." Either way they had him. The judge heard the case and gave the vagrant the maximum penalty of thirty days or $300 fine.

The judge then stood up, took off his robe, laid it down on his chair, walked down in front of the bench and put his arm around the shoulders of his old fraternity brother. He told him that as judge, in order to uphold the law, he had to give him the maximum penalty, because he was guilty. But because he cared about him, he wanted to pay the fine for him. So the judge took out his wallet and handed his old fraternity brother $300.

For God to be "just," He has to uphold the law that says "the soul who sins will die." On the other hand, because He loves us, He wants to pay that death penalty for us. I cannot pay the death penalty for you, because I have a death penalty of my own that I have to worry about, since I, too, have sinned. If I were sinless, I could die in your place. I guess God could have sent down millions of sinless beings to die for us. But what God chose to do was to send down one Person, who was equal in value, in God's eyes, to all of the people who will ever live, and yet who would remain sinless. Jesus Christ died physically and spiritually in order to pay the death penalty for you and me. The blood of Christ washes away all of our sins, and with it the death penalty that resulted from our sin.

The judge's old fraternity brother could have taken the $300 and said, "Thank you," or he could have told the judge to keep his money and that he would do it on his own. Similarly, each person can thank God for allowing Christ to die in his place and receive Christ as his own Savior, or he can tell God to keep His payment and that he will make it on his own. What you do with that question determines where you will spend eternity.

Referring to Christ, the book of John says this:

HOW TO BECOME A CHRISTIAN

12 But as many as received Him, to them He gave the right to become children of God, even to those who believe in His name, . . .
—John 1

16 "For God so loved the world, that He gave His only begotten Son, that whoever believes in Him should not perish but have eternal life. . . ."
—John 3

Here we see that if we believe in Christ we won't perish, but we will have everlasting life and the right to become children of God. Right now you can tell God that you believe in Christ as the Son of God, that you are sorry for your sins and that you want to turn from them. You can tell Him that you want to accept Christ's payment for your sins, and yield your life to be controlled by Christ and the Holy Spirit. (You must accept Christ as your Savior *and your Master.*)

If you pray such a prayer, Christ will come and dwell within your heart and you will know for sure that you have eternal life.

If you have any questions about what you have just read, I would encourage you to go to someone that you know, who really knows Jesus Christ as his Savior, and ask him for help and guidance. After you receive Christ, I would encourage you to become a part of a group of believers in Christ who study the Scriptures together, worship God together and have a real love relationship with each other. This group (body of believers) can help nurture you and build you up in your new faith in Jesus Christ.

If you have received Christ as a result of reading these pages, I would love to hear from you. My address is at the end of this book.

Welcome to the family of God.

James McKeever

Appendix B

THE STAR OF DAVID AND THE MENORAH

I have mixed emotions about including this appendix concerning the star of David. It could brand me as some type of a nut and discredit this entire book, and yet I feel compelled to include it for your sake.

The Bible warns us not to be involved with the occult and not to use or wear occultic symbols. A book that I ran across recently investigated the history of the star of David and concluded that David never saw nor used the six-pointed star. Rather, it said that it first came into use in the State of Israel with Solomon, when he stopped following God and began to follow the pagan and occultic gods of his foreign wives. The author, O.J. Graham, feels that the "star of David" was an occult symbol and not one given by God to the Jewish people. I do not know whether or not this is true, but I thought that I should at least let you read his research.

The menorah, the candlestick with seven lamps (or candles) shown on the next page, was the national symbol of Israel all through the Old Testament, and it still is even today. In fact, outside of the Knesset is a giant menorah that Britain gave to the newly-formed State of Israel.

254 APPENDIX B

Figure B.1

Since I am a strong supporter of the State of Israel, many years ago I bought a gold "star of David" with a cross on it, which hung on a chain. I wore it around my neck for a few weeks to give public evidence of my support for the State of Israel. Even though my support for the nation did not wane at all, I began to feel uneasy in my spirit about wearing the symbol, and I discarded it. There are many Christian believers wearing a similar symbol, either in a pin or on a necklace, who supposedly do so to show their support of the Israel of God, which in their minds is the State of Israel. According to O.J. Graham, it is possible that these Christians are wearing an occultic symbol unknowingly.

If this is of any concern or interest to you, you might want to read the excerpts from this book, *The Six-Pointed Star*, contained in this appendix. If you are really interested in the subject, you could get the book from the publisher (New Puritan Library, 91 Lytle Road, Fletcher, NC 28732). The remainder of this appendix is excerpts taken from this book by O.J.

THE STAR OF DAVID AND THE MENORAH 255

Graham, wherein he investigates the origin of the Star of David:

FACT:
"The Star of David is not of Jewish origin—and the ancient Israelites never used it as their religious symbol" (M. Hirsch Goldberg, *The Jewish Connection*).

M. Hirsch Goldberg goes on to say,

"Perhaps most ironic, the very sign of the Jew in today's world—the six-pointed Star of David—is not really the historic symbol of Jewry, nor was it used as a religious sign by the Israelites. It became the emblem of the Jewish people in 1897, when the Zionist conference convened by Theodor Herzl chose it as the insignia of their movement. But even though each of the Twelve Tribes in the Land of Israel had its own symbol, *not one tribe* [author's italics] used the Star of David. . . ."

"Construction workers apparently were digging in Ramle which is a town near Tel Aviv in Israel and they found the six-pointed star imbedded into a mosaic floor which was about 1,200 years old. However, it was established that the floor was Moslem, not Jewish."

The date of that find would have been around A.D. 776. The *Universal Jewish Encyclopedia* describes the six-pointed star as "two equilateral triangles that are interlaced so as to form a hexagonal star, every point of which touches a circle of the same radius as each one of their six sides." This description is important, as we shall see in chapter four when we go into the occult origins of this symbol.

The *Universal Jewish Encyclopedia* declares that the six-pointed star is of ancient origin, according to the Rosicrucians, and that it was known to the ancient Egyptians, Hindus, Chinese and Peruvians.

Pause a minute and note the words "ancient Egyptians." Where were the children of Israel taken from by

Moses? Out of Egypt. It is intriguing here to mention that in the book of Acts, reference is made to a certain star.

> *"Yea, ye took up the tabernacle of Moloch and the star of your god Remphan, figures which ye made to worship . . ."* (Acts 7:43).

This star was taken along through the wilderness by some of the Hebrew children. Where is this confirmed in the Old Testament? In the book of Amos. The original Hebrew reads:

> *"Did ye bring unto Me sacrifices and offerings in the wilderness forty years, O house of Israel? So shall ye take up Siccuth your king and Chiun your images, the STAR of your god, which ye made to yourselves. Therefore will I cause you to go into captivity beyond Damascus, saith He, whose name is the Lord God of hosts"* (Amos 5:25-26).

We shall deal with the names Remphan and Chiun in chapter four. However, this serves to confirm that there was a particular star known to the ancient Egyptians and mentioned during the exodus of the Hebrew children under Moses.

The *Universal Jewish Encyclopedia* lists the following mentions of the six-pointed star:

"on an Arabic amulet;
in Byzantine magic texts;
in medieval books of magic as a pentagraph;
in German folklore;
in the relics of the Templars: as the 'stone of the wise';
in alchemy: as the stone-mason's sign (but in a somewhat different form);
in the coat of arms of the Freemasons: as the 'Order of the Seal of Solomon,' in Abyssiania [sic] (from 1874 on);
in old town hall of Vienna;

on or in Churches at Aquileia, Brandenburg, Stendal, Hanover, Luneburg and Bad Gastein;

in South Germany it was put on the signboards of taverns by the Pythagoreans to tell their comrades they had found hospitality at that tavern while on a begging tour."

This encyclopedia states that it was from the 16th century on, during the time of the Cabalist, Isaac Luria, that the symbol began to be used by Jewish people. Many times it was seen next to the menorah which, until the 16th century, had been accepted as the "Shield of David." After this, however, the six-pointed star began replacing the menorah on synagogues and on Jewish religious articles.

Quotes the *Universal Jewish Encyclopedia:*

"It is only in Jewish sources that the interlaced triangles are called 'Shield of David,' as non-Jewish sources call the symbol the 'Seal of Solomon.'"

The *Jewish Encyclopedia* attests to the fact that Isaac Luria was indeed a Cabalist (1533-72) and claimed that "one man could be master of the terrestrial world." "The writing of amulets, conjuration of devils, mystic jugglery with numbers and letters increased as the influence of this school spread." In the 16th century in Italy, a school was founded and this source states that the Hasidim took up Luria's teachings and made them into a system. There was opposition by some, including Mordecai Corcos, but the encyclopedia reports that even Corcos's work against it was never printed. . . .

Star of which David?

. . . David became king of Israel and was the greatest king that Israel ever had.

Solomon was his son. But unlike Solomon, David was never an idolater. He was loyal to the Lord in his testimony and witness. David's great sin was with Bathsheba, and the subsequent murder of her husband, Uriah the Hittite, to cover his adulterous relationship (II Samuel 11-12). The Scriptures bear proof of his later penitence in Psalm 51.

Why then is the six-pointed star called the Star or Shield of David? Is this reference to David, king of Israel, or some other David?

If the reference is to King David, is this because he was Solomon's father? We have definite evidence that this six-pointed star or hexagram was called the Seal of Solomon after Solomon went into idolatry as told in I Kings 11:6-10.

Why would this involve King David? David was not alive when Solomon took this star upon himself. There is no record whatsoever that David, king of Israel, had any connection with this star, nor with what it represents.

Who, then, is this reference made to?

Arthur Koestler wrote that the six-pointed star is a magical emblem which dates back only to the 12th century A.D. At that time, an Ashkenazic Jew, named Menahem ben Duji, tried to convince his people he was the Messiah. He changed his name to David al-Roy, amassed some troops in Khazaria and Kurdistan, and was assassinated on his way to "liberate" Palestine. From the 13th century on, the six-pointed star was attributed to him and first appeared on a Jewish flag in Prague in 1527.

The *Encyclopaedia Britannica* identifies the six-pointed star as a "magical sign." Although it does not have the information on David al-Roy, the *Britannica* says: "Practical [magic] cabala popularized the use of the Magen David as a protection against evil spirits."

The *Universal Jewish Encyclopedia* mentions another David in Vol XII. It tells of a third-century C.E. (A.D.) tombstone of one Leon ben David on the synagogue at Tell (Capernaum) in Galilee. The encyclopedia discloses that according to the teachings of the Rosicrucians, this symbol was known to the ancient Egyptians, Hindus,

Chinese and Peruvians. This star was also found on a Hebrew seal discovered in Sidon dated seventh century B.C.E. (B.C.) . . .

What Solomon left behind was not only the division of the twelve tribes of Israel, but evidence of his idolatry. His foreign wives led him into the worship of the goddess Astoreth, otherwise called Astarte (meaning star). The six-pointed star or hexagram, which came to be called the "seal of Solomon" when King Solomon took it upon himself, was the chief article of this pagan worship.

The Seal of Solomon and Occultism

"And Solomon did evil in the sight of the Lord, and went not fully after the Lord as did David his father. Then did Solomon build an high place for Chemosh, the abomination of Moab, in the hill that is before Jerusalem, and for Molech, the abomination of the children of Ammon. And likewise did he for all his strange wives, which burnt incense and sacrificed unto their gods. And the Lord was angry with Solomon, because his heart was turned from the Lord God of Israel who had appeared unto him twice and had commanded him concerning this thing, that he should not go after other gods; but he kept not that which the Lord commanded" (I Kings 11:6-10).

This was the consequence of his disobedience:

"Wherefore the Lord said unto Solomon, Forasmuch as this is done of thee, and thou hast not kept my covenant and my statutes, which I have commanded thee, I will surely rend the kingdom from thee, and will give it to thy servant. Notwithstanding in thy days I will not do it for David thy father's sake; but I will rend it out of the hand of thy son. Howbeit I will not rend away all the kingdom; but will give one tribe to thy son for David my servant's sake; and for Jerusalem's sake which I have chosen" (I Kings 11:11-13).

And God kept His word. Solomon was the last king of united Israel. . . .

King Solomon built an altar for Ashteroth, worshiped her, and also practiced Moloch rituals. It was at this time that the hexagram or six-pointed star came to be called the "Seal of Solomon."

How do the dictionaries define "hexagram"?

> "The root word hex is defined as (1) an evil spell, (2) a witch (v.t., to bewitch)" (*Funk & Wagnall's Dictionary*).

> "Hex (heks) n. Something supposed to bring bad luck; v.t. to cause to have bad luck; hexa—combining form meaning six" (*Webster's New World Dictionary*).

The *Encyclopaedia Judaica* has this to say:

> "It is not clear in which period the hexagram was engraved on the seal of Solomon mentioned in the Talmud (Git 68a) as a sign of his dominion over the demons, instead of the name of God which originally appeared on his ring."

It goes on to say that the Seal of Solomon or hexagram was used widely in Arabic magic. However, use of the six-pointed star was restricted within Jewish groups.

The *Jewish 44 Almanac* in its article, "Metamorphoses of a Tree: 10 Jewish Symbols and Their Meanings," states that it is only since the tenth through the fourteenth centuries that the Seal of Solomon began appearing in Jewish magical texts. The first use was in the mystical work of Sefer ha-Gevul (Book of Boundary), authored by the grandson of the Spanish Jewish mystic, Nahmanides.

This source also reports that alchemists used the symbol to depict the union of fire and water and in this context, after 1724, it began to be called the "Shield of David."

THE STAR OF DAVID AND THE MENORAH 261

The above citation is also from the Cabala and this is confirmed by the *Jewish Encyclopedia* under the section "Cabala."

Indeed, Solomon left his name on the six-pointed star as proof of his involvement with Ashteroth and Moloch. . . .

The next reference is the book *Man, Myth and Magic: An Illustrated Encyclopedia of the Supernatural.* This work admits that the six-pointed star "contains occult power."

In the book *An Illustrated Encyclopedia of Traditional Symbols,* by J.C. Cooper, it is called the hexagram and affiliation is made with the Chinese occult symbol of ying and yang.

Next source? *Symbols Around Us* by Sven Tito Achen. Here the author calls it the hexagram and talks about it being made the symbol of Zionism. They mention that it is called the Seal of Solomon by the Muslims and that alchemists made use of it. It is also mentioned that during the Nazi regime, the Jews were forced to wear it as a "badge of shame."

In the book *The History and Practice of Magic, Vol. II,* it is called the Talisman of Saturn. There is a diagram of the six-pointed star in the reverse; the obverse contains a pentagram, or five-pointed star.

In the book titled *A Witch's Grimoire of Ancient Omens, Portents, Talismans, Amulets and Charms,* by Gavin & Yvonne Frost, the six-pointed star is featured as well and bears support of its occultism. . . .

The six-pointed star, as we have seen, is an occult symbol. *Webster* defines *occultism* as "hidden, secret, mysterious, from the Latin word *occulere,* to conceal . . . of the mystic arts such as magic, astrology, etc."

Many believers are untaught about the dangers of the occult. They do not realize they must stop wearing jewelry with occult symbols and renounce all occult dabbling.

—pp. 12-37

262 APPENDIX B

This ends the quote from the book *The Six-Pointed Star*. As an added footnote, if a Christian wanted to wear some symbol to support either the State of Israel or God's Israel, I would suggest that he utilize the seven-branched lampstand, called the menorah, which was the symbol of Israel throughout the Old Testament. God told Moses to make it, and it is recorded that he did so:

31 "Then you shall make a lampstand of pure gold. The lampstand and its base and its shaft are to be made of hammered work; its cups, its bulbs, and its flowers shall be of one piece with it.

32 "And six branches shall go out from its sides; three branches of the lampstand from its one side, and three branches of the lampstand from its other side.

33 "Three cups shall be shaped like almond blossoms in the one branch, a bulb and a flower, and three cups shaped like almond blossoms in the other branch, a bulb and a flower—so for six branches going out from the lampstand;

34 and in the lampstand four cups shaped like almond blossoms, its bulbs and its flowers.

35 "And a bulb shall be under the first pair of branches coming out of it, and a bulb under the second pair of branches coming out of it, and a bulb under the third pair of branches coming out of it, for the six branches coming out of the lampstand.

36 "Their bulbs and their branches shall be of one piece with it; all of it shall be one piece of hammered work of pure gold.

37 "Then you shall make its lamps seven in number; and they shall mount its lamps so as to shed light on the space in front of it.

38 "And its snuffers and their trays shall be of pure gold.

39 "It shall be made from a talent of pure gold, with all these utensils.

40 "And see that you make them after the pattern for them, which was shown to you on the mountain. . . ."
—Exodus 25

We have a menorah in our home, which we proudly display. When I see it, it reminds me that I am part of Israel today—I am one of God's chosen people. I think it is a wonderful symbol to remind Christians of their glorious birthright, along with the Old Testament saints, who are also part of Israel.

Appendix C

MODERN JUDAISM IS VERY DIFFERENT FROM BIBLICAL JUDAISM

When we think of the Jews worshiping in the synagogue on Saturday, we assume that their Judaism is the Judaism of the Old Testament. This is far from the case. They are so different that in some ways they do not even deserve to be compared with each other.

In no way is this an attempt to put down Judaism or to cast any disparaging light on Jewish leaders. It is simply an attempt to factually and, hopefully, objectively look at the evolution of Judaism through the centuries to see the significant changes that have occurred.

In fact, the Judaism that was practiced during the time of Jesus Christ was far, far different from the Judaism practiced during King David's time. I had often wondered why Jesus Christ condemned so harshly the Jewish religious leaders, the Pharisees. After studying what had happened to Judaism between King David's time and the time of Jesus Christ, I can begin to see why He did so.

According to the Pharisees, it was okay to commit *indirect* murder: for example, tying your neighbor up and letting him starve to death or luring him into a tight room and letting him die of suffocation. In neither of these cases did a person murder him directly. This is one of the reasons that the Jewish religious leaders wanted the Romans to kill Jesus—it was indirect and, therefore, they were not guilty. The Pharisees endorsed the taking of three-year-old brides, as well as child sex with girls three years and one day, and older. According to the Pharisees, sex between a man and another man was prohibited, but a boy did not become a man until he was a certain age and, thus, sex with a younger boy was okay, because he was not a man. They said it was not adultery if one slept with the wife of a minor. To the Pharisees, their written law (which, in the time of Christ, was called the *"Tradition of the Elders"* and today is called the *"Talmud"* had higher authority than the Bible. The *Torah* is the first five books of the Bible, while the *Talmud* is a piece of literature produced solely by man. However, on page 637 of *The Universal Jewish Encyclopedia* we read this:

> *"Thus the ultimate authority for orthodoxy is the Babylonian Talmud. The Bible itself ranks second to it in reality, if not in theory."*

So, by the time of Christ, the Pharisees' written regulations allowed them to do essentially what they wanted to do, and this took precedence over God's laws and God's commands. Here are some of the things that Jesus had to say about the Pharisees and to them:

> **20** "For I say to you, that unless your righteousness surpasses that of the scribes and Pharisees, you shall not enter the kingdom of heaven. . . .
> —Matthew 5

> **11** "How is it that you do not understand that I did not speak to you concerning bread? But beware of the leaven of the Pharisees and Sadducees."
> **12** Then they understood that He did not say to beware of the leaven of bread, but of the teaching of the Pharisees and Sadducees.
> —Matthew 16

13 "But woe to you, scribes and Pharisees, hypocrites, because you shut off the kingdom of heaven from men; for you do not enter in yourselves, nor do you allow those who are entering to go in.

14 ["Woe to you, scribes and Pharisees, hypocrites, because you devour widows' houses, even while for a pretense you make long prayers; therefore you shall receive greater condemnation.]

15 "Woe to you, scribes and Pharisees, hypocrites, because you travel about on sea and land to make one proselyte; and when he becomes one, you make him twice as much a son of hell as yourselves...."

—Matthew 23

25 "Woe to you, scribes and Pharisees, hypocrites! For you clean the outside of the cup and of the dish, but inside they are full of robbery and self-indulgence...."

—Matthew 23

27 "Woe to you, scribes and Pharisees, hypocrites! For you are like whitewashed tombs which on the outside appear beautiful, but inside they are full of dead men's bones and all uncleanness.

28 "Even so you too outwardly appear righteous to men, but inwardly you are full of hypocrisy and lawlessness...."

—Matthew 23

29 "Woe to you, scribes and Pharisees, hypocrites! For you build the tombs of the prophets and adorn the monuments of the righteous,

30 and say, 'If we had been living in the days of our fathers, we would not have been partners with them in shedding the blood of the prophets.'

31 "Consequently you bear witness against yourselves, that you are sons of those who murdered the prophets.

32 "Fill up then the measure of the guilt of your fathers.
33 "You serpents, you brood of vipers, how shall you escape the sentence of hell? . . ."
—Matthew 23

I believe the reason that Christ so harshly condemned the Pharisees (the rabbis) was that they had so distorted God's revelation, God's truth and God's requirements for a holy and righteous life. Let's turn back the pages of history and see how all of this distortion got started.

THE BABYLONIAN CAPTIVITY

While the Jews were living in the wilderness, their religion was centered around the tabernacle. After they moved into the promised land and Solomon built the temple, their religion was centered around the temple. When that was destroyed and the Jews were carried off into Babylonian captivity, their religion could no longer be centered around the temple. Thus, the Jewish leaders had to create a new form of religion by which they could exist in a foreign country without a temple and without sacrifices. I am sure that this was well-intended and necessary at first, but as they began to apply human reasoning, as opposed to God's revelation, man's basic sinful nature began to creep in and the writings began to change such that they would justify the acts of the Jewish leaders. Now this is a supposition on my part, but I believe their writings themselves will verify this.

You also need to realize that when the Jews returned from Babylon during the time of Ezra and Nehemiah to rebuild first the temple, and then Jerusalem, only a very small portion of the Jews returned. The vast majority of them remained in Babylon. After the 70 A.D. crushing of Jerusalem, many of the Jews who were there fled back to Babylon. It was there that the *Talmud* was actually completed, about five centuries

MODERN JUDAISM VS. BIBLICAL JUDAISM

after the time of Christ. Yet much of it existed during the time of Christ, either as the *"Traditions Of The Elders"* or oral tradition, which was later written down in the final document of the *Talmud*.

The *Talmud* itself is a group of 63 books which have 524 chapters. It is basically made up of the Pharisees' customs, opinions, laws and traditions. Even though it has been the mainstay of the Jewish religion for almost two thousand years, it has only recently been translated into English.

Today you can get a copy of the *Talmud*, in 18 volumes, for $375 (Press Ltd., 5 Essex St., New York, NY 10002). The Jews today prefer that Gentiles not read the *Talmud*, but read books about the *Talmud*, and I can see why.

As we begin to look at some of the writings in the *Talmud* itself, you need to realize that these are basically composed of writings of various Jewish rabbis, and it will frequently give the name of the Pharisee (rabbi) who is talking. We will look at the *Talmud* itself in just a moment, but first let's discuss the Pharisees who created the *Talmud*.

PHARISEES

In his book, *Israel Our Duty . . . Our Dilemma*, Theodore Pike had this to say about the early days of the Pharisees:

> Have you ever wondered where the Pharisees came from? They are unknown to the Old Testament, but are everywhere in the New. The history of the Pharisees begins like this:
> When King Nebuchadnezzar conquered Jerusalem in 597 B.C. and led the Jews across the desert to Babylon, the Jews suddenly found themselves without their cherished temple and all the rituals that went with it. In order to help the Jews adjust to life in a foreign environment, a class of teachers arose called the scribes or

"sopherim." The scribes created new laws and regulations which "built a fence around Judaism," making possible the continuance of the Jewish religion.

In the beginning this system may have been harmless enough, but it was soon abused, especially in Palestine during the several centuries before Christ. The interpretations of the scribes began to possess a unique legal authority in themselves—even about the Old Testament—which meant in contradiction to it. Thus (as *The Universal Jewish Encyclopedia* frankly admits), "A method of exegesis (Midrash) had to be evolved that would permit the interpretation of the Torah beyond its literal meaning." When the law of the Torah was unavoidably opposed to rabbinic interpretation, they "attempted whenever possible not to abolish it, but to introduce some legal fiction whereby the authority of the law was upheld and yet at the same time rendered null and void for all practical purposes."

Perverting God's Law

Now the manner whereby the scribes were able to "interpret" Scripture in contradiction to it and yet boldly profess their allegiance to every jot and tittle of it is very significant. It is unique to rabbinic hypocrisy.

The problem of the Pharisees was this: How could the Pharisees uphold the letter of the Mosaic law which they cherished and yet do exactly what they wanted? Their solution is one of the most amazing feats of evasion that could be imagined.

First, the Pharisees said that as an architect uses blueprints to construct a building, so God used the letters of the Hebrew alphabet to create the universe, including the "Torah" or first five books of the Old Testament. The Torah, the Pharisees believed, contained two distinct layers of interpretation: a literal surface interpretation, and a much more profound mystical interpretation hidden in the letters of the Hebrew alphabet. . . .

The Pharisees believed that only they had the key to understanding all the information hidden in the Hebrew alphabet and the Scriptures. They believed that their most eminent rabbis knew how to decipher the "true" meanings of Scripture because they had previously lived in Heaven and were only now recalling what God had told them. The Talmud relates how Moses ascended to Heaven and there beheld Rabbi Akiba (still unborn) expounding the Torah in a wondrous manner. (Menachoth 29b.) . . .

A Secret Tradition

By such occult methods and a good measure of sheer imagination, the rabbis claimed to be the possessors of a secret "oral" law which "Moses handed down to Joshua, Joshua to the Elders, the Elders to the Prophets, the Prophets to the Men of the Great Synod and the Men of the Great Synod to the Rabbis. . . . " (Aboth 1:1). Despite God's testimony that He had made a covenant with Israel because of the *written* law, the scribes claimed that "The Holy One, blessed be He, only made a covenant with Israel on account of the Oral Torah; as it is said, 'For after the tenor of these words I have made a covenant with thee and with Israel.'" (Gittin 60b.)

As custodians and interpreters of this secret tradition, the Pharisees invested themselves with tremendous authority. By majority decision, their most eminent rabbis could overturn anything Moses had said. If a particular rabbi was acclaimed by his fellow Pharisees as the greatest of that generation, then "he is, by virtue of his position as chief of the courts of justice, invested with the same authroity as Moses (Sifre, Deut. 153; R.H. 25ab). . . ."

A New Tradition

Like Korah, the Pharisees claimed that because "all the congregation are holy, every one of them, and the Lord is among them," those teachers chosen from among them innately possessed a divine unction. Thus the authority of the Pharisaic creed no longer resided in God or special prophets or even in the written Torah, but in those bearers of the "oral tradition" chosen from the "holy congregation." The ancient prophets, as well, inhibited the Pharisees and their followers no longer, for the Pharisaic Masters claimed direct succession to Moses and the same authority as Moses. From the day the Temple was destroyed by Nebuchadnezzar, the Talmud says, the prophetic gift was taken from the prophets and given to the Sages. At that time, Rabbinic tradition relates, many prophets arose in Israel, double the number of those who left Egypt, which would be about 1,200,000!

It is to these, the Jews and their leaders, "to the genius of its own people," *The Jewish Encyclopedia* tells us, "that we must turn for the secret of its (Judaism's) power. It has grown out of the soul of the Jewish people. . . . Whereas Buddhism centers in the Buddha and Christianity in the Christ, Judaism centers in no one personality." "In Judaism the center of gravity is the Jewish people."

From the onset of the domination of the religious life of Israel by the scribes and Pharisees, even unto the present, the religion of Israel no longer consisted of obedience to a revelation of the past. Judaism became the "progressive religious expression of the Jewish people." The rabbis, having acquired greater authority than the Bible, were persons of immeasurable power. One of the features of rabbinism, we are told, was "the development of new codes of laws based on and supplementary to the Torah." Let us turn then to a consideration of these new laws and the men who made them. . . .

—Big Sky Press, P.O. Box 203, Oregon City, OR 97045, pp. 15-19

THE TALMUD

Let's first see what the *Talmud* has to say about indirect murder. This was the thinking that ultimately allowed them to encourage the Romans to crucify Jesus Christ. In the *Talmud*, we find in *Sanhedrin 76b-77a* that "indirect" murder was permitted:

> Raba said: If one bound his neighbour and he died of starvation, he is not liable to execution. Raba also said: If he bound him in the sun, and he died, or in a place of intense cold and he died, he is liable; but if the sun was yet to appear, or the cold to make itself felt, he is not. Raba also said: If he bound him before a lion, he is not; before mosquitoes, [who stung him to death] he is. R. Ashi said: Even before mosquitoes, he is not liable, because these go and others come.
>
> It has been stated: If one overturned a vat upon a man [who then died of suffocation], or broke open a ceiling above him, Raba and R. Zera [differ]: One ruled that he is liable, the other that he is not. It can be proved that it was Raba who ruled that he is not liable, for he said: If one bound his neighbour and he dies of starvation, he is not liable. On the contrary, it can be shewn that R. Zera ruled that he is not liable. For R. Zera said: If one led his neighbour in to an alabaster chamber and lit a candle therein, so that he died [of the fumes], he is liable. Now, the reason is only that he lit a candle that he is liable; but had he not lit a candle [and the prisoner died of the natural heat and lack of air], he would be exempt!—I will tell you: In that case, without a candle, the heat would not have commenced [its effects] [77b] immediately [he placed him therein]; but in this case [of placing the upturned vat over him] the heat commences immediately.
>
> —*The Babylonian Talmud*
> The Soncino Press

274 APPENDIX C

I think from this first quote from the *Talmud* you can see two Pharisees (rabbis Raba and R. Zera) speaking and creating the laws by which the Pharisees and Judaism were governed.

The *Talmud* also says it is okay for a priest to marry and have sex with a girl who is three years and one day old. This is found in *Yebamoth 60b:*

> It was taught: R. Simeon b. Yohar stated: A proselyte who is under the age of three years and one day is permitted to marry a priest, for it is said, *But all the women children that have not known man by lying with him, keep alive for yourselves,* and Phinehas surely was with them. And the Rabbis—[These were kept alive] as bondmen and bondwomen. If so, a proselyte whose age is three years and one day should also be permitted! . . .
> R. Jacob b. Idt stated in the name of R. Joshua b. Levi: The *halachuh* is in agreement with R. Simeon b. Yohai. Said R. Zera to R. Jacob b. Idi: Did you hear this explicitly or did you learn it by a deduction? What [could be the] deduction?—As R. Joshua b. Levi related: There was a certain town in the Land of Israel the legitimacy of whose inhabitants was disputed, and Rabbi sent R. Romanos who conducted an enquiry and found in it the daughter of a proselyte who was under the age of three years and one day, and Rabbi declared her eligible to live with a priest.

In another place, the *Talmud* deals with intercourse with children and with someone who is asleep. This is what it says in *Kerithoth 11a-11b:*

> IF ONE IS AWAKE AND THE OTHER ASLEEP, THE LATTER IS EXEMPTED. Is indeed in our instance a sleeping person guilty? Said Rab Judah in the name of Rab: This is meant: In the case of all forbidden connections, if one is awake and the other asleep, the latter is exempted and the former guilty, in

our instance even the one awake is exempted, because they depend upon one another. . . .

"When I said it before Samuel he said: "Injured by a piece of wood" does not apply to flesh. Some teach this teaching by itself; [As to] a small boy who has intercourse with a grown-up woman, Rab said, he makes her [as though she were] injured by a piece of wood; whereas Samuel said: "Injured by a piece of wood" does not apply to flesh. R. Oshaia objected: WHEN A GROWN-UP MAN HAS HAD INTERCOURSE WITH A LITTLE GIRL, OR WHEN A SMALL BOY HAS INTERCOURSE WITH A GROWN-UP WOMAN, OR WHEN A GIRL WAS ACCIDENTALLY INJURED BY A PIECE OF WOOD—[IN ALL THESE CASES] THEIR KETHUBAH IS TWO HUNDRED [ZUZ]; SO ACCORDING TO R. MEIR. BUT THE SAGES SAY: A GIRL WHO WAS INJURED ACCIDENTALLY BY A PIECE OF WOOD—HER KETHUBAH IS A MANEH! Raba said. It means this: When a grown-up man has intercourse with a little girl it is nothing, for when the girl is less than this, it is as if one puts the finger into the eye; but when a small boy has intercourse with a grown-up woman he makes her as a little girl who is injured by a piece of wood," and [with regard to the case of] "a girl injured by a piece of wood," itself, there is the difference of opinion between R. Meir and the Sages.

In the *Talmud*, if a man has sex with the wife of a minor or the wife of a heathen, it is not adultery. In *Sanhedrin 52b* it says:

GEMARA. Our Rabbis taught: [*And the man that committeth adultery with another man's wife, even he that committeth adultery with his neighbour's wife, the adulterer and the adulteress shall surely be put to death*]. "*The man*" excludes a minor, "*that committeth adultery with another man's wife*" excludes the wife of a minor; "*even he that committeth adultery with his* neighbour's *wife*" excludes the wife of a heathen; "*shall surely be put to death*", by strangulation.

As you can see in this quote from the *Talmud,* the Pharisees circumvented God's laws by creating laws of their own and definitions of their own. As would be expected in a fleshly document, there is a lot of bickering and disagreement, as opposed to a document which contains a revelation of God. The chief rabbi's opinion is the one that prevails.

HOW RELEVANT IS THE TALMUD TO MODERN JUDAISM?

Here again, we would like to turn to the work done by Theodore Pike in his book, *Israel Our Duty ... Our Dilemma.* By quoting him again, this does not mean that I agree with all of his work or all of his conclusions. In this area, he has done his research. Let us see what he has to say in his chapter on the relevance of the *Talmud* to modern Judaism (pages 39-45):

After presenting an introduction to the perversions of the Pharisees, the overwhelming question of course is, How seriously is the Talmud taken by Jews today?
There is no simple answer because Judaism like any other major religion contains various shades of opinion. The Hassidic and Orthodox on the right, in theory at least, take every letter of the Talmud as the word of God. The Conservative, very similar to the Orthodox, admit a greater leeway in adjusting the Talmud to modern forms of worship and social conventions. The Reform movement reserves the right to spiritualize or set aside opinions and practices of their pharisaic tradition which clash with modern life and learning.
Since Reform Judaism has been around for about 200 years, it represents a small but potent contrast to the great majority of religious Jews, who as either Conservative or Orthodox take the Talmud as their final author-

ity. This contrast is made more poignant by the rigidly Orthodox position of the State of Israel which completely rejects the Reform or "Progressive" point of view. In fact, it blames the Reform movement for the assimilation and lack of fervor which plague modern Judaism.

> *There are very few Reform or Conservative congregations in the State of Israel. Orthodoxy is the official religious position in Israel with the majority of the rabbis belonging to the old school of talmudic jurists.* . . .

Another factor which lessens the contradiction in which modern Jews find themselves is present Jewish ignorance of many of the seamy aspects of their sacred traditions. Only a minority of Jews even *knows* of pederasty in the Talmud. Modern Jews are almost as much victims of ignorance and misinformation concerning their beliefs as modernistic Christians. In fact the present stage of distortion and whitewashing of the true nature of Rabbinic Judaism is so pervasive that it could almost constitute a separate Jewish tradition in itself—a third great phase of Judasim. Thus, the first phase, established at Sinai, comprised the highest ethical system known to man. The second phase, Rabbinic Judaism, involved the complete perversion by the Pharisees of everything the former dispensation had tried to establish. The third phase, which we are in now, consists of the marketing of a white-washed facsimile of Judaism for the benefit of the unsuspecting world, but which bears little resemblance to what went before it, just as Rabbinic Judaism bore little resemblance to the old Hebrew religion. . . .

Because of the obsolescence of such rabbinic traditions as child marriages, our point in focusing upon the perversions of the Pharisees has not been to implicate modern Jews in such practices. Rather, it is to demonstrate that at the very fountainhead of Rabbinic Judaism exists a massive confusion of ethics—not just in such things as blasphemy, murder, or sexual aberration, but as we have seen and will see, in all areas of social importance.

> *But if thine eye be evil, the whole body shall be full of darkness. If therefore the light that be in thee be darkness, how great is that darkness! (Matthew 6:23)* . . .
>
> Modern apologists of Judaism continuously hold up such phrases as "the exalted ethics of Judaism," "the flawless logic of Judaism," as if Judaism rested on pillars of marble. The truth, as the preceding passages from the Talmud have shown, is that Rabbinic Judaism rests upon a foundation only as stable and trustworthy as those whom Christ described as "liars," "murderers," "blind guides," and "whited sepulchres"—a sleazy substratum laid out upon the broad boulevards of Babylon. How much better for Judaism (even if it did not accept Christianity) to simply go back to the pure commandments of Moses, forgetting everything the Pharisees so tragically added!" . . .

I certainly agree with the conclusion above by Mr. Pike, purely on moral grounds. Yet it still would not help the Jews to have eternal life or become part of Israel, even if their religion was pure. That only comes through Jesus Christ. I do not necessarily agree with all of Mr. Pike's conclusions, but I do want to thank him for bringing this information to my attention.

THE CHRISTIAN, THE TALMUD AND THE JEW

As one studies the various religions of the world, one sees that religions are normally of high moral and ethical standards, even if they will not get one to God. However, the *Talmud* has some portions which, in my opinion, are of questionable moral value. In addition, in the portion of it called, "Toldth Jesu," there are some very bad and immoral things said about Jesus Christ. In fact, many of the things contained in the terrible movie,

"The Last Temptation of Christ" (such as Christ having sex with Mary) are stated in this document.

Space does not permit a further analysis of the *Talmud*, which unfortunately take precedence over the Holy Scriptures, in many Jewish minds. We trust that we have presented enough here to help give you a feeling of the two later stages of Judaism for a better evaluation of it.

Let me state one final time: we do not want anyone to become anti-Jewish or anti-Semitic. We are to love the Jews. We are to try to help them find a right relationship with God through the only way possible, Jesus Christ. There is no other way, certainly not through the *Talmud*, which is the controlling influence of Judaism.

Appendix D

MEET THE AUTHOR

Dr. James McKeever is an international consulting economist, lecturer, author, world traveler, and Bible teacher. His financial consultations are utilized by scores of individuals from all over the world who seek his advice on investment strategy and international affairs.

Dr. McKeever is the editor and major contributing writer of the *McKeever Strategy Letter*, an economic and investment letter with worldwide circulation and recognition. The *Hulbert Financial Digest*, an independent newsletter-rating service, rated this newsletter the *Number One*, most profitable newsletter in the nation three of the last four years (1985, 1986 and 1988)! It has shown an average profit of 66.25 percent per year over the last eleven years (1978-1988).

Dr. McKeever has been a featured speaker at monetary, gold and tax haven conferences in London, Zurich, Bermuda, Amsterdam, South Africa, Australia, Singapore and Hong Kong, as well as all over the North American continent and Latin America.

As an economist and futurist, Dr. McKeever has shared the platform with such men as Ronald Reagan, Gerald Ford, William Simon, William Buckley, Alan Greenspan, heads of foreign governments, and many other outstanding thinkers.

For five years after completing his academic work, Dr. McKeever was with a consulting firm which specialized in financial investments in petroleum. Those who were following his counsel back in 1954 invested heavily in oil.

For more than ten years he was with IBM, where he held several key management positions. During those years, when IBM was just moving into transistorized computers, he helped that company become what it is today. With IBM, he consulted with top executives of many major corporations in America, helping them solve financial, control and information problems. He has received many awards from IBM, including the "Key Man Award" and the "Outstanding Contribution Award." He is widely known in the computer field for his books and articles on management, management control and information sciences.

In addition to this outstanding business background, Dr. McKeever is an ordained minister. He has been a Baptist evangelist, pastor of Catalina Bible Church for three and a half years (while still with IBM) and a frequent speaker at Christian conferences. He has the gift of teaching, an in-depth knowledge of the Bible, and has authored eleven best-selling Christian books, seven of which have won the "Angel Award."

Dr. McKeever is president of Omega Ministries, which is a nonprofit organization established under the leading of the Holy Spirit to minister to the body of Christ by the traveling ministry of anointed men of God, through books, cassettes, seminars, conferences, and video tapes. He is the editor of the widely-read newsletter, *End-Times News Digest* (published by Omega Ministries), which relates the significance of current events to biblical prophecy and to the body of Christ today. The worldwide outreach of Omega Ministries is supported by the gifts of those who are interested.

DETAILED OUTLINE

1. **GIVE AWAY YOUR BIRTHRIGHT?** 21
   - Who or What is Israel? 22
   - Esau Acted Foolishly 23
   - Christians Today are Just Like Esau 26

2. **THE TWO COVENANTS** 29
   - The Old Covenant versus the New Covenant . 30
   - The Old Covenant has Ended 36
   - Other Passages Which Show that the New Covenant Replaced the Old Covenant ... 39
   - Circumcision is a Key 43
   - Jesus and the New Covenant 53

3. **OTHERS INCLUDED IN ISRAEL** 55
   - Promises Made to Abraham and His Offspring 55
   - Ruth, Rahab and Others 56
   - Foreign Wives Assimilated into Israel 60
   - Many Became Jews 61
   - Return from the Babylonian Captivity 63
   - Assimilating Proselytes 64
   - Jews from Every Nation 66
   - Aliens Being Merged into "Jews" Today 69

4. **HEBREWS EXCLUDED FROM ISRAEL** 71
   - Hebrews Expelled from Israel 71
   - Exclusion in the Book of Leviticus 72
   - Hebrew Prophets Cut Off from Israel 75
   - Hebrews Who Did Not Listen to Spiritual Leaders Cut Off 76
   - Jesus Excluded Some Hebrews from Israel ... 78
   - Summary and Conclusion 79

5. **WHO IS ISRAEL TODAY?** 81
   - Promises to Abraham 82
   - The Rules Change 85
   - The Church is Israel in Song 93
   - The Evidence is Overwhelming 98
   - Proof from Galatians 6:16 101
   - Summary and Conclusion 106

6. **UNFULFILLED PROMISES
   AND PROPHECIES** 107
   I Will Bless Those Who Bless You
      and Curse Those Who Curse You 113
   What About the Unfulfilled Prophecies? ... 116

7. **EZEKIEL 36-37—
   THE GATHERING OF ISRAEL** 119
   Problems with Prophecy 119
   Ezekiel 36 123
   Ezekiel 37 129
   Summary and Conclusion 132

8. **EZEKIEL 38-39—GOG-MAGOG BATTLE** ... 133
   The Gog-Magog War 134
   The Great Plain of the Earth 140
   Summary and Conclusion 143

9. **JERUSALEM MADE DESOLATE** 145
   Recent Mideast Events 145
   What is Desolation? 146
   The Times of the Gentiles 148
   The Next Mideast War 150
   The World Destroyed by Fire 152

10. **THE TEN LOST TRIBES** 155
    The Dispersal of the Tribe of Dan 158
    The Ten Tribes Who Went into Captivity ... 162

11. **THE ONE "FOUND TRIBE"** 167
    Will the Real Jews Please Stand Up? 170
    Summary and Conclusion 181

12. **WHAT ABOUT THE STATE OF ISRAEL?** ... 183
    The Zionist Movement 184
    The State of Israel 189
    What about the Return of the State
       of Israel to that Land? 191
    What is the Significance of the Formation
       of the State of Israel in 1948? 194
    Summary on Israel and the Covenants 199
    The Fig Tree and Israel 201

The Tribulation Did Not Start in 1981 202
   Where Did This 1988 Teaching Get its Start? 204
      A Close Look at the Fig Tree 208
   A Quick Review 214
   Beware of False Teachings 214
   Why are These Things Important? 215
   We must be Willing to Change 216

13. **WILL ALL OF ISRAEL BE SAVED?** 219
   Will All of the Hebrews be Saved? 219
   Romans 9 & 10 223
   Romans 11 227
   Will All Israel be Saved? 231

14. **CLAIM YOUR BIRTHRIGHT** 235
   The Covenants and Old Testament Israel ... 235
   Unfulfilled Promises and Prophecies 238
   Biological Descendants of Abraham 239
   Claim Your Birthright! 241

Appendices

A. **HOW TO BECOME A CHRISTIAN** 247

B. **THE STAR OF DAVID AND THE MENORAH** 253
      Star of which David? 257
      The Seal of Solomon and Occultism ... 259

C. **MODERN JUDAISM IS VERY DIFFERENT
   FROM BIBLICAL JUDAISM** 265
   The Babylonian Captivity 268
   Pharisees 269
      Perverting God's Law 270
      A Secret Tradition 271
      A New Tradition 271
   The Talmud 273
   How Relevant is the Talmud
      to Modern Judaism? 276
   The Christian, The Talmud and the Jew 278

D. **MEET THE AUTHOR** 281

TO THE AUTHOR

Some of the materials available from Dr. James McKeever are shown in summary on the reverse side. Please indicate your area of interest, remove this page and mail it to Omega Publications.

Dr. McKeever would appreciate hearing any personal thoughts from you. If you wish to comment, write your remarks below on this reply form.

Comments:

ORDER FORM

Omega Publications BC-121
P.O. Box 4130
Medford, OR 97501

$ _____ Please send me _____ copies of your popular *Victory Bible Reading Plan* ($1)

Please send me the following books by Dr. McKeever:
(Prices subject to change without notice)

Qty

____	$____	*The Rapture Book* ($6.95)
____	____	*You Can Overcome* ($6.95)
____	____	*Become Like Jesus* ($6.95)
____	____	*Financial Guidance* ($7.95)
____	____	*Believe it or not . . . It's in the Bible* ($7.95)
____	____	*The AIDS Plague* (Revised and Expanded—$6.95)
____	____	*The Future Revealed* ($6.95)
____	____	*Revelation for Laymen* ($5.95)
____	____	*Claim Your Birthright* (7.95) (Hardback—$12.95)

Please send me more information about:

☐ Dr. McKeever speaking at our church or Christian conference
☐ Cassette tapes
☐ Video tapes

Please send the materials I have indicated to:

Name _____

Address _____

City, State _____ Zip _____